Wisdom of Solomon

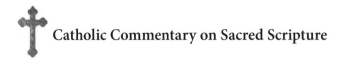 Catholic Commentary on Sacred Scripture

Wisdom
of Solomon

Mark Giszczak

Baker Academic
a division of Baker Publishing Group
Grand Rapids, Michigan

© 2024 by Mark Giszczak

Published by Baker Academic
a division of Baker Publishing Group
www.bakeracademic.com

Printed in the United States of America

Library of Congress Cataloging-in-Publication Data
Names: Giszczak, Mark, author.
Title: Wisdom of Solomon / Mark Giszczak.
Description: Grand Rapids, Michigan : Baker Academic, a division of Baker Publishing Group, [2024] |
    Series: Catholic commentary on sacred scripture | Includes bibliographical references and index.
Identifiers: LCCN 2023020260 | ISBN 9781540963697 (paperback) | ISBN 9781540967275 (casebound) |
    ISBN 9781493444281 (ebook) | ISBN 9781493444298 (pdf)
Subjects: LCSH: Bible. Wisdom of Solomon—Commentaries. | Bible. Wisdom of Solomon—Study and
    teaching. | Wisdom—Biblical teaching.
Classification: LCC BS1755.53 .G57 2024 | DDC 229/.307—dc23/eng/20230705
LC record available at https://lccn.loc.gov/2023020260

Nihil Obstat:
Father Michael Rapp, S.S.L.
Censor Librorum
March 10, 2023

Imprimatur:
Most Reverend Samuel J. Aquila, S.T.L.
Archbishop of Denver
Denver, Colorado, USA
March 10, 2023

Baker Publishing Group publications use paper produced from sustainable forestry practices and post-consumer waste whenever possible.

24   25   26   27   28   29   30   7   6   5   4   3   2   1

To my mother
Rebecca C. Giszczak
Wisdom 7:11–12

Contents

Illustrations

Editors' Preface

The Church has always venerated the divine Scriptures just as she venerates the body of the Lord. . . . All the preaching of the Church should be nourished and governed by Sacred Scripture. For in the sacred books, the Father who is in heaven meets His children with great love and speaks with them; and the power and goodness in the word of God is so great that it stands as the support and energy of the Church, the strength of faith for her sons and daughters, the food of the soul, a pure and perennial fountain of spiritual life.

Second Vatican Council, *Dei Verbum* 21

Did not our hearts burn within us while he talked to us on the road, while he opened to us the Scriptures?

Luke 24:32

The Catholic Commentary on Sacred Scripture Old Testament series aims to serve the ministry of the Word of God in the life and mission of the Church. Since the Second Vatican Council, Catholics have demonstrated an increasing hunger to study Scripture in depth and in a way that reveals its relationship to liturgy, evangelization, catechesis, theology, and personal and communal life. This series responds to that desire by providing accessible yet substantive commentary on the books of the Old Testament, drawn from the best of contemporary biblical scholarship as well as the rich treasury of the Church's tradition. These volumes seek to offer scholarship illumined by faith, in the conviction that the ultimate aim of biblical interpretation is to discover what God has revealed and is still speaking through the sacred text. Central to our approach are the principles taught by Vatican II: first, the use of historical and literary methods to discern what the biblical authors intended to express; second, prayerful theological reflection to understand the sacred text "in accord with the same Spirit by whom it was written"—that is, in light of the content and unity of the whole Scripture, the living tradition of the Church, and the analogy of faith (*Dei Verbum* 12).

The Catholic Commentary on Sacred Scripture is written for those engaged in or training for pastoral ministry and others interested in studying Scripture to understand their faith more deeply, to nourish their spiritual life, or to share the good news with others. With this in mind, the authors focus on the meaning of the text for faith and life rather than on the technical questions that occupy scholars, and they explain the Bible in ordinary language that does not require "translation" for preaching and catechesis. Although this series is written from the perspective of Catholic faith, its authors draw on the interpretation of Protestant and Orthodox scholars and hope these volumes will serve Christians of other traditions as well.

A variety of features are designed to make the commentary as useful as possible. Each volume includes the biblical text of the Revised Standard Version, Second Catholic Edition (RSV-2CE). This translation follows in the English Bible tradition largely embodied in the King James Version and conforms to Vatican guidelines given in *Liturgiam authenticam* (2001). Each unit of the biblical text is followed by a list of references to relevant Scripture passages, Catechism sections, and uses in the Roman Lectionary. The exegesis that follows aims to explain in a clear and engaging way the meaning of the text in its original historical context as well as its perennial meaning for Christians. "Reflection and Application" sections help readers apply Scripture to Christian life today by responding to questions that the text raises, offering spiritual interpretations drawn from Christian tradition or providing suggestions for the use of the biblical text in catechesis, preaching, or other forms of pastoral ministry. "In the Light of Christ" sections illustrate how certain passages prefigure, prophesy, or point forward to Christ and the new covenant.

Interspersed throughout the commentary are Biblical Background sidebars that present historical, literary, or theological information and Living Tradition sidebars that offer pertinent material from the postbiblical Christian tradition, including quotations from Church documents and from the writings of saints and Church Fathers. The Biblical Background sidebars are indicated by a photo of urns that were excavated in Jerusalem, signifying the importance of historical study in understanding the sacred text. The Living Tradition sidebars are indicated by an image of Eadwine, a twelfth-century monk and scribe, signifying the growth in the Church's understanding that comes by the grace of the Holy Spirit as believers study and ponder the word of God in their hearts (see *Dei Verbum* 8).

A glossary is located in the back of each volume for easy reference. The glossary explains key terms from the biblical text as well as theological or exegetical terms, which are marked in the commentary with a cross (†). A list of suggested resources, an index of pastoral topics, and an index of sidebars are included to enhance the usefulness of these volumes. Further resources can be found at the series website, www.CatholicScriptureCommentary.com.

It is our desire and prayer that these volumes be of service so that more and more "the word of the Lord may speed forward and be glorified" (2 Thess 3:1) in the Church and throughout the world.

Mary Healy
Mark Giszczak
Peter S. Williamson

Abbreviations

†	indicates that the definition of a term appears in the glossary
AB	Anchor Bible
ABD	*Anchor Bible Dictionary*. Edited by D. N. Freedman. 6 vols. (New York, 1992)
ANF	*The Ante-Nicene Fathers*. Edited by Alexander Roberts and James Donaldson. 1885–87. 10 vols. (Reprint, Peabody, MA: Hendrickson, 1994)
ANRW	*Aufstieg und Niedergang der römischen Welt: Geschichte und Kultur Roms im Spiegel der neueren Forschung*. Part 2, *Principat*. Edited by Hildegard Temporini and Wolfgang Haase (Berlin: de Gruyter, 1972–)
BDAG	Danker, Frederick W., Walter Bauer, William F. Arndt, and F. Wilbur Gingrich. *A Greek-English Lexicon of the New Testament and Other Early Christian Literature*. 3rd ed. (Chicago: University of Chicago Press, 2000)
ca.	circa
Catechism	*Catechism of the Catholic Church* (2nd edition)
CSEL	Corpus Scriptorum Ecclesiasticorum Latinorum
DS	Denzinger-Schönmetzer, *Enchiridion Symbolorum, definitionum et declarationum de rebus fidei et morum* (1965)
ESV-CE	English Standard Version (Catholic Edition)
FC	Fathers of the Church
LCL	Loeb Classical Library
LXX	Septuagint
NABRE	New American Bible Revised Edition
NETS	New English Translation of the Septuagint
OTP	*Old Testament Pseudepigrapha*. Edited by J. H. Charlesworth. 2 vols. New York: Doubleday, 1983–85.
Philo	Translated by F. H. Colson, G. H. Whitaker, and J. W. Earp. 10 vols. LCL (Cambridge, MA: Harvard University Press, 1929–62)
PL	Patrologia Latina. Edited by J.-P. Migne. 217 vols. (Paris, 1844–61)
RSV	Revised Standard Version
RSV-2CE	Revised Standard Version, Second Catholic Edition (Ignatius)
SBLSCS	Society of Biblical Literature Septuagint and Cognate Studies
t.	Tosefta

Books of the Old Testament

Gen	Genesis	Tob	Tobit	Dan	Daniel
Exod	Exodus	Jdt	Judith	Hosea	Hosea
Lev	Leviticus	Esther	Esther	Joel	Joel
Num	Numbers	Job	Job	Amos	Amos
Deut	Deuteronomy	Ps(s)	Psalms	Obad	Obadiah
Josh	Joshua	Prov	Proverbs	Jon	Jonah
Judg	Judges	Eccles	Ecclesiastes	Mic	Micah
Ruth	Ruth	Song	Song of Songs	Nah	Nahum
1 Sam	1 Samuel	Wis	Wisdom of	Hab	Habakkuk
2 Sam	2 Samuel		Solomon	Zeph	Zephaniah
1 Kings	1 Kings	Sir	Sirach	Hag	Haggai
2 Kings	2 Kings	Isa	Isaiah	Zech	Zechariah
1 Chron	1 Chronicles	Jer	Jeremiah	Mal	Malachi
2 Chron	2 Chronicles	Lam	Lamentations	1 Macc	1 Maccabees
Ezra	Ezra	Bar	Baruch	2 Macc	2 Maccabees
Neh	Nehemiah	Ezek	Ezekiel		

Books of the New Testament

Matt	Matthew	Eph	Ephesians	Heb	Hebrews
Mark	Mark	Phil	Philippians	James	James
Luke	Luke	Col	Colossians	1 Pet	1 Peter
John	John	1 Thess	1 Thessalonians	2 Pet	2 Peter
Acts	Acts	2 Thess	2 Thessalonians	1 John	1 John
Rom	Romans	1 Tim	1 Timothy	2 John	2 John
1 Cor	1 Corinthians	2 Tim	2 Timothy	3 John	3 John
2 Cor	2 Corinthians	Titus	Titus	Jude	Jude
Gal	Galatians	Philem	Philemon	Rev	Revelation

Introduction to Wisdom of Solomon

The Wisdom of Solomon is an invitation to a pursuit of God that involves both the mind and the heart. Because it was the last book of the Old Testament to be written, Wisdom serves as a bridge from the Old Testament to the New. In a unique way, this book integrates faith and reason in its approach to God, bringing together the insights of both Greek philosophy and God's revelation to Israel. It encourages us to seek †wisdom, which is to seek God. If we respond to the invitation, we are promised royal authority, glory, and †immortality. The book also previews the experience of God's judgment after †death, promising the reward of immortality to the righteous and punishment to the wicked. It explains that wisdom is not merely practical knowledge but a gift from God that brings us to know him. Using examples from biblical history—primarily from the exodus—Wisdom shows how God teaches us through cause and effect to choose righteousness and reject wickedness.

The Wisdom of Solomon belongs to the "wisdom literature" of the Old Testament, a collection of books devoted to the practical application of God's principles for human life (Proverbs, Sirach) and to considering the puzzling questions posed by it (Job, Ecclesiastes). While these books collect everyday advice on self-discipline, daily work, and personal relationships, they are fundamentally oriented toward God. The path of wisdom begins with "fear of the Lord" (Prov 9:10) and ultimately "leads upward to life" (Prov 15:24). Wisdom itself is hard to define. A nonbiblical Jewish text that is contemporaneous with Wisdom of Solomon, *4 Maccabees*, offers the following: "Wisdom, I submit, is knowledge of things divine and human, and of their causes."[1] Similarly, St. Thomas Aquinas will name wisdom as the highest of intellectual virtues "because wisdom

---

1. *4 Maccabees* 1.16 (trans. H. Anderson, *OTP* 2:545).

considers the Supreme Cause, which is God."[2] In its essence, wisdom has three distinct yet related meanings: (1) God's perfect knowledge, (2) the knowledge of causes that human beings can come to possess, and (3) the habitual seeking of knowledge with integrity of heart. The Wisdom of Solomon proposes a way of knowing God that begins with honest seeking after truth, leads to embracing what is found on this path, and eventually arrives at union with wisdom itself in God.

Because of this overlap between divinity and wisdom, the statements about wisdom's identity in relation to God can be confusing in this book. On the one hand, wisdom is the *path* to God: readers are invited to embrace "the most sincere desire for instruction" (Wis 6:17). On the other hand, wisdom is the *destination*: "a holy and disciplined spirit" (1:5), who "knows and understands all things" (9:11). As in other Old Testament texts, wisdom is personified as a woman. While wisdom is not explicitly identified with God, she is close at his side (9:9), is given by God (9:17), and carries out his saving will (10:1–21).

The book of Wisdom is philosophical in that it invites its audience to love wisdom, and it is historical in that it reflects on the past. It is a call to leave behind the false reasoning of the ungodly and seek true wisdom from above. It invites readers to understand biblical events from God's perspective, to reflect on his wonderful deeds and draw insight from how he has dealt with his people. If we seek wisdom and learn the lessons that God teaches through salvation history, we will one day obtain glory and immortality in union with him.

Title and Canonical Status

The Wisdom of Solomon is sometimes called "The Book of Wisdom," or simply "Wisdom." Since the book was extant only in Greek, it was included in the †Septuagint but never in the Hebrew Bible. St. Paul might allude to the book, which would seem to indicate his approval of its content (compare, e.g., Rom 9:21 and Wis 15:7). While it enjoyed some authority in early Judaism, it was included only in the Christian canon. It is thus grouped with the other deuterocanonical books of the Old Testament, which are regarded as canonical by the Catholic and Orthodox Churches but excluded from the canon by Protestants. While Origen (ca. 185–254) and St. Jerome (ca. 347–420) express some doubt about its canonicity, it is included in the Muratorian Canon (ca. 170–200) and enthusiastically approved by St. Augustine (354–430). Its canonicity is recognized by the Council of Hippo (393) and the Council of Carthage (397), and definitively affirmed by the Council of Trent (1545–63). It appears

---

2. St. Thomas Aquinas, *Summa Theologica* I-II, q. 66, a. 5, trans. Fathers of the English Dominican Province (New York: Benziger Brothers, 1947–48), 1:869.

in the Lectionary eight times in the three-year Sunday cycle and eight times in the two-year weekday cycle.

Who Wrote Wisdom?

The Wisdom of Solomon does not disclose the name of its author. While part of it is clearly written in Solomon's voice (6:22–9:18; perhaps also 1:1–15), Solomon is certainly not the author of the book. Solomon's voice appears prominently in first-person statements that refer to elements of his biography known from 1 Kings 2–11, such as his prayer for wisdom (Wis 9:1–18) and the command to build the temple (9:8). This book was written in the Greek language during the †Hellenistic era (dated from the death of Alexander the Great in 323 BC to the rise of the Roman Empire in the late first century BC). Written nine centuries after Solomon, the book is pseudonymous, attributed to the great king yet obviously not written by him. This customary practice of writing books and attributing them to renowned individuals was a way of honoring them and invoking their authority. Here Solomon's voice invites the reader to join him on the great quest for wisdom.

The author was a philosophically inclined, law-observant Jew (Wis 12:21–22). This learned teacher of both Hebrew and Greek traditions likely lived in the largest Jewish community at the time. That community dwelt in Alexandria in Egypt and produced a considerable amount of literature, including the Greek Septuagint translation of the Old Testament, *3 and 4 Maccabees*, and the *Letter of Aristeas*. In addition, we have fragments from the second-century BC Jewish philosopher Aristobulus, who lived in Alexandria (see the sidebar "Aristobulus," p. 103). Likewise, the many works of the prolific first-century AD Jewish writer †Philo (ca. 20 BC–50 AD) come from this city. This robust Jewish literary culture in Alexandria, the writer's evident familiarity with Greek philosophy, and the extensive references to Egypt and Egyptian worship (chaps. 11–19)—perhaps even to Roman emperor worship (14:16–22)—combine to place the Wisdom of Solomon in late Hellenistic Alexandria. While some scholars have suggested the possibility that Aristobulus or Philo might be the author of the book, it is best to admit that his name remains unknown.

Alexandria

Alexandria in Egypt was the greatest city of Hellenistic civilization. Though Alexander the Great (356–323 BC) founded it in 331 BC, the bulk of the city was built after his death. Filled with Greek colonists who arrived at its Mediterranean harbor, the city soon became the most populous city of its time. Its great

Photo: Andreas Wolochow / Shutterstock.com

Figure 1. Detail of Alexander the Great (356–323 BC) from Pompeii. Alexander founded the city of Alexandria and named it after himself.

lighthouse was one of the Seven Wonders of the Ancient World. Alexandria was adopted as the capital of the Ptolemaic kingdom, whose rulers, along with a community of scholars, gathered and maintained the largest collection of scrolls in the world at the Museum and Great Library of Alexandria. Under the patronage of Ptolemy II Philadelphus (308–246 BC), among other rulers, Alexandria became the premier center of Greek culture, learning, and literary production in the Hellenistic period (323–30 BC).

The city also contained the largest Jewish community in the world, which organized itself into a semiautonomous *politeuma* (self-governing community) that consisted of many synagogues, including a great basilica-synagogue of legendary proportions.[3] Though the Jews enjoyed the peace, privilege, and education that the Hellenistic world offered, they were not totally assimilated into the Greek citizenry. When the Ptolemaic kingdom was incorporated into the Roman Empire (30 BC), the emperor Augustus (63 BC–AD 14) imposed a poll tax (*laographia*) that divided the inhabitants of Alexandria into two groups: those who were exempt from the tax and those who had to pay it.[4] The Greek citizens were exempt, while the Egyptians, as second-class citizens, were forced to pay. However, the Jews, who had previously enjoyed a certain equality with the Greeks, were now reduced in status and forced to pay the tax. By law, they were regarded as beneath the Greeks and on par

3. See *t. Sukkah* 4.4.

4. John J. Collins, *Between Athens and Jerusalem: Jewish Identity in the Hellenistic Diaspora* (Grand Rapids: Eerdmans, 2000), 115–17.

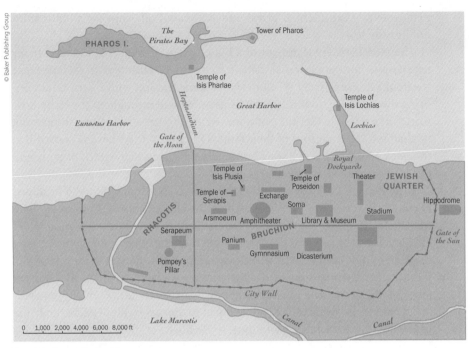

Figure 2. Map of Alexandria.

with the Egyptians. The Jews objected to this degradation of their status, while the Greeks supported it. The conflict later developed into a full-scale persecution against the Jews of Alexandria in AD 38, which prompted a Jewish delegation that included the famous Philo to visit the emperor Caligula (reigned AD 37–41) in Rome to plead their case.[5] These concerns over the status of the Jews form the background for Wisdom's emphatic distinction between the righteous and unrighteous, the wise and the foolish, the Hebrews and the Egyptians.

Purpose and Audience

The purpose of the Wisdom of Solomon depends on the audience it was written for. Since it is addressed to kings and rulers (1:1; 6:1) in the voice of King Solomon, commentators have sometimes argued that the book is directed to Gentile readers, perhaps even Gentile rulers. Its balance of universal concern (18:4) and a particular focus on the Jewish people is similar to Philo's insistence to Gentile readers that Jewish religion is compatible with a more universal

---

5. Though Caligula rebuffed their requests, soon after his death the Jews of Alexandria launched an armed revolt that resulted in a strong letter from the new emperor Claudius (reigned AD 41–54) reaffirming the equality and rights of the Jews. See Josephus, *Jewish Antiquities* 19.5.2.

perspective—that the high priest, indeed, makes offerings for all humanity, not just the Jews.[6]

The pluralistic environment of a big city like Alexandria presented many temptations for young Jewish people to lose their faith and assimilate. Since the book's praise of Lady Wisdom shares some features with inscriptions honoring the popular goddess Isis, who was celebrated throughout the Hellenistic world, it is possible that the book was written to urge young Jewish men not to abandon the traditions of their fathers for Isis.[7] Others have proposed that the book was directed at Jews who had already given in to Greek paganism in order to gain political power.[8]

Regardless of the exact situation, the book of Wisdom appears to be aimed at convincing Jews who were tempted by the allurements of the cosmopolitan milieu of Alexandria not to give up the faith but to regard their tradition as not only intellectually defensible but truly wiser than the other options presented by the surrounding culture—the worship of idols and the pursuit of mere pleasure. If the book was written after the Roman poll tax was imposed on the Alexandrian Jews (24 BC), it could be seen as an argument not just for the rationality of Jewish belief but for the status of the Jews as equal to the tax-exempt Greeks. Only the Jews would catch the biblical allusions, so the book's original audience was likely Jewish. Yet these Jews lived in a complex, pluralistic cultural situation, which would make them eager to hear well-crafted philosophical arguments for their faith.

The first five chapters of Wisdom combat philosophical and carnal temptations that appear culturally Greek (e.g., 1:16–2:24), while chapters 10–19 are directed against the Egyptians, who oppressed the Hebrews in the exodus period and practiced the worst forms of idolatry in their worship of animals (11:15; 13:10). In response to these aberrations, Wisdom argues for the intellectual validity of faith, for the philosophical soundness of keeping the law of God. It argues against both the absurdity of idolatry and the folly of hedonism. The book is an attempt at integration, bringing together Jewish tradition and Greek philosophy.

Date

Our ability to date the Wisdom of Solomon is limited by the available evidence—namely, (1) quotations of the Septuagint, (2) a possible allusion to Roman emperor worship, (3) the unique vocabulary of the book, and (4) the earliest unambiguous quotations of the book.

6. See Philo, *On the Life of Abraham* 98; *On the Life of Moses* 1.149; *On the Special Laws* 2.162–63; C. T. R. Hayward, *The Jewish Temple: A Non-Biblical Sourcebook* (London: Routledge, 1996), 135.

7. James M. Reese, *Hellenistic Influence on the Book of Wisdom and Its Consequences*, Analecta Biblica 41 (Rome: Biblical Institute Press, 1970), 40–50.

8. A. T. S. Goodrick, *The Book of Wisdom with Introduction and Notes* (London: Rivingtons, 1913; repr., New York: Cambridge University Press, 2012), 5–6.

First, the Septuagint, the first Greek translation of the Old Testament, began with a translation of the Pentateuch alone under the sponsorship of Ptolemy II Philadelphus (308–246 BC), according to the legendary *Letter of Aristeas*. By 132 BC, there were Greek translations not only of the Pentateuch but of "the prophecies, and the rest of the books" as well (see the prologue to Sirach). Wisdom quotes the Septuagint of Isaiah and Job,[9] placing it clearly after these books had been translated into Greek, which likely happened no earlier than 200 BC. The earliest possible date for Wisdom then would be around the middle of the second century BC, since a few years would need to pass for the translations to be copied, disseminated, and then quoted.

Second, several scholars have perceived in Wis 14:16–20 a deliberate

Figure 3. Marble bust of Serapis from the Serapeum of Alexandria. The cult of this syncretic Hellenistic-Egyptian deity, a combination of Osiris and Apis with Greek features, became popular in Alexandria.

Public Domain / Wikimedia Commons / Jastrow

allusion to the imperial worship of the emperor Caligula (AD 37–41), who placed his statue in every temple and synagogue in the Roman Empire and even threatened to put his statue in the Jewish temple in Jerusalem. However, such a severe sacrilege would have likely provoked a far stronger reaction than is evidenced in any text in the Wisdom of Solomon, so it cannot be as late as Caligula.

Third, the vocabulary of the book has been studied in detail to reveal that a few dozen words it employs are not attested before the Roman period (30 BC–AD 395) and that some of the terms it uses fit very well within the vocabulary of that time.[10]

Fourth, though the Wisdom of Solomon might be alluded to in the New Testament (see "Connections to the New Testament" below), it is not unambiguously quoted until St. Irenaeus (ca. 140–98).[11] It is more frequently quoted by Clement of Alexandria (ca. 150–215) and Origen (ca. 185–254).

---

9. Isa 3:10, quoted in Wis 2:12; Isa 44:20, quoted in Wis 15:10; Job 9:12, 19, quoted in Wis 12:12.

10. David Winston, *The Wisdom of Solomon*, AB 43 (Garden City, NY: Doubleday, 1979), 22–23; James M. Reese, *The Book of Wisdom, Song of Songs*, Old Testament Message 20 (Wilmington, DE: Michael Glazier, 1983), 17.

11. Irenaeus's *Against Heresies* 4.38.3 quotes Wis 6:19.

Figure 4. Pillar of Pompey in Alexandria, erected by the emperor Diocletian ca. AD 300.

These data combine to convince major commentators to place the book in the Roman period, which began in 30 BC. Chrysostom Larcher suggests 31–10 BC.[12] David Winston chooses the reign of Caligula, AD 37–41.[13] The book likely finds its place early in the Roman period, sometime after Egypt is annexed in 30 BC but before Caligula's reign.

Literary Form and Features

St. Jerome says that the style of Wisdom of Solomon is "redolent of Greek eloquence."[14] The book is written in good Greek philosophical style, perhaps the best Greek in the biblical canon. It freely combines rhetorical modes, Hebrew stylistic concepts, and Greek rhetorical techniques to develop its ideas. In this sense, the book is truly a unique fusion of literary strategies. The overall approach is exhortatory, so the book has been classified as a "protreptic," that is, a discourse designed to convince—in this case, to convince the reader to pursue wisdom. James M. Reese observes that "the entire book contains only 6952 words, but employs a vocabulary of 1734 different words, of which 1303 appear only once."[15] This unusually wide vocabulary includes many original compound words and 335 words that appear nowhere else in the Septuagint.[16]

The author displays his skill not only in his use of rare words but in his mastery of literary techniques. Many scholars have noted the †diatribe style, in which an imaginary debate partner is given voice and then refuted (see Wis 2:1–24). The early chapters of the book frequently use Hebrew poetic parallelism, where an idea is presented in one line and repeated with slight modification in the next (e.g., 1:5). Similarly, the author offers many comparisons, labeled †synkrises in Greek terminology, especially in the latter half of the book (chaps. 10–19). The

---

12. Chrysostom Larcher, *Le livre de la sagesse ou la sagesse de Salomon*, Études Bibliques Nouvelle série 1 (Paris: Gabalda, 1983), 1:141–61.
13. Winston, *Wisdom of Solomon*, 23.
14. Jerome, *Prologue to Wisdom* (PL 28:1242).
15. Reese, *Hellenistic Influence*, 3.
16. Reese, *Hellenistic Influence*, 3.

book mentions many persons and nations but never includes proper names. This technique is called antonomasia and forces the reader to guess at the subject being discussed (see the sidebar "Why Omit Names?," p. 61). Other notable rhetorical devices employed include hyperbaton, an emphatic separation of words that naturally belong together, which occurs some 240 times in Wisdom;[17] litotes, an ironic understatement (e.g., "You were not unable," 12:9); †inclusio, where elements at the beginning and ending of a section are repeated; chiasm, a concentric structure (see chap. 9); anaphora, a repeated use of a pronoun (found in chap. 10, where "she" is repeated many times); antithesis, where contrasting ideas are juxtaposed; and †sorites, a playful syllogism (e.g., 6:17–20). The very breadth of Greek literary devices and the use of Hellenistic philosophical style (see especially 13:1–9) reveal that this book was composed according to the most sophisticated principles available in the Alexandrian intellectual milieu, but with such dexterity that a truly original literary form resulted.

Structure

For over a century, scholars have largely agreed on the structure of the Wisdom of Solomon.[18] Essentially, the book has three parts:

Part 1—Life and Death (1:1–6:21)
Part 2—Solomon's Pursuit of Wisdom (6:22–9:18)
Part 3—Book of History (10:1–19:22)

Part 1, "Life and Death" (sometimes called the Book of †Eschatology), focuses on the search for wisdom, the comparison of the righteous and the wicked, and the final judgment. "Eschatology" here refers to what happens to a person after death rather than to what will happen at the end of history.

Part 2 of the book of Wisdom centers on the character of Solomon himself, his quest for wisdom, and his prayer to the Lord for wisdom. It offers us an ideal model of the wisdom seeker and constitutes the heart of the book. Chapter 10 functions as a transition from the quest for wisdom into the highly structured Part 3, "Book of History," which retells the story of the exodus in a veiled form, drawing out the lessons God wanted to teach through that era. This section shows that God uses creation to bless the righteous and to correct the wicked, according to the principle that "one is punished by the very things by which he sins" (11:16).

This widely agreed-upon tripartite structure is the most important aspect of the book's arrangement, but a few additional structural features are worth noting. First,

---

17. Reese, *Hellenistic Influence*, 26.

18. There has been agreement since the seminal article establishing the tripartite structure: W. Weber, "Die Komposition der Weisheit Salomos," *Zeitschrift für wissenschaftliche Theologie* 48 (1904): 145–69.

the book is divided into two parts by reason and faith: chapters 1–9 are primarily philosophical, urging the reader to embrace the search for wisdom through human reason, but chapters 10–19 are primarily theological, reflecting on the lessons of salvation history from the vantage point of faith. Second, the author has a fondness for concentric or chiastic structures. Chapter 9, for example, has a concentric structure, with Solomon's prayer for the sending of wisdom as the heart and center of the whole composition.[19] Third, the latter half of the book is characterized by seven antitheses (though some argue for only five), which reveal how God blesses his faithful ones and punishes the wicked by the very same created things:

1. Water from the Rock versus River of Blood (11:1–14)
2. Unappetizing Animals versus Delicious Quail (16:1–4)
3. Lethal Creatures versus Saving Bronze Serpent (16:5–14)
4. Storms of Wrath versus Manna from Heaven (16:15–29)
5. Plague of Darkness versus Pillar of Light (17:1–18:4)
6. Death of the Firstborn versus Israel's Deliverance from Death (18:5–25)
7. Drowning in the Sea versus Being Saved by the Sea (19:1–9)

Fourth, the development of these antitheses is interrupted by a long digression on God's power and the folly of idolatry (11:15–15:19). Overall, the book is easily divided into major sections, and the author employs structural elements throughout to develop his composition and emphasize certain points.

Connections to the New Testament

The New Testament does not explicitly quote the Wisdom of Solomon. However, commentators have long proposed many allusions to Wisdom in the New Testament. Certain passages appear to be parallel. For example, Wisdom's portrayal of the taunting and death of the righteous man (2:17–20) is apparently alluded to in Matthew's portrayal of Jesus's crucifixion (Matt 27:39–43). Similarly, Paul's discussion of the armor of God (Eph 6:11–17) shares many commonalities with Wis 5:17–20, but perhaps only because both texts are dependent on Isa 59:17. Other passages share metaphors, terminology, and theology. In particular, the description of wisdom here is like the portrayal of Jesus as the divine Word in the New Testament. Both are preexistent (Wis 8:3; 9:4; John 1:1–2), involved in creation (Wis 7:22; 8:6; John 1:3), and reflections of God (Wis 7:26; Col 1:15; Heb 1:3).[20] Jesus is even identified as "wisdom from God" (1 Cor 1:30 ESV-CE).

19. For a further examination of concentric structures in Wisdom, see Michael Kolarcik, "The Book of Wisdom," in *The New Interpreter's Bible*, ed. Leander E. Keck, 12 vols. (Nashville: Abingdon, 1997), 5:444–45.

20. See José María Casciaro, ed., *Wisdom Books*, trans. Michael Adams, Navarre Bible (New York: Scepter, 2004), 306.

Certain terms appear in close proximity in similar ways, such as "grace and mercy,"[21] "elect,"[22] and "signs and wonders."[23]

Here is a summary of some of the most important correspondences between Wisdom and the New Testament:

	Wisdom	New Testament
Taunting the righteous	2:17–20	Matt 27:39–43
The armor of God	5:17–20	Eph 6:11–17
Reflection of God	7:26	Col 1:15; Heb 1:3
Wisdom and the Holy Spirit	7:27–28 9:11–15	1 Cor 2:7–16
Vessels of wrath and the patience of God	12:8–11, 20	Rom 9:22
Idolatry	chaps. 13–15	Rom 1:18–32
The potter	15:7–8	Rom 9:21

While these examples are representative, one author has identified 111 allusions to the Wisdom of Solomon in the New Testament,[24] while another has found 146.[25] It is possible "that St. Paul had read the Book of Wisdom and knew it well."[26] While some argue that Paul's views militate against the teaching of Wisdom,[27] it seems likely that Wisdom "belonged to the mental furniture of the NT writers."[28] However, there is no definitive proof of the New Testament's dependence on Wisdom, and the apparent allusions could be explained as references to common ideas in Judaism at the time.

The Wisdom of Solomon in Christian Tradition

Christian interpreters have found compelling prefigurements of Christ in the Wisdom of Solomon. The persecuted righteous man of chapter 2 foreshadows Jesus. The "paltry piece of wood" (10:4) through which wisdom saves the world and the blessed wood "by which righteousness comes" (14:7) prefigure the cross. The New Testament and early Christian writers identify Jesus with the "pure

---

21. Wis 3:9; 4:15; 1 Tim 1:2; 2 Tim 1:2; Heb 4:16; 2 John 1:3.

22. Wis 3:9; 4:15; 1 Tim 5:21; 2 Tim 2:10; 2 John 1:1, 13.

23. Wis 8:8; 10:16; 19:8; Matt 24:24; Mark 13:22; John 4:48; Acts 2:19, 22, 43; Rom 15:19.

24. Lee Martin McDonald, *The Biblical Canon: Its Origin, Transmission, and Authority* (Grand Rapids: Baker Academic, 2011), 452–64.

25. Craig A. Evans, *Ancient Texts for New Testament Studies* (Grand Rapids: Baker Academic, 2005), 343–406.

26. Goodrick, *Book of Wisdom*, 403.

27. Jonathan Linebaugh, *God, Grace and Righteousness in Wisdom of Solomon and Paul's Letter to the Romans: Texts in Conversation* (Boston: Brill, 2013).

28. J. A. F. Gregg, *The Wisdom of Solomon in the Revised Version with Introduction and Notes*, Cambridge Bible for Schools and Colleges (Cambridge: Cambridge University Press, 1922), lx.

emanation of the glory of the Almighty" (7:25; e.g., Heb 1:3; James 2:1) and the "reflection of eternal light" (Wis 7:26; e.g., 2 Cor 4:6; Col 1:15).

Relatively few commentaries have been written about the Wisdom of Solomon in Christian history. Commentaries include those authored by the monk Rabanus Maurus (ca. 780–856); the Seraphic Doctor of the Church, St. Bonaventure (1217–74); the English Dominican Robert Holcot (1290–1349); and the great Jesuit biblical scholar Cornelius à Lapide (1568–1637). While Wisdom has been included in the canon from ancient times, it is one of the least-studied books of the Bible.

Theological Themes

Since the Wisdom of Solomon owes a debt to Greek philosophy, it contains many unique doctrinal perspectives that are only latent in the other books of the Old Testament. These ideas resurface in the New Testament and are incorporated into Christian teaching. For example, it emphasizes the immortality of the soul (Wis 2:23–3:4). It highlights personal judgment after death, after which each soul awaits punishment or reward (3:4, 10). These new developments pave the way for the New Testament doctrine of eternal life. Wisdom alone among the books of the Bible names the four cardinal virtues (8:7). It adopts the Greek conception of the Word (†*Logos*) as the animating principle for creation, identifying this entity as wisdom. Its portrayal of wisdom as near to God or even semidivine blurs the line between God and his wisdom, which sets the stage for the development of trinitarian theology. It defines God as "him who exists" (13:1), denoting his nature as pure existence. It explains wisdom as a means to access God, the path to union with God (7:14). It insists that desiring and honoring wisdom leads to sharing in God's eternal reign (6:20–21; see also 3:8). Lastly, it interprets history as a †divine pedagogy, wherein God teaches wisdom through the consequences of human action (12:2). The Wisdom of Solomon consistently invites its readers to follow the path to God, which is the path of wisdom. This path ultimately leads to immortality and union with God.

Wisdom for Today

The Wisdom of Solomon stands at the very end of the Old Testament era and on the cusp of the New. It is the last Old Testament book to be written. Its meditation on salvation history allows us to take a deep breath and look back on the Old Testament before proceeding to the New. On the one hand, the book is retrospective, recalling the lessons of the past and interpreting biblical history. On the other hand, it invites us to a new vision for Christian life not merely as an ethical or devotional enterprise but as an intellectual one: a pursuit of wisdom. While St. Paul calls us to "run that you may obtain" the prize and to imitate him as he imitates Christ (1 Cor 9:24; 11:1), the Wisdom of Solomon calls us to be like Solomon in his love and zeal for wisdom (Wis 7:8–10). Readers are invited to follow him in the quest for wisdom. Since Jesus is the fulfillment of the Old Testament, the true †*Logos*, he is the goal of the search for wisdom. Jesus is wisdom incarnate.

Because the book was composed in the multicultural environment of Hellenistic Alexandria, we can learn from it how to be faithful to God's call amid contemporary global, pluralistic culture. On the one hand, the author adopts the best literary techniques and philosophical insights of his era and incorporates them into his biblical faith, while on the other hand, he evaluates and critiques the polytheistic and †hedonistic elements of the culture around him. We too can value the best insights the world has to offer, while rejecting its false enticements and ideas.

The Wisdom of Solomon offers us a hopeful vision for human life with God now and in the hereafter. While we might tend to evaluate human history as a series of failures and disappointments, the sadness of sin dominating our perspective, Wisdom invites us to a more hopeful outlook where we notice God's hand guiding all events toward his providential purposes. In addition, we can embrace wisdom as both the way and the destination, as Jesus tells us, "I am the way, and the truth, and the life" (John 14:6). We get to wisdom by wisdom. And in the end, we can have hope even after death, that "the souls of the righteous are in the hand of God" (Wis 3:1). The ultimate goal of wisdom-seeking is union with God forever in heaven.

Part 1

Life and Death

Wisdom 1:1–6:21

Love Righteousness

Wisdom 1:1–15

The wise remind us to begin with the end in mind. Thus, the first chapter of Wisdom begins with an exhortation to "love righteousness" (1:1) and then concludes by explaining why: "righteousness is immortal" (v. 15). The thoughtful reader will put the pieces together: love of righteousness leads us through righteousness to †immortality. This opening exhortation helps us meditate on genuine devotion to God by examining the obstacles human beings can put in the way of wisdom: sinful thoughts (vv. 4–5), words (vv. 6–11), and actions (v. 12). Only by loving, thinking of, and seeking the Lord can one rise above sin, embrace righteousness, and find the path to immortality.

Love Righteousness (1:1–5)

¹Love righteousness, you rulers of the earth,
think of the Lord with uprightness,
and seek him with sincerity of heart;
²because he is found by those who do not put him to the test,
and manifests himself to those who do not distrust him.
³For perverse thoughts separate men from God,
and when his power is tested, it convicts the foolish;
⁴because wisdom will not enter a deceitful soul,
nor dwell in a body enslaved to sin.
⁵For a holy and disciplined spirit will flee from deceit,
and will rise and depart from foolish thoughts,
and will be ashamed at the approach of unrighteousness.

OT: Wis 6:1; 10:16; Deut 6:16; Josh 24:14; Ps 2:10; Sir 15:7
NT: Matt 5:6; Acts 2:40; Rom 2:15; Phil 2:15; Titus 1:8; Heb 12:10
Catechism: testing God, 2119
Lectionary: 1:1–7: Ordinary Time, Week 32, Monday (Year I)

1:1   The book opens with three commands: love, think, seek. The author, speaking in the voice of Solomon the great king of Israel, invites his fellow kings, the **rulers of the earth** (see Ps 2:10), to three distinct yet united actions. He proposes a way of life for all his readers, whether royal or not. To **love righteousness** is to love God, to embrace the path of wisdom. Righteousness, sometimes translated "justice," is about giving to each person his or her due. It means to do the right thing in every situation. Proverbs 1–9 characterizes the search for wisdom as a romance, a wooing of Lady Wisdom and a rejection of Lady Folly. Here the author invites his hearers to this kind of loving pursuit. This romance can also be characterized as a journey of the mind. One must **think of the Lord**, in the same way that Psalm 1 depicts the righteous man meditating on the law of God day and night. The mind is not passed over but is fully engaged in the romance. The Greek for **with uprightness** here means something like "with friendship" or "with goodwill." In addition, to truly find God one must **seek him** with singled-hearted devotion. Here, the author commands his audience to embark on this integrating process of seeking God with intellect, will, and emotions. Indeed, this very first verse begins with **love** and ends with **heart** (though not in the Greek word order), putting the focus on integration and **sincerity**. This Greek word translated "sincerity" can mean "simplicity" or even "singleness." To find God one must not be double-minded, but of a firm and single mind. To follow him requires a genuine commitment.

1:2   If God invites us to seek him, he wants to be **found**. Yet putting God **to the test** throws an obstacle in the way of seeking him. Testing God is forbidden by a command in the Pentateuch (Deut 6:16), which will be cited by Jesus (Matt 4:7; Luke 4:12). It involves attempting to force God's hand, to demand he prove himself by a miracle. This type of challenge comes from a lack of faith, but God makes himself manifest only **to those who do not distrust him**. Here Wisdom regards unbelief as a roadblock to finding God but implies that faith is the key, foreshadowing a central New Testament teaching.

1:3   Again, one's thinking is the focus: **perverse** (literally, "crooked") **thoughts** create a separation between us and God. On the other hand, pure thoughts can lead us to God; thus St. Paul teaches his audience to think about true, honorable, just, and pure things (Phil 4:8). Here Wisdom calls for a conversion of mind: false, foolish, and twisted thoughts foul the waters of the mind and prevent one from seeking God, but a true seeking of wisdom requires purity of intention.

Referring back to the first part of verse 2, the author explains what happens when the power of God **is tested**. Simply, **it convicts**, or "reproves," **the foolish**. Trying to force God to act will lead to humiliation. Paradoxically, this reproof could lead the foolish to learn their lesson and thus find God.

1:4–5   Now the author turns from speaking of God to introducing **wisdom** as **a holy and disciplined spirit** that might or might not enter a human **soul** or **body**. The Greek could be rendered "the holy spirit of discipline" (NABRE),

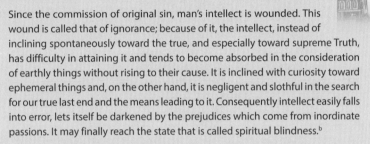

The Wounded Intellect   LIVING TRADITION

The famous twentieth-century Catholic philosopher and close friend of Pope St. Paul VI, Jacques Maritain, said, "The disease afflicting the modern world is above all a disease of the intellect."[a] The book of Wisdom shows how ancient this disease is. A great Dominican theologian, Réginald Garrigou-Lagrange, explains how the human mind is led astray by sin:

> Since the commission of original sin, man's intellect is wounded. This wound is called that of ignorance; because of it, the intellect, instead of inclining spontaneously toward the true, and especially toward supreme Truth, has difficulty in attaining it and tends to become absorbed in the consideration of earthly things without rising to their cause. It is inclined with curiosity toward ephemeral things and, on the other hand, it is negligent and slothful in the search for our true last end and the means leading to it. Consequently intellect easily falls into error, lets itself be darkened by the prejudices which come from inordinate passions. It may finally reach the state that is called spiritual blindness.[b]

a. Jacques Maritain, *St. Thomas Aquinas* (New York: Meridian, 1960), 89.
b. Réginald Garrigou-Lagrange, *The Three Ages of the Interior Life*, vol. 1 (St. Louis: Herder, 1947), 353–54.

picking up an Old Testament theme (Ps 51:11; Isa 63:10–11) and foreshadowing the New Testament identification of the Holy Spirit (Matt 1:18, 20; John 20:22; Acts 2:4). Here the unity of God and his wisdom begins to be displayed, a theme that will continually mark the pages of the Wisdom of Solomon. To seek wisdom is to seek God.

As with the problem with perverse thoughts in verse 3, moral failings likewise prevent one from truly possessing wisdom. Wisdom is simply incompatible with **sin** and **deceit**. Sin disposes us toward ignorance, while humble truth-seeking leads to God. In verse 5, the author presents a triple lineup of problematic ways of thinking: **deceit, foolish thoughts**, and **unrighteousness**. These sinful modes of thought are opposites of wise thinking. Deceit opposes honesty. Foolish thoughts (literally, "thoughts without understanding") are opposed to intelligence. And unrighteousness is the opposite of righteousness, which verse 1 tells us to love. Righteousness and unrighteousness thus bookend the first part of Wisdom's opening exhortation (vv. 1–5).

Wisdom, Lover of Humanity (1:6–11)

> [6]**For wisdom is a kindly spirit**
> **and will not free a blasphemer from the guilt of his words;**

because God is witness of his inmost feelings,
and a true observer of his heart, and a hearer of his tongue.
⁷Because the Spirit of the Lord has filled the world,
and that which holds all things together knows what is said;
⁸therefore no one who utters unrighteous things will escape
    notice,
and justice, when it punishes, will not pass him by.
⁹For inquiry will be made into the counsels of an ungodly man,
and a report of his words will come to the Lord,
to convict him of his lawless deeds;
¹⁰because a jealous ear hears all things,
and the sound of murmurings does not go unheard.
¹¹Beware then of useless murmuring,
and keep your tongue from slander;
because no secret word is without result,
and a lying mouth destroys the soul.

OT: Wis 1:16; 7:22–23; Exod 20:5; Ps 139:7–12; Sir 39:19; Jer 17:10
NT: 1 Cor 2:10–11; Eph 4:29–31; Phil 2:14; Col 1:17; 3:8; James 3:5–8
Catechism: blasphemy, 2148

1:6   In these verses, the author explains the spiritual nature of wisdom, which accounts for God's knowledge of all things and serves to warn his readers against sinful speech. The audience is called upon to think of God "with uprightness" (v. 1), as **wisdom is a kindly** (*philanthrōpos*) **spirit** in relation to humanity. The term *philanthrōpos* means "loving of humanity," here demonstrating that wisdom acts benevolently, seeking our good, sometimes through punishment. Wisdom convicts **a blasphemer from the guilt of his words**, literally "from his lips." Blasphemy is a sin of speech that entails speaking evil of God. While God is also **a hearer** of the blasphemer's **tongue**, more importantly he knows one's **inmost feelings** and **heart**. God is here named as **witness** (*martys*) and **observer**.

1:7–8   God's omniscience is made possible by his omnipresence, since the **Spirit of the Lord has filled the world**, like the "eyes of the LORD, which range through the whole earth" (Zech 4:10). God's knowledge is all-encompassing, so his **justice** is inescapable and will not bypass the unrighteous. This personified figure of justice is reminiscent of the so-called angel of death, which mercifully did bypass the houses of faithful Israelites (Exod 12; Wis 18:2–25). God's kindness and justice are two sides of the same coin. While he graciously welcomes the repentant with mercy, he "will by no means clear the guilty" (Exod 34:7).

1:9–10   Verses 9–10 preview the final judgment, when the Lord will judge everyone's **counsels, words**, and **deeds**. The word translated "counsels" could be rendered "schemings" or "machinations." The author plots a trajectory from inner thoughts to sinful words and finally to **lawless deeds**. Sinful action is preceded by sinful talking, which is preceded by sinful thinking. **A jealous**

Soul (Greek *psychē*)   **BIBLICAL** **BACKGROUND**

The Greek word *psychē* appears twenty-five times in the Wisdom of Solomon. It is usually translated "soul" but can also be rendered "life" or "self." It refers to the innermost self, which can be directed toward good or evil (1:4, 11; 2:22; 4:11). In the †Septuagint, *psychē* translates Hebrew *nephesh*, which means "soul" or "breath." Wisdom depicts human beings as embodied souls: "A perishable body weighs down the soul" (9:15); Solomon has both a "good soul" (8:19) and an "unde-filed body" (8:20). This book breaks new ground in the Old Testament by clearly teaching that the souls of the just continue to live in God's presence after †death (3:1–9). The Church teaches that "'soul' signifies the *spiritual principle* in man" (Catechism 363).

ear—namely, God—hears all things, another poetic description of his omni-science. Early in Israel's history, he defined himself as "a jealous God" (Exod 20:5), and Wisdom develops this idea to explain his all-embracing knowledge and justice. The **sound of murmurings** against God, another sin of speech, was one of the principal sins of the Israelites during the exodus and wilderness wanderings (Exod 16:7–12; Num 17:5, 10).

The fact that God knows everything now leads to a warning in verse 11. **Be-**   1:11
ware could be translated reflexively as "keep yourself from" **useless murmuring**. This second mention of the exodus-era sin of speech teaches that such sinful talk, even if a **secret word**, is without benefit. It does not accomplish anything except to separate us from God. Instead of helping us, it **destroys the soul**. In a similar vein, Jesus warns that "what you have whispered in private rooms shall be proclaimed upon the housetops" (Luke 12:3), but he also teaches that God rewards those who do good in secret (Matt 6:4, 6, 18).

Invite Not Death (1:12–15)

> ¹²Do not invite death by the error of your life,
> nor bring on destruction by the works of your hands;
> ¹³because God did not make death, and
> he does not delight in the death of the living.
> ¹⁴For he created all things that they might exist,
> and the creatures of the world are wholesome,
> and there is no destructive poison in them;
> and the dominion of Hades is not on earth.
> ¹⁵For righteousness is immortal.

OT: Wis 2:23–24; 11:23–25; Ezek 18:23; 2 Macc 7:28
NT: Acts 7:41; 1 Cor 15:55–56; 2 Pet 3:9; Rev 9:20
Catechism: God did not make death, 413; death is a consequence of sin, 1008; God holds us in existence, 27; creation is good, 299
Lectionary: 1:13–15; 2:23–24: 13th Sunday in Ordinary Time (Year B)

1:12   In this conclusion to the opening exhortation of the book, the author warns his readers not to **invite death**. The verb for "invite" means to "zealously seek" (NETS), as though the sinner exhibits desire for †death by his straying from the path of wisdom. While wisdom-seeking is commended, death-seeking is warned against. The warning is not just against foolish behavior but against the terrible results brought on **by the works of your hands**, a biblical euphemism for idols (13:10; Deut 4:28; Isa 37:19; Acts 7:41). The verse offers a tight parallelism between **death** and **destruction**, and also between **error** and idolatry. The adoration of idols brings on death.

1:13   In verse 13, the opening principle is expanded with an explanation that **God did not make death**. This allusion to the story of Adam and Eve laments the sad reality that their sin, not God, brought about death's "entrance into human history" (Catechism 400; see also Rom 5:12). Human death is the result of sin, not of God's design. God intended for Adam and Eve to live forever, but by their sin, they chose death (Catechism 1008). They invited it by their error. Even though God permits death, he did not create it, nor does he **delight in the death of the living**. This verse is a reminder of the biblical teaching that God's plan for humanity leads to life (see Ezek 18:23, 32; 33:11). The second word translated "death" in this verse is *apōleia*, which elsewhere means destruction, defined as "the death of an ultimate judgment that signifies a broken relationship with both God and the cosmos."[1] Even more so, it is "an everlasting state of torment and death."[2] But this negative destiny was not God's purpose for creation.

1:14–15   Now the author continues the development by alluding to Gen 1:31, where all of creation is declared "very good." God creates a good world, but it can be corrupted by human error and sin. He creates all things **that they might exist**: being is better than nonbeing. While error leads to destruction, **the creatures of the world are wholesome** (Greek *sōtērios*)—that is, having a tendency toward safety or preservation. Created living things have a survival instinct, a life-preserving nature to them. Once things exist, God "at every moment, upholds and sustains them in being" (Catechism 301). By nature, **there is no destructive poison in them**, meaning they are good and wholesome. The last line of verse 14 insists that the **dominion of Hades is not on earth**, meaning

1. Michael Kolarcik, "The Book of Wisdom," in *The New Interpreter's Bible*, ed. Leander E. Keck, 12 vols. (Nashville: Abingdon, 1997), 5:455.
2. Albrecht Oepke, "ἀπόλλυμι, ἀπώλεια, Ἀπολλύων," in *Theological Dictionary of the New Testament*, ed. Gerhard Kittel, Geoffrey W. Bromiley, and Gerhard Friedrich, 10 vols. (Grand Rapids: Eerdmans, 1964), 1:397.

that life reigns here, not death. †Hades was the Greek god of the underworld, whose name became synonymous with his kingdom (see the sidebar "Hades," p. 161). Later, Jesus will say that "the gates of Hades" will not prevail against the Church (Matt 16:18), and he will even declare that his disciples will not be harmed "if they drink any deadly poison" (Mark 16:18 ESV-CE), signifying the defeat of death, a defeat foreseen by the concluding line of this opening exhortation: that **righteousness is immortal**. This undying quality can be obtained by those who love righteousness and seek God sincerely (Wis 1:1), thus treading the path of wisdom.

Ungodly Reasoning

Wisdom 1:16–2:24

After the opening exhortation to love righteousness, the author takes us on a very jarring journey into the mind of the ungodly. This section presents the unsound reasoning of the wicked, which begins with †nihilism—the idea that life is meaningless (1:16–2:5); leads to †hedonism—the view that pleasure is all that matters (2:6–11); and descends into a depravity that brings the wicked to persecute the righteous (2:12–20), all of which shows their spiritual blindness (2:21–24). This glimpse into the reasoning of the wicked is the photonegative of wisdom-seeking. Instead of loving righteousness and seeking the Lord, the ungodly are loving wickedness and seeking †death. It is a cautionary tale of what not to do.

The Ungodly Covenant with Death (1:16–2:5)

¹⁶But ungodly men by their words and deeds summoned death;
considering him a friend, they pined away,
and they made a covenant with him,
because they are fit to belong to his party.
²:¹For they reasoned unsoundly, saying to themselves,
"Short and sorrowful is our life,
and there is no remedy when a man comes to his end,
and no one has been known to return from Hades.
²Because we were born by mere chance,
and hereafter we shall be as though we had never been;
because the breath in our nostrils is smoke,
and reason is a spark kindled by the beating of our hearts.
³When it is extinguished, the body will turn to ashes,
and the spirit will dissolve like empty air.

40

⁴Our name will be forgotten in time,
and no one will remember our works;
our life will pass away like the traces of a cloud,
and be scattered like mist
that is chased by the rays of the sun
and overcome by its heat.
⁵For our allotted time is the passing of a shadow,
and there is no return from our death,
because it is sealed up and no one turns back."

OT: Gen 47:9; 1 Chron 29:15; Job 14:1–2; Ps 39:4–6; Eccles 8:8; Isa 28:15–18
NT: James 4:14

The first verse introduces the erroneous thinking of **ungodly men**, describing   **1:16** their **words and deeds** as expressing a longing for ⁺death. In contrast to the ⁺immortality of the righteous, the unrighteous **summoned death**.[1] They have three types of affiliation with death: friendship, **covenant**, and belonging **to his party**. While Moses could count God as a friend (Exod 33:11), the wicked here long for death as **a friend**. They have the whole concept of friendship backward: a friend should be "an elixir of life" (Sir 6:16), not death itself! The covenant here recalls Judah's "covenant with death, and with Sheol" (Isa 28:15), an alliance with foreign powers that Isaiah criticized. The author, however, is working in moral, not political, terms: **by their words and deeds** the ungodly commit themselves to a permanent and irrevocable relationship with death. One's thoughts lead to words, which lead to deeds. These three are aligned here on a destructive trajectory. The idea of death's **party** or "portion" (Greek *meris* in both cases) will recur in Wis 2:24 and so mark the beginning and end of the unit (1:16–2:24). That the wicked are death's "portion" is in contrast to Israel's being the Lord's "portion" (Deut 32:9; Zech 2:12). The author is setting up a dichotomy, a choice to be in one group or the other. While the righteous have been exhorted to love, think of, and seek wisdom, here the foolish are depicted as adopting false love, false thinking, and a self-destructive pursuit of death.

Now in 2:1, we get to hear the unsound reasoning of the ungodly in their   **2:1–5** own voice. This imaginary depiction of their inner thoughts could be categorized as ⁺diatribe, a technique of Greek rhetoric in which an opponent's views are given voice and then refuted. Their thoughts begin with a ⁺nihilistic meditation on death, for which **there is no remedy** and from which **no one has been known to return**. Similar to other despairing reflections on death in the biblical tradition (2 Sam 14:14; Job 14:1–2; Eccles 8:8), this verse also matches common Greco-Roman views of death: an inevitable and irreparable fate for all. It foreshadows the true test case for a nihilistic viewpoint: resurrection

---

1. The Greek here just says "him," referring back to "death" in 1:12–13, but the Latin includes "death," which is added for clarity in most modern translations.

from the dead. The wicked imply that if someone did return from death, then that would supposedly change their minds (see Luke 16:30). From reflecting on death, the thoughts of the ungodly now turn to birth, the beginning of life. They attribute all of human life to **mere chance**, not to any sort of divine intention. That is, our coming to be, our earthly existence, and our passing on into death are a random set of events without intelligent cause. For them, life is a roll of the dice.

To the wicked, death is the doorway into a permanent and meaningless state of nonexistence, for **hereafter we shall be as though we had never been.** Their understanding of birth and death as chance events is now matched by their view of human nature as merely material: human **reason** is only a **spark** that arises from the body. The soul has no real existence of its own but will be **extinguished** and **dissolve.** Even those who hope for a quasi-immortality in the memories of their families and friends **will be forgotten in time** (see Eccles 1:11; 2:16; 9:5). The nihilistic reasoning of the ungodly is forceful and complete: **no one will remember.**

Using a multitude of metaphors and lines of attack, Wisdom depicts the specious reasoning of the ungodly in all its force. To be sure, many people, both ancient and modern, have thought this way, viewing life as ultimately without meaning and death as the inevitable and final conclusion of the human story.

Let Us Enjoy (2:6–11)

> 6"Come, therefore, let us enjoy the good things that exist,
> and make use of the creation to the full as in youth.
> 7Let us take our fill of costly wine and perfumes,
> and let no flower of spring pass by us.
> 8Let us crown ourselves with rosebuds before they wither.
> 9Let none of us fail to share in our revelry,
> everywhere let us leave signs of enjoyment,
> because this is our portion, and this our lot.
> 10Let us oppress the righteous poor man;
> let us not spare the widow
> nor regard the gray hairs of the aged.
> 11But let our might be our law of right,
> for what is weak proves itself to be useless."

OT: Wis 12:16; Exod 22:21–23; Lev 19:32; Eccles 2:24; Isa 22:13; 56:12
NT: 1 Cor 15:32; 1 Tim 5:1

2:6–8   Now that the ungodly have established their perspective on the ephemeral nature of life and the finality of †death, they proceed to explain their life's project: seeking

Epicureanism

BIBLICAL BACKGROUND

The philosopher Epicurus (341–270 BC) taught that the soul dissipates at death, and therefore the purpose of life is to seek pleasure and avoid pain. Epicurean philosophers are often faulted with promoting the kind of †hedonism mentioned in Wis 2:6–9, but their actual view was more nuanced: seeking to reasonably optimize their experience of life and even focus on mental pleasure. The author of Wisdom is criticizing the faulty logic of hedonism in general rather than a particular philosophical school.

pleasure. To **enjoy the good things that exist** seems harmless enough, but the †hedonistic vision presented here holds personal pleasure as the highest good. No greater sense of fulfillment or meaning is attainable, only a philosophy of *carpe diem*, "seize the day," will do. These aging pleasure-seekers attempt to go back and enjoy life **as in youth**. Indeed, their goals have an adolescent quality: **wine, perfumes**, spring flowers, and rosebud crowns. These tokens do depict in caricature the entertainments enjoyed by the upper classes in the culture of the time: lavish feasts, expensive wines, and so forth. The book of Ecclesiastes also, at times, recommends a kind of *carpe diem* approach to life,[2] but there the commendation is tempered by receiving the goods of creation as gifts from God and by an evaluation of earthly life as vain and toilsome.

The first line of verse 9 could read "Let no meadow be free from our wantonness" (NABRE), alluding perhaps to sexual indulgence.[3] The revelers leave behind **signs of enjoyment**, such as "torn wreaths, smashed cups."[4] Their jaded view of life leads them to see merrymaking as their **portion** (Greek *meris*) and their **lot**. The key word *meris* connects back to Wis 1:16 (death's "party," *meris*) and forward to 2:24 (the devil's "party," *meris*), hinting at the corrupt alliances that characterize such pleasure-seekers. Here the empty inheritance of the ungodly is the silliness of **revelry**, while the true portion or inheritance of the righteous—namely, †immortality—will be far greater.   2:9

The revelers' thoughts now take a dark turn. What had been fun and gaiety in the pursuit of pleasure now becomes vindictive oppression of **the righteous poor man**. This startling shift from pleasure-seeking to abuse of power shows the inevitable progression of selfishness. It begins as a seemingly private matter   2:10–11

2. Eccles 2:24; 3:12–13; 5:18; 8:15; 9:7; 11:9–10.

3. See J. R. Busto Saiz, "The Meaning of Wisdom 2:9a," in *VII Congress of the International Organization for Septuagint and Cognate Studies, Leuven 1989*, ed. Claude E. Cox, SBLSCS 31 (Atlanta: Scholars Press, 1991), 355–59.

4. Paul Heinisch, *Das Buch der Weisheit*, Exegetisches Handbuch zum Alten Testament 24 (Münster in Westalen: Aschendorff, 1912), 46 (my translation).

but quickly moves to the seeking of pleasure at the expense of others.[5] While God wants us to care for the vulnerable and honor **the aged**, self-seeking people tend to exploit them. The hedonists adopt a "**might** makes **right**" view.[6] In their opinion, the **weak** are **useless** and therefore expendable. This twisted thinking was not foreign to a Greek culture that practiced infanticide by exposing to the elements babies who were unwanted because of their weakness or disability. Such disregard for life has similarly informed dictatorial and oppressive regimes in recent times. Eventually, Wisdom will upend the "might makes right" doctrine of the hedonists by contrasting it to God's might: "Your strength is the source of righteousness" (12:16). The seeming power of human oppressors will fade away in the face of God's "sovereignty over all" (12:16).

Let Us Lie in Wait (2:12–20)

> [12]"Let us lie in wait for the righteous man,
> because he is inconvenient to us and opposes our actions;
> he reproaches us for sins against the law,
> and accuses us of sins against our training.
> [13]He professes to have knowledge of God,
> and calls himself a child of the Lord.
> [14]He became to us a reproof of our thoughts;
> [15]the very sight of him is a burden to us,
> because his manner of life is unlike that of others,
> and his ways are strange.
> [16]We are considered by him as something base,
> and he avoids our ways as unclean;
> he calls the last end of the righteous happy,
> and boasts that God is his father.
> [17]Let us see if his words are true,
> and let us test what will happen at the end of his life;
> [18]for if the righteous man is God's son, he will help him,
> and will deliver him from the hand of his adversaries.
> [19]Let us test him with insult and torture,
> that we may find out how gentle he is,
> and make trial of his forbearance.
> [20]Let us condemn him to a shameful death,
> for, according to what he says, he will be protected."

OT: Wis 5:4–5; Gen 37:20; Ps 22:8; Prov 1:11; Isa 3:10 LXX; Jer 11:19
NT: Matt 9:4; 11:27; 27:43; Luke 22:70; John 5:18; 10:36
Lectionary: 1:13–15; 2:23–24: 13th Sunday in Ordinary Time (Year B); 2:1a, 12–22: Votive Mass of the Mystery of the Holy Cross, Fourth Friday of Lent (Years I and II); 2:23–3:9: Ordinary Time, Week 32, Tuesday (Year I)

---

5. It is possible that the author is painting a portrait of Gentile oppression of the Jews in his time.
6. This doctrine is discussed in Plato, *Republic* 338c.

Paideia

Paideia is a key term in Wisdom (1:5; 2:12; 3:11; 6:17; 7:14). It indicates education, discipline, upbringing, or training. Elsewhere in the Greek Old Testament, the word is used to translate the Hebrew term *musar*, which means discipline or correction. Greek culture upheld *paideia* as an ideal to aspire to, that one might be properly educated and formed as a human being in order to achieve a level of ethical and intellectual maturity. Wisdom incorporates the concept of *paideia* into the Jewish wisdom tradition, essentially combining Greek and Jewish ideals of moral formation. In addition, the author will pair *paideia* with observance of the Mosaic law (2:12) in order to show that piety toward God's law goes hand in hand with the pursuit of wisdom, and indeed the two are the same. This teaching agrees with Sirach's perspective that "in all wisdom there is the fulfillment of the law" (Sir 19:20). The New Testament uses *paideia* to refer to Christian formation (Eph 6:4; 2 Tim 3:16; Heb 12:7–11).

The reasoning of the ungodly has progressed from a reflection on the final- **2:12** ity of †death, to an embrace of †hedonism, to a rejection of the weak, and now finally to active persecution of the **righteous man** precisely because of his righteousness. **He is inconvenient** because he **opposes, reproaches,** and **accuses** the wayward for their sins. While the author is not drawing a direct line of connection, one cannot avoid thinking of the biblical prophets here. Isaiah, Jeremiah, and the other prophets consistently rebuke the nation for their disobedience to God's law and their straying from his ways. Here, Wisdom highlights two types of moral error: **sins against the law** and **sins against our training,** which perfectly match the priorities of †Hellenistic Judaism. On the one hand, "sins against the law" refers to transgressions of the law of Moses, the ancient ancestral law of the Jews. On the other hand, "sins against our training [*paideia*]" refers to rejecting the lessons learned in the context of family and, more precisely, Greek education. The erring ones have strayed both from the Jewish ideal of law observance and from the Greek educational ideal of *paideia*.

In verse 13, the righteous man's asserted identity is in focus. According to **2:13–15** the ungodly, the righteous man claims **to have knowledge of God** and to be **a child of the Lord.** These two claims are synonymous. "Knowledge of God" refers primarily to covenantal friendship with God (see Hosea 4:1; 6:6), not to information about him. The righteous man's claim to know God is a claim to be in relationship with him. The righteous man also embodies the true identity of God's people Israel, called by God "my first-born son" (Exod 4:22). God's fatherhood grants the righteous man a filial identity, so that his obedience is rooted in love (see also Isa 63:16; Jer 31:9; Hosea 11:1). Yet the very existence of the righteous person is offensive to the ungodly. For them, **the very sight of him is a burden**. The righteous man is nonconformist: **his ways are strange**. The Jews were known for their distinctive laws and practices (Esther 3:8), so the righteous man again appears to be representative of the nation. Jews were sometimes persecuted in the Hellenistic world for their nonconformist observance of Mosaic customs like sabbath-keeping, circumcision, and rejection of idolatry.

2:16   Despite their ridicule of the righteous, the wicked are self-conscious, resentful of what the righteous man thinks of them: **we are considered by him as something base**. The Greek word for "base" is typically used to indicate debased coinage; here it labels the wicked as counterfeit or fraudulent in the mind of the righteous. Debased coinage also recalls the biblical metaphor of impurities that must be separated from pure metals (Ps 119:119; Isa 1:25; Ezek 22:18). The statement **he avoids our ways as unclean** refers to the fact that Jews would avoid contact with Gentiles in many settings in order not to become ritually and morally impure. The latter part of verse 16 highlights the hope of the righteous: **he calls the last end of the righteous happy**. This wording alludes to the budding doctrine of †immortality in Wisdom (1:16; 2:22–23): the righteous look forward to eternal happiness. Both verses 13 and 16 affirm that God is father of the righteous in line with a wider Old Testament theme (Sir 23:1–4; Isa 63:16; Mal 2:10).

2:17–20   The thinking of the ungodly takes a final, ugly turn toward violence. If the righteous believes himself to be a child of God, observes strange customs, rejects the practices of the wicked, and looks forward to a happy eternity, the only way to cut him down to size is to torture and kill him. The ungodly thus plan to **test** the veracity of the righteous man's hope and character by torturing and killing him. That they question whether **the righteous man is God's son** shows their resentment at the identity of the righteous. The wicked are attempting to put God to the test by doing violence to his righteous one, exactly the opposite of the sincere seekers of God who do not put him to the test (Wis 1:2). Those who have divine sonship also enjoy divine protection (see Ps 91:9–13), but that does not mean they cannot be killed. Testing the beliefs of the righteous turns into a direct trial of the righteous in verse 19: **Let us test him with insult and torture**. His virtues, gentleness and **forbearance**, are being pushed to the limit to try to find his breaking point. Examples of the torture of Jews for their beliefs in this era appear in 2 Macc 6–7, which narrates the martyrdoms of Eleazar and seven Jewish brothers and their mother. Finally, in Wis 2:20, the twisted logic of the ungodly reaches its inevitable conclusion: the murder of the righteous. Yet paradoxically, even in the face of death the righteous **will be protected**. Rather than exempting the righteous from death, the ultimate protection God offers is life after death.

> ## In the Light of Christ (2:12–20)
>
> This passage on the persecution of the righteous foreshadows the plots against the life of Jesus. Like the ungodly here, his enemies harbored evil intentions in their hearts against him (Matt 9:4). Like the righteous man of Wis 2:12–20, Jesus claimed to be God's Son (Matt 27:43; Luke 22:70; John 5:18) and to know God (Matt 11:27; John 7:29). Like the righteous in Wis 2:12, Jesus was unsparing in his reproach of the religious authorities of his day (Matt 23:13–29; Mark 7:8–13). He did not accept the prevailing moral standards of his time but called people to repent (Luke 13:1–5) and held them to account for hypocrisy (see Matt 15:1–9). His opponents were offended by his teachings and even by his very existence. They felt the need to kill him so they could persist in their erring ways (John 7:1; 8:37). Like the righteous in Wis 2:16, Jesus pointed to the happy end of the righteous (Matt 25:46). And like the righteous in Wis 2:19, Jesus was tested "with insult and torture." He too was condemned "to a shameful death" (v. 20). Wisdom foreshadows the life of the righteous Son of God, who represents the people of God and passes the ultimate test of †death. Only through Jesus's victory over death are the righteous fully vindicated.

The Blindness of the Wicked (2:21–24)

²¹Thus they reasoned, but they were led astray,
for their wickedness blinded them,
²²and they did not know the secret purposes of God,
nor hope for the wages of holiness,
nor discern the prize for blameless souls;
²³for God created man for incorruption,
and made him in the image of his own eternity,
²⁴but through the devil's envy death entered the world,
and those who belong to his party experience it.

OT: Wis 1:16; Gen 1:26–27; 3:4; Ps 18:24; Prov 11:18; Sir 17:3
NT: Matt 15:14; John 8:44; Rom 5:12; 6:23; 1 Cor 9:24; Phil 3:14
Catechism: death enters human history, 400
Lectionary: 1:13–15; 2:23–24: 13th Sunday in Ordinary Time (Year B); 2:1a, 12–22: Votive Mass of the Mystery of the Holy Cross, Fourth Friday of Lent (Years I and II); 2:23–3:9: Ordinary Time, Week 32, Tuesday (Year I)

Sin and ignorance go together. Thus, the ungodly are **blinded** by their own   2:21–22
wickedness. In their thoughts, **they were led astray,** wandering off the path of
reason like errant sheep. Wisdom explains that this happened because **they did
not know the secret purposes of God**. The word *mystērion*, translated as "secret

The Devil's Envy

The Life of Adam and Eve (ca. 100 BC–AD 500) is an ancient expansive retelling of the stories of Gen 1–3 that is preserved in Greek and Latin. Its content could be of Jewish or Christian origin, and its date is disputed. In it, the devil describes his envy:

> And the devil sighed and said, "O Adam, all my enmity and envy and sorrow concern you, since because of you I am expelled and deprived of my glory which I had in the heavens in the midst of angels, and because of you I was cast out onto the earth."[a]

Theophilus of Antioch, a late second-century bishop, explains the devil's envy as follows:

> When, then, Satan saw Adam and his wife not only still living, but also having children, he was carried away with spite because he had not succeeded in putting them to death. When he saw that Abel was pleasing to God, he worked on the heart of his brother Cain, and caused him to kill his brother Abel. This is the way that death found a beginning in this world and made its way into every race of man even to this day.[b]

a. *Life of Adam and Eve* 12.1 (trans. M. D. Johnson, *OTP* 2:262).
b. Theophilus of Antioch, "Theophilus to Autolycus," *ANF* 2:105 (translation modified).

purposes," appears to indicate God's plan of †immortality for the righteous.[7] In the New Testament, *mystērion* will similarly be used to indicate God's plan of salvation (see Rom 16:25; Eph 3:3–9; Col 1:26–27). The **wages of holiness** refer to the immortality the righteous will enjoy, the opposite of †death, which St. Paul refers to as the "wages of sin" (Rom 6:23). The idea of immortality as a **prize** also anticipates the Apostle's encouragement to seek the "prize of the upward call" (Phil 3:14; see also 1 Cor 9:24).

2:23–24   In verse 23, the author switches from speaking about immortality to **incorruption**, an Epicurean term (see the sidebar "Epicureanism," p. 43) that refers to the nondecaying material out of which the Greek gods were thought to be composed. This gift—to become incorruptible like God—is offered to **man**, who is made in the image of God. The text could read **the image of his own eternity** or "the image of his own character" (ESV-CE). Either way, humanity is created in God's likeness; a Godlike destiny is therefore fitting. Wisdom is making a subtle point: "Human beings are not created immortal; they are created *for* immortality."[8] Eternal life is a gift of God.

7. See *1 Enoch* 103.2.
8. Michael Kolarcik, "The Book of Wisdom," in *The New Interpreter's Bible*, ed. Leander E. Keck, 12 vols. (Nashville: Abingdon, 1997), 5:465.

However, the **devil's envy** brought **death** into **the world**. Envy is a sinful sadness over the good fortune of others. The devil was envious of the greatness of God and of the good life given to humanity. Here for the first time in the Bible, the serpent in Genesis is explicitly identified as the devil (Greek *diabolos*). This brief verse reveals Wisdom's interpretation of salvation history as the struggle of righteous wisdom seekers to obtain their immortal destiny and to avoid the death spiral of the ungodly, **who belong to** the devil's **party**. This last use of the word for "party, portion, inheritance" (see 1:16; 2:9) illustrates how the wicked are the opposite of the righteous. The righteous are God's "portion," but the devil's "portion" are those who experience death because of their own wickedness (see John 8:44).

The Just and the Unjust

Wisdom 3:1–4:20

After putting the thoughts of the ungodly on display, Wisdom reflects on the happy end of the righteous. They will enjoy immortal life with God, sharing in his reign, while the wicked are punished (3:1–13a). Foreseeing possible objections to this view, the author reflects on the righteous who cannot have children: the barren woman and the eunuch (3:13b–19). He then develops this idea of childlessness with virtue in contrast with the children of illicit unions (4:1–6). He answers yet another objection, insisting that the righteous can enjoy the satisfaction of a life well lived even if they die early (4:7–15), in contrast with the dishonorable fate of the unrighteous at the final judgment (4:16–20). By comparing the final ends of the just and the unjust, Wisdom invites us to choose between two paths.

In the Hand of God (3:1–13a)

---

¹But the souls of the righteous are in the hand of God,
and no torment will ever touch them.
²In the eyes of the foolish they seemed to have died,
and their departure was thought to be an affliction,
³and their going from us to be their destruction;
but they are at peace.
⁴For though in the sight of men they were punished,
their hope is full of immortality.
⁵Having been disciplined a little, they will receive great good,
because God tested them and found them worthy of himself;
⁶like gold in the furnace he tried them,
and like a sacrificial burnt offering he accepted them.

> [7]In the time of their visitation they will shine forth,
> and will run like sparks through the stubble.
> [8]They will govern nations and rule over peoples,
> and the Lord will reign over them for ever.
> [9]Those who trust in him will understand truth,
> and the faithful will abide with him in love,
> because grace and mercy are upon his elect,
> and he watches over his holy ones.
> [10]But the ungodly will be punished as their reasoning deserves,
> who disregarded the righteous man and rebelled against the Lord;
> [11]for whoever despises wisdom and instruction is miserable.
> Their hope is vain, their labors are unprofitable,
> and their works are useless.
> [12]Their wives are foolish, and their children evil;
> [13a]their offspring are accursed.

OT: Wis 2:23; 4:17; Job 12:10; Prov 17:3; Sir 2:5; 41:5–6; Dan 12:3
NT: Matt 13:43; John 10:28; Rom 8:18; 1 Cor 6:2; 2 Cor 4:17; 1 Pet 1:6–7; Rev 20:4
Lectionary: 3:1–9: Masses for the Dead (Christian Burial, All Souls), Common of Martyrs; 2:23–3:9: Ordinary Time, Week 32, Tuesday (Year I)

This most famous passage in the Wisdom of Solomon puts forward the Old Testament's strongest statement regarding life after †death, giving us hope for loved ones who have died. It is commonly read at funeral Masses.

The author builds on the idea that only the members of the devil's party ex- 3:1–3
perience death (2:24). In contrast, **the souls of the righteous are in the hand of God**. The death of the righteous then is not death in its fullest sense but a kind of pseudodeath: **they seemed to have died**. Wisdom appears to delineate two notions of death: physical death experienced by all and a spiritual death experienced only by the wicked (1:16; 2:5; 2:24). While †immortality is a key idea throughout Wisdom, the mention of "souls" illustrates how immortality is envisioned here as a nonbodily afterlife in God's presence. God's "hand" typically symbolizes his power in the Bible, while here it seems to point to the safety and protection he offers to the righteous. Though the wicked torture the righteous on earth (2:19), ultimately **no torment will ever touch them**.

The wicked had sought the death of the righteous one, thinking that they could win a victory over him by killing him, but now we learn that though the righteous one's death appeared to be **an affliction** or his **destruction**, in fact the righteous **are at peace**. "Peace" here indicates reconciliation with God and rest from the assaults of the wicked (see Ps 4:8). While Wisdom develops the notion of immortality in a Greek philosophical mode, it is by no means foreign to the biblical tradition. Many earlier texts envision some kind of after-death experience of life (1 Sam 25:29), peace (Isa 57:1–2), and vision of God (Job 19:26). These vague hopes come into clearer focus here in Wisdom. Death can no longer be considered entirely negative or final. Rather, the righteous enter death as a doorway to another, better existence with God.

3:4   Now the author continues reflecting on the fact that the death of the righteous is misperceived by others. Death appears to be a punishment, yet the **hope** of the righteous is **full of immortality**. Again, this text could be inspired by the actual persecution and martyrdom of Jews in the †Hellenistic age, especially as recorded in the books of Maccabees, where one of the dying retorts to the persecutor: "You dismiss us from this present life, but the King of the universe will raise us up to an everlasting renewal of life, because we have died for his laws" (2 Macc 7:9). While 2 Maccabees emphasizes bodily resurrection, Wisdom highlights the immortality of the soul.

3:5–6   The book of Wisdom regards the suffering of the righteous as discipline from God. This common biblical theme, often displayed in historical terms where the suffering of the nation at the hands of foreign powers is viewed as a trial from God, here is applied on a personal level (Judg 13:1; 1 Sam 12:9; 2 Macc 6:12). The purpose of punishment, testing, and even persecution is the purification of the righteous. **God tested them and found them worthy**, just as "God tested Abraham" by commanding him to sacrifice his son, Isaac (Gen 22:1). The righteous are refined **like gold in the furnace**, a common biblical metaphor (Ps 66:10; Prov 17:3; Isa 48:10; Zech 13:9). However, the notion of the persecuted righteous being akin to a **sacrificial burnt offering** is relatively new (though see Ps 51:17). The death of a martyr is accepted by God as a form of worship, an idea that foreshadows New Testament teaching on offering one's life as a spiritual sacrifice (Rom 12:1; Phil 4:18; 1 Pet 2:5) and forms the basis of the Christian understanding of martyrdom (Phil 2:17; 2 Tim 4:6; Rev 6:9).

3:7–8   The death of the righteous brings on **the time of their visitation**—that is, God's visitation of the righteous (2:20; 3:9). Finally, they are vindicated and **will shine forth** like the stars (see Dan 12:3). Thus, the righteous are not destroyed by death but transformed by it. They are made like God, divinized in divine radiance. They **will run like sparks through the stubble**, an allusion to their participation in God's judgment of the ungodly (Isa 10:17; Obad 1:18; Zech 12:6). The vindication of the righteous includes the punishment of the wicked. The fact that the righteous **will govern nations and rule over peoples** signifies both their ultimate victory over the wicked and their share in God's just government. This theme of God's faithful people sharing God's governance is a consistent element in Scripture's teaching about the end of history (Dan 7:22; Matt 19:28; 1 Cor 6:2; Rev 20:4).

3:9   The righteous are identified as **those who trust in him** and **the faithful**. Faith enables them to understand the truth and to **abide with him in love**. Trust in God leads to understanding, and faith leads to love. The final end of the righteous in communion with God satisfies the desires of both the will and the intellect. Truth and love, in the end, are inseparable. The righteous enjoy

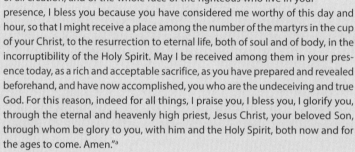

Excerpt from *The Martyrdom of Polycarp*

LIVING TRADITION

The earliest extant Christian martyrdom story, *The Martyrdom of Polycarp* (ca. 155), depicts St. Polycarp offering himself to God as a sacrifice:

> So they did not nail him, but tied him instead. Then, having placed his hands behind himself and having been bound, like a splendid ram chosen from a great flock for sacrifice, a burnt offering prepared and acceptable to God, he looked up to heaven and said: "O Lord God Almighty, Father of your beloved and blessed Son Jesus Christ, through whom we have received knowledge of you, the God of angels and powers and of all creation, and of the whole race of the righteous who live in your presence, I bless you because you have considered me worthy of this day and hour, so that I might receive a place among the number of the martyrs in the cup of your Christ, to the resurrection to eternal life, both of soul and of body, in the incorruptibility of the Holy Spirit. May I be received among them in your presence today, as a rich and acceptable sacrifice, as you have prepared and revealed beforehand, and have now accomplished, you who are the undeceiving and true God. For this reason, indeed for all things, I praise you, I bless you, I glorify you, through the eternal and heavenly high priest, Jesus Christ, your beloved Son, through whom be glory to you, with him and the Holy Spirit, both now and for the ages to come. Amen."[a]

a. *The Martyrdom of Polycarp* 14, in *The Apostolic Fathers: Greek Texts and English Translations*, ed. and trans. Michael W. Holmes, 3rd ed. (Grand Rapids: Baker Academic, 2007), 321–23.

such rewards because **grace and mercy are upon his elect**. They will enjoy God's favor at his "visitation" (Wis 3:7).

After describing the destiny of the righteous (3:1–9), in verses 10–12 the author focuses on the destiny of the wicked. As in chapter 2, the false **reasoning** of the unrighteous leads them to persecute **the righteous man** and so to rebel **against the Lord**. Their false reasoning is not merely an intellectual mistake but is evidence of a rebellion that deserves to be punished. Like the foolish depicted elsewhere in the Bible (Prov 1:7), the wicked despise **wisdom and instruction**. The sad consequence of rejecting the path to wisdom is to become **miserable**. The author expands on what kind of misery he means: **Their hope is vain, their labors are unprofitable, and their works are useless**. The plans of the fool come to nothing. Only by embracing the path to wisdom can one overcome this futility.

In elaborating the sad consequences of rebellion against the Lord, Wisdom describes the effects of unrighteous men's choices on their families: **Their wives are foolish, and their children evil**. "Foolish" means that the wives share in the sinful rebellion of their husbands, and "evil" refers to the regrettable state of being born into a family that has rejected God. The fact that **their offspring**

3:10–11

3:12–13a

are accursed accords with the biblical notion that the curse of sin is inherited (Exod 20:5; Num 14:33; Sir 41:5–7; Jer 32:18), a teaching that is qualified to emphasize personal responsibility (Ezek 18:20). In contrast to the righteous barren woman who has eschewed the bed of sin and yet has "fruit" at the judgment (Wis 3:13b), perhaps the wives and children here are metaphors for sin and its consequences.

In the Light of Christ (3:1–13a)

When Jesus cries out from the cross, "Father, into your hands I commit my spirit!" (Luke 23:46), he is alluding to Ps 31:5. Likewise, Wisdom uses this vocabulary of being in God's hand to describe being safe in his presence after †death. It also foreshadows Good Friday: Jesus's death, though very real, is reversed by his resurrection. Like the righteous described by Wisdom, he only "seemed to have died" (Wis 3:2). Also like them, Jesus is regarded as "punished" (3:3–4; Isa 53:5–6), but by his suffering, Jesus was tested and found worthy (Wis 3:5). Jesus's death is accepted by God as a sacrificial offering (3:6; see Isa 53:10; Heb 10:12). He shines with divine light after his resurrection (Wis 3:7; see Acts 9:3; 26:13) and is given governing authority at God's right hand (Wis 3:8; Rom 8:34).

In the midst of a Greek philosophical culture that promoted the idea of the †immortality of the soul, Wisdom receives the Jewish biblical tradition of bodily resurrection but does not present a fully developed teaching on the afterlife. These differing Greek and Jewish views will eventually be integrated in the Church's profession of the resurrection of the dead:

In death, the separation of the soul from the body, the human body decays and the soul goes to meet God, while awaiting its reunion with its glorified body. God, in his almighty power, will definitively grant incorruptible life to our bodies by reuniting them with our souls, through the power of Jesus' Resurrection. (Catechism 997)

Blessed Is the Barren (3:13b–19)

13bFor blessed is the barren woman who is undefiled,
who has not entered into a sinful union;
she will have fruit when God examines souls.
14Blessed also is the eunuch whose hands have done no lawless
deed,
and who has not devised wicked things against the Lord;

> for special favor will be shown him for his faithfulness,
> and a place of great delight in the temple of the Lord.
> ¹⁵For the fruit of good labors is renowned,
> and the root of understanding does not fail.
> ¹⁶But children of adulterers will not come to maturity,
> and the offspring of an unlawful union will perish.
> ¹⁷Even if they live long they will be held of no account,
> and finally their old age will be without honor.
> ¹⁸If they die young, they will have no hope
> and no consolation in the day of decision.
> ¹⁹For the end of an unrighteous generation is grievous.

OT: Wis 4:1; 2 Sam 12:14; Sir 23:25; Isa 54:1–17; 56:3–5
NT: Matt 17:17; 19:12; Luke 11:29
Catechism: children as supreme gift of marriage, 1652; infertility and spiritual fecundity, 2379

In the Old Testament, children were considered to be visible blessings from God,   **3:13b**
a "reward" for the righteous (Gen 33:5; Ps 127:3) and the means through which
one lived on after †death (2 Sam 18:18; Sir 44:11–13). Sterility was commonly
thought of as a punishment for sexual sin.[1] Thus, barren women and eunuchs,
two classes of people who could not have children, were considered cursed (Gen
16:2) or outsiders. Eunuchs, for example, were specifically excluded from temple
worship and priestly service because of their lack of bodily wholeness (Deut 23:1;
see also Lev 21:20). But now the book of Wisdom, with its new teaching about
the life after death that God has in store for the righteous, turns conventional
thinking on its head by proclaiming both barren women and eunuchs who are
righteous as *blessed* by God!

First, **the barren woman** is proclaimed **blessed** because she is **undefiled**,
bearing the spiritual **fruit** of a righteous life rather than children, who would be
natural "fruit of the womb." She has **not entered into a sinful union**—literally,
she has not had "intercourse with transgression." One who has "intercourse
with transgression" gives birth to sin. Wisdom is here drawing on Isaiah's depiction of Jerusalem as a barren woman restored to fertility by God when the
exiles return (Isa 54) to illustrate the divine approval that the righteous barren
woman will enjoy at her judgment.

Second, **blessed also is the eunuch**. Again, this surprising turnaround for   **3:14**
persons viewed as most unfortunate would startle the original audience. Since
they lacked children of their own, eunuchs could be trusted to seek their master's benefit rather than that of their own households and were therefore often
employed in royal palaces in a variety of roles, such as overseeing the harem
(Esther 2:14–15). Here Wisdom emphasizes the eunuch's **hands**, representing

---

1. Gen 20:18; 30:23; Isa 4:1; Luke 1:25; *1 Enoch* 98.5. See David Winston, *The Wisdom of Solomon*,
AB 43 (Garden City, NY: Doubleday, 1979), 131.

deeds, and his thoughts (**who has not devised wicked things**), drawing our attention back to one of the central threads of the book: the unity of thought and action. Instead of being cursed, as was supposed, the righteous eunuch will enjoy **special favor** and **a place of great delight in the temple**. These extraordinary promises highlight the great reversal of expectations. The idea that the faithful eunuchs would receive a reward in the temple reflects Isaiah's prophecy of the same (Isa 56:5). Since eunuchs were not eligible to enter the temple on earth (Deut 23:1), the heavenly temple is likely what is in view. There, the righteous but childless will enjoy the rewards prepared for them.

3:15   Next the author summarizes the blessing of God, from **root** to **fruit**, on the faithful unable to bear children. Their **good labors** flow forth from the **root of understanding**, showing the organic unity of the moral life. Again, right thinking leads to right acting. The Greek word for "labors" connotes the strenuous, even painful nature of this work. The barren woman and the eunuch may not experience the temporal blessing of children, but they enjoy spiritual fruitfulness because of their virtue.

3:16–19   In an era when few people believed in an afterlife, one's hope rested on one's children and their futures. The message here is that sin is a flimsy foundation and that the posterity of the wicked will come to nothing. If their plans are built on disobedience to God, they will be frustrated. At verse 16, the author contrasts the spiritual "fruit" of the righteous barren with the **children of adulterers** who **will not come to maturity**. For example, the first child of David and Bathsheba, conceived in adultery, died shortly after birth as a punishment for David's sin (2 Sam 12:14–19). The comparison proposed by Wisdom alludes to the punishment of sin that is passed down (Exod 20:5), contrasting the spiritual fruitfulness of those who are righteous but childless with the sterility of those who are wicked but have **offspring**. Again, the author upends conventional thinking that regarded the barren as cursed, teaching the opposite: that the adulterers who appear to be blessed because they have children are actually cursed because of their sin. Minor children are not the exclusive focus here, since the text mentions those who **live long** or reach **old age**. In the last verse of this section, Wisdom summarizes the lesson that **the end of an unrighteous generation is grievous**. Sin has sad, long-lasting consequences, and the way it plays out in people's lives is cause for grief.

This passage must be read, not in isolation, but rather in balance with everything else the Bible teaches about children. In fact, Ezekiel teaches that "the son shall not suffer for the iniquity of the father" (Ezek 18:20), and biblical law forbids executing children for their fathers' crimes (Deut 24:16; 2 Kings 14:6). Some children of sinful unions go on to be faithful to the Lord in extraordinary ways, such as St. Brigid of Ireland (d. 525), born of a concubine slave, and the Slovenian martyr Blessed Lojze Grozde (1923–43), born out of wedlock.

In the Light of Christ (3:13b–19)

Jesus offers a special teaching on eunuchs—a term he uses figuratively to refer to persons who have renounced marriage—that forms the foundation of the Church's practice of celibacy:

> Not all men can receive this precept, but only those to whom it is given. For there are eunuchs who have been so from birth, and there are eunuchs who have been made eunuchs by men, and there are eunuchs who have made themselves eunuchs for the sake of the kingdom of heaven. He who is able to receive this, let him receive it. (Matt 19:11–12)

Isaiah 56:3–5 and Wis 3:14–15 teach that faithful eunuchs are particularly blessed by God, a principle that the Lord applies to all celibates in a surprising way. Vatican II taught that virginity and celibacy "for love of the kingdom of heaven [have] always been held in high esteem by the Church as a sign and stimulus of love, and as a singular source of spiritual fertility in the world."[2] Celibacy has a special role in the life of the Church as an †eschatological sign of undivided devotion to the Lord.

Childlessness with Virtue (4:1–6)

> ¹Better than this is childlessness with virtue, for in the memory
>   of virtue is immortality, because it is known both by God and
>   by men.
> ²When it is present, men imitate it,
> and they long for it when it has gone;
> and throughout all time it marches crowned in triumph,
> victor in the contest for prizes that are undefiled.
> ³But the prolific brood of the ungodly will be of no use,
> and none of their illegitimate seedlings will strike a deep root
> or take a firm hold.
> ⁴For even if they put forth boughs for a while,
> standing insecurely they will be shaken by the wind,
> and by the violence of the winds they will be uprooted.
> ⁵The branches will be broken off before they come to maturity,
> and their fruit will be useless,
> not ripe enough to eat, and good for nothing.

---

2. *Lumen Gentium* 42, in *Vatican Council II: The Conciliar and Post Conciliar Documents*, vol. 1, electronic ed. of the new revised ed., Vatican Collection (Northport, NY: Costello, 1992), 401.

> ⁶**For children born of unlawful unions**
> **are witnesses of evil against their parents when God examines**
> **them.**

OT: Ps 21:10; Prov 10:7; Sir 16:1–3; 23:25; 40:15; Isa 40:24
NT: 1 Cor 4:16; 11:1

4:1–2   After considering the lamentable fate of the unrighteous, Wisdom turns back to the childless righteous, declaring their lot to be **better**. The author uses a key term from Greek philosophy, *aretē*, translated **virtue**. *Aretē* signifies excellence of character, the balanced and integrated living out of all the virtues.[3] The author then defines [†]**immortality** as **the memory of virtue**. That is, the righteous are **known both by God and by men**. While the wicked were sad that no one would remember them (Wis 2:4), the righteousness of the upright will be remembered. Nevertheless, immortality is more than being recalled with nostalgic fondness by friends and family—it is being known by God forever.

Virtue can feel like a distant, abstract concept, but **when it is present** people are drawn to **imitate it**. It is easier to practice righteousness when one has the example of godly people to follow. They are sadly missed when they are not to be found. Here Wisdom depicts virtue as **crowned in triumph**, marching in parade as a **victor in the contest for prizes**. The author likely has in mind Greek athletic contests, wherein winners were awarded crowns of leaves. The Greek philosophical tradition also conceived of the ethical life as a kind of battle which could result in victory. Unlike the rewards of this world, which are always tainted by selfish ambition and compromise, the rewards of virtue **are undefiled**.

4:3–6   Returning to earlier themes, verses 3–6 reflect on the **prolific brood of the ungodly**, declaring them useless and insecurely rooted. Using the common biblical metaphor of a fruit tree (Ps 1:3; Prov 11:30; Jer 17:8), the author describes how in all stages of its growth, from seedling to branch to harvest time, the "tree" of the unrighteous will be unfruitful. When the **wind** of divine judgment comes, they will not be able to stand but **will be uprooted**. When the harvest comes, **their fruit** will be unripe and **good for nothing**. Again, it is best to consider this as a description of the spiritual sterility of wickedness, not as a condemnation of **children born of unlawful unions**. Rather than the children bearing guilt themselves, their existence is evidence of the guilt of their parents. In the time of divine judgment, they will be **witnesses of evil against their parents**. This meditation extends and concludes the inspired author's comparison of virtuous childlessness and unrighteous fertility: the barren can be blessed by God, while those with many children can suffer from spiritual fruitlessness. The point is not to stigmatize children born out of wedlock, who are not at fault, but to commend a godly way of life.

---

3. Aristotle, *Nichomachean Ethics* 2.6.15.

In the Light of Christ (4:1–6)

Wisdom describes how people imitate virtue when it is present. St. Paul takes up this idea when he urges his hearers to "be imitators of me, as I am of Christ" (1 Cor 11:1). We need virtuous people like the saints to pattern our lives after. They help us understand how to apply the principles of godly living in daily life.

Wisdom depicts the moral life in athletic terms: "crowned in triumph, victor in the contest for prizes" (4:2). The New Testament likewise draws on the imagery of Greek athletic competition to describe pursuing the Christian life as a kind of footrace that would result in being "crowned" (1 Cor 9:24; 2 Tim 4:8; Heb 12:1). St. Paul calls Christians "more than conquerors through him who loved us" (Rom 8:37; see also 1 John 5:4–5). In Revelation, Jesus promises the best reward "to him who conquers": the prize of communion with God forever (Rev 2:7, 11, 17, 26).

The Righteous Man at Rest (4:7–15)

⁷But the righteous man, though he die early, will be at rest.
⁸For old age is not honored for length of time,
nor measured by number of years;
⁹but understanding is gray hair for men,
and a blameless life is ripe old age.

¹⁰There was one who pleased God and was loved by him,
and while living among sinners he was taken up.
¹¹He was caught up lest evil change his understanding
or guile deceive his soul.
¹²For the fascination of wickedness obscures what is good,
and roving desire perverts the innocent mind.
¹³Being perfected in a short time, he fulfilled long years;
¹⁴for his soul was pleasing to the Lord,
therefore he took him quickly from the midst of wickedness.
¹⁵Yet the peoples saw and did not understand,
nor take such a thing to heart,
that God's grace and mercy are with his elect,
and he watches over his holy ones.

OT: Wis 3:3; Gen 5:21–24; Job 32:9; Sir 44:16; Isa 57:1–2; Dan 13:45–51
NT: Heb 11:5; 2 Pet 2:7 ·
Catechism: spiritual maturity in children, 1308

4:7–9   At this point, Wisdom has professed a happy end for the **righteous** and explained how this outcome applies to the cases of the barren woman and the eunuch. Now he will confront one more question: What if the righteous **die early**? As with the previous considerations, this question is firmly situated in conventional human thinking. †Death is the ultimate negative event, the thing to be avoided at all costs. But the author's interpretation of death differs from the typical view. According to him, the death of the righteous is an entrance into eternity, into **rest**. He will build his case from the biblical wisdom tradition and from one specific example.

First, he insists that **old age is not honored for length of time**. On the contrary, **understanding is gray hair**. That is, one earns honor by wisdom and understanding, not mere length of **years**. While literal old age and understanding often go together, the author is happy to separate the concepts, arguing that the young can be wise and the aged can be foolish. For him, actual understanding and **a blameless life** are accounted as "old age" from God's vantage point. Thus, one could be young and yet possess the honor of old age. For example, the young Daniel is accorded the privilege or status of an elder (Dan 13:50). Ancient Greek and Roman literature also took up this theme of the youthful wise.[4] Wisdom thus qualifies the earlier biblical praise for old age (Prov 16:31; 20:29), insisting that it is virtue, not mere years, which make old age venerable.

4:10–14   Next, the author gives us an example of the principle he is advocating: Enoch. Genesis recounts how "Enoch walked with God; and he was not, for God took him" (Gen 5:24). Despite the brevity of this account, Enoch's strange fate of being taken up by God made him a figure for endless speculation and comment in the Jewish tradition. His fate is an early indication of belief in the afterlife. Enoch's story is vastly expanded by the pseudepigraphal work *1 Enoch*.

Wisdom will consistently leave out the names of figures being discussed, so that the reader must guess as to whom the author is referring, especially in chapters 10–19 (see the sidebar "Why Omit Names?," p. 61). When saying that he **pleased God**, Wisdom alludes to the †Septuagint translation of Gen 5:24, which reads that Enoch "was well pleasing to God, and he was not found, because God transferred him" (NETS). The author explains that God snatched Enoch away from earth before he could be corrupted by it (Wis 4:11). The next verse describes the **fascination of wickedness** as a potential intellectual temptation, what the Christian tradition names as the vice of curiosity. This is paired with

---

4. For example, Menander states, "Not from white heads has wisdom always sprung; Nature gives it to some men while they're young" (John Maxwell Edmonds, *The Fragments of Attic Comedy*, vol. IIIB [Leiden: Brill, 1961], 811; frag. 639). Also, †Philo says, "Those who have passed a long span of years in the existence of the body without goodness or beauty of life must be called long-lived children who have never been schooled in the learning worthy of grey hairs; but he who is enamoured of sound sense and wisdom and faith in God may be justly called elder" (*On Abraham* 271 [Colson, Whitaker, and Earp, LCL 6:457]).

Child Saints

As quoted in the Catechism (1308), St. Thomas Aquinas teaches,

> Age of body does not determine age of soul. Even in childhood man can attain spiritual maturity: as the book of *Wisdom* says: "For old age is not honored for length of time, or measured by number of years" [Wis 4:8]. Many children, through the strength of the Holy Spirit they have received, have bravely fought for Christ even to the shedding of their blood.[a]

Similarly, St. Pius X is reputed to have said, "There will be children among the saints."[b] The Church has in fact canonized many children in recent times, such as St. Dominic Savio (died age fourteen), St. Maria Goretti (age eleven), Ss. Francisco and Jacinta Marto (ages ten and nine, respectively), as well as many child martyrs of China, Japan, Spain, Korea, Uganda, and Mexico.

a. *Summa Theologica* III, q. 72, a. 8.
b. Luigi Borriello, "Anche i bambini possono essere santi," *Rivista di Vita Spirituale* 56 (2002): 443–68.

Why Omit Names?

Wisdom, in 4:10–14, omits the name of Enoch and later will leave out the names of the Egyptians, the Hebrews, Adam, Noah, Abraham, and others (see especially chap. 10). This practice, which might seem strange to us, was in fact a rhetorical device called antonomasia that was used by other Greek authors. Like a riddle or an inside joke, it forces the reader to guess what the author is talking about, rewarding those who recognize the references and stoking the curiosity of those who do not.

roving desire, which denotes a more bodily lust. Sinful desire—intellectual or bodily—twists the human mind away from God. But Enoch was **perfected in a short time**, so God took him as though he had already achieved the goal of **long years**—namely, moral uprightness. Thus, Wisdom interprets Enoch's early death not as a tragedy but as a divine rescue from a wicked world, an honor.

Sadly, however, **the peoples saw and did not understand**. Even though   4:15
people knew Enoch's story, they did not **take such a thing to heart**. The correct interpretation of Enoch's story is that early death is not necessarily tragic but can be God's way of extricating the righteous from the wicked world before it is too late. This segment concludes (v. 15b) with a repetition of an earlier lesson (3:9b), that **God's grace and mercy are with his elect**. His provident care protects those he has chosen even when they die.

The Anguish of the Unrighteous (4:16–20)

¹⁶The righteous man who has died will condemn the ungodly who
  are living,
and youth that is quickly perfected will condemn the prolonged
  old age of the unrighteous man.
¹⁷For they will see the end of the wise man,
and will not understand what the Lord purposed for him,
and for what he kept him safe.
¹⁸They will see, and will have contempt for him,
but the Lord will laugh them to scorn.
After this they will become dishonored corpses,
and an outrage among the dead for ever;
¹⁹because he will dash them speechless to the ground,
and shake them from the foundations;
they will be left utterly dry and barren,
and they will suffer anguish,
and the memory of them will perish.

²⁰They will come with dread when their sins are reckoned up,
and their lawless deeds will convict them to their face.

OT: Wis 2:22; 3:2; Job 18:17; Ps 37:13; Isa 14:19; 2 Macc 7:14
NT: Matt 12:41–42; Luke 11:31; Acts 1:18

4:16   These verses close out the logic of chapters 3–4, finish the refutation of the
ungodly reasoning in chapter 2, and set the stage for the description of the final
judgment in the next chapter. God will bring about a great reversal in the end.
Those who appear to be useless and foolish because of their attentiveness to God
will be vindicated after †death. Wisdom does not adopt the wicked's negative
view that death is a final end (2:5), but instead teaches that even after death the
righteous **will condemn the ungodly who are living**. And the righteous youth
who die before their time will also, by their example, **condemn the prolonged
old age of the unrighteous man**. This talk of condemnation might strike us
as terribly vindictive, but it is a common biblical theme. For example, one of
the youthful Maccabean martyrs condemns the evil Seleucid king to his face
(2 Macc 7:14). St. Stephen condemns the Sanhedrin for their obstinace (Acts
7:51–53). Jesus even forecasts how the "men of Nineveh" and the "queen of
the South" will judge his generation (Matt 12:41–42). As the righteous have a
share in God's rule (Wis 3:8), they also share in his judgment. God reverses the
expectations of the wicked. Those who prosper despite their sin in this life will
be judged unworthy in the next.

4:17–20   On this side of eternity, however, the wicked **will not understand** the Lord's
purposes for the righteous man (see Wis 2:22). They will witness his death and

consider him accursed (3:2). The death of the righteous appears to indicate their undoing, but in fact it is their destiny. They are truly **safe**. The unrighteous, in their ignorance of God's intentions, will scornfully laugh at the righteous, but the Lord, in turn, **will laugh them to scorn**, a quotation of Ps 2:4. That is, he will judge the wicked, who will not enjoy God's presence after death but instead **will become dishonored corpses**, a figurative way of describing their condemnation. Biblical tradition regarded burial with one's ancestors a happy fate, but a lack of burial with the probability of the corpse's mutilation was a terrible judgment (Ps 79:2–3; Isa 66:24; 2 Macc 5:10). The author develops the theme of God's judgment of the unrighteous with multiple forceful concepts: they will be dashed, shaken, dried out, **suffer anguish**, and be forgotten. While the "memory of virtue is †immortality" (Wis 4:1), **the memory** of the wicked **will perish**. The final verse describes how the wicked will finally be called to account for **their sins** and **deeds** at the final judgment, which will be the subject of the next chapter.

Reflection and Application (3:1–4:20)

Wisdom 3–4 prompts us to think about our end and to remember the inevitability of our own deaths. For the righteous, †death can be a moment of triumph, of joy, of entering God's presence for all eternity—what we all long for. But for the wicked, death is a time of fearful judgment. Most people today prefer to keep thoughts of death at arm's length to make ourselves feel safe. However, in previous generations, Christian homes would typically have a *memento mori*—an artistic token of death such as a skull—in plain sight. These symbolic reminders provided occasion for reflection, something that would call to mind the end of one's earthly journey and perhaps help a person to live more wisely in the present. Wisdom would have us seek to bear spiritual fruit in this life in order that we might share in God's triumphant reign in the next.

The Judgment of the Ungodly and the Reward of the Righteous

Wisdom 5:1–23

The final judgment of the wicked, mentioned at the end the preceding chapter (4:20), is now on full display with the righteous facing their oppressors after †death. The erroneous thinking of the ungodly, illustrated in chapter 2, is now thoroughly refuted by God's vindication of the righteous. Wisdom 5:1–2 sets the scene of this confrontation, while in verses 3–13 the voice of the unrighteous returns—this time in anguish and thoroughly aware of their terrible mistake. After a brief summary (v. 14), the author turns to the glorious destiny of the righteous and describes God's final defeat of his enemies at the end of the chapter (vv. 15–23).

The Judgment of the Ungodly (5:1–14)

---

¹Then the righteous man will stand with great confidence
in the presence of those who have afflicted him,
and those who make light of his labors.
²When they see him, they will be shaken with dreadful fear,
and they will be amazed at his unexpected salvation.
³They will speak to one another in repentance,
and in anguish of spirit they will groan, and say,
⁴"This is the man whom we once held in derision
and made a byword of reproach—we fools!
We thought that his life was madness
and that his end was without honor.
⁵Why has he been numbered among the sons of God?
And why is his lot among the saints?

⁶So it was we who strayed from the way of truth,
and the light of righteousness did not shine on us,
and the sun did not rise upon us.
⁷We took our fill of the paths of lawlessness and destruction,
and we journeyed through trackless deserts,
but the way of the Lord we have not known.
⁸What has our arrogance profited us?
And what good has our boasted wealth brought us?
⁹All those things have vanished like a shadow,
and like a rumor that passes by;
¹⁰like a ship that sails through the billowy water,
and when it has passed no trace can be found,
nor track of its keel in the waves;
¹¹or as, when a bird flies through the air,
no evidence of its passage is found;
the light air, lashed by the beat of its pinions
and pierced by the force of its rushing flight,
is traversed by the movement of its wings,
and afterward no sign of its coming is found there;
¹²or as, when an arrow is shot at a target,
the air, thus divided, comes together at once,
so that no one knows its pathway.
¹³So we also, as soon as we were born, ceased to be,
and we had no sign of virtue to show,
but were consumed in our wickedness."
¹⁴Because the hope of the ungodly man is like chaff carried by the
     wind,
and like a light hoarfrost driven away by a storm;
it is dispersed like smoke before the wind,
and it passes like the remembrance of a guest who stays but a day.

OT: Job 9:25–26; Ps 1:4; Prov 4:18–19; 30:19; Isa 59:9–13; Ezek 33:10
NT: Matt 13:43; Col 1:12
Catechism: the Last Judgment, 1038–41

Now the author describes **the righteous man** on the day of judgment. He **will   5:1
stand with great confidence** to face down his oppressors before the bar of divine
justice. At first, the Judge does not appear, and the scene depicts a confrontation between the righteous and the wicked, as if the defendant is brought into a
courtroom only to see the victim of his crime in the gallery. The biblical perspective on social justice looms large in Wisdom's description of divine judgment
of the individual. The people of God were the underdogs of the ancient world.
They were routinely sidelined, overlooked, overtaxed, oppressed, and otherwise
persecuted by powerful nations: Assyria, Babylon, Persia, Greece, Rome. For
them, justice has the distinctive flavor of vindication, when the oppressed are

finally released from slavery, political domination, and unfair treatment. While the persecuting nations may **make light of his labors**, the righteous man keenly feels the injustice of his situation.

5:2–3   Earlier, the ungodly had laughed at the righteous man and even tested him "with insult and torture" (Wis 2:19), thinking that a shameful †death would prove how wrong he was. However, in this scene after death, the wicked see the righteous man, and **they will be shaken with dreadful fear**. They will be **amazed** when they see the one they mocked experiencing **unexpected salvation**. Watching him suffer and die brought peace of mind to the ungodly, confirming their false reasoning. But now that they see him standing at the judgment, they are rightly seized with terror. Their faults are now on display, and their faulty ideas have been overturned. The presence of the righteous man is living proof that he was right, and they were wrong. In response, **they will speak to one another in repentance**. Their regret overwhelms them. The soliloquy of the wicked that ensues exposes the foolishness of their moral reasoning. It is followed by a description of the triumph of the righteous (vv. 15–16) and God overwhelming his enemies—both tokens of final judgment. Earlier, the thoughts of the wicked attracted them to sin (2:1–20), but now they are afflicted by biting regret in the face of full knowledge.

5:4–5   The speech of the ungodly begins: **This is the man whom we once held in derision**. They speak about the righteous man and their previous negative reaction to him. **We thought that his life was madness**, when in fact his devotion to God was perfectly sane. This verse anticipates God's fight "against the madmen" (v. 20). Wickedness is the truly insane choice. Though the death of the righteous was **without honor** among men, now he is honored by God and **numbered among the sons of God** and **saints** or "holy ones" (NABRE), a term that probably refers to the angels who dwell with God (see Job 38:7; Ps 89:5, 7).

5:6–7   Finally, the wicked realize that when the righteous man they scorned was avoiding their "ways" (Wis 2:16), it was they who had **strayed from the way of truth**. Their sinful pleasure-seeking was a fool's errand, which brought darkness upon them rather than **the light of righteousness**. This passage may allude to Mal 4:2, where the prophet predicts, "For you who fear my name the sun of righteousness shall rise, with healing in its wings." The happy fate of the righteous will not be shared by those who devote themselves to **the paths of lawlessness and destruction**. The **way of the Lord**, the way of wisdom, is often described in Scripture as a level, straight path, while the path of the fool is rocky, twisted, and even **trackless**. The book of Wisdom here contrasts observance of God's law to the lawless ways of the wicked. Righteousness is ordered and directed, leading us to God, while wickedness opposes God's order, introducing confusion and chaos.

5:8–13   While the wicked had thought of themselves as pleasure-seekers, enjoying the "good things" of life (Wis 2:6), now they realize that their **arrogance** and

boasted wealth have brought them no profit in the end. What seemed like success was mere self-seeking, which at the final judgment is worthless. **All those things**—their enjoyments, their money, their pride—**have vanished like a shadow**. They are realizing too late how vacuous their pursuits have been. What follows is a powerful poetic meditation on the fleeting nature of human life apart from God. It picks up on the Old Testament theme of how short and ephemeral our life is: "The grass withers, the flower fades" (Isa 40:7). The soliloquy of the wicked employs three metaphors for this purpose: **a ship**, **a bird**, and **an arrow**. Each passes through water or air, but leaves **no trace**, **nor track**, **no sign** behind. Yet they realize that **we also, as soon as we were born, ceased to be**. That might sound strange, but they realize that the only human thing of enduring worth is **virtue**. Only righteousness is immortal (Wis 1:15), but they have none since they were **consumed** in **wickedness**.

Arriving at this realization after death means it is too late for the wicked to   5:14
alter their course, to change their ways and build a lasting legacy of virtue. Yet it is not too late for us, the readers of Wisdom. The final verse of the section comments on the prospects of the ungodly, declaring their hope to be **like chaff**, **like a light hoarfrost, like smoke**, or like a one-night **guest**. They devoted their time to worthless pursuits, so their lives fade without record, and they stand condemned at the final judgment, groaning with regret over their foolish lives. The dramatic scene here is meant as a warning. We do not want to come to the end of life full of regret and anguish, but rather we desire to "stand with great confidence" (5:1) among God's holy ones, the angels and saints.

The Reward of the Righteous (5:15–23)

> [15]But the righteous live for ever,
> and their reward is with the Lord;
> the Most High takes care of them.
> [16]Therefore they will receive a glorious crown
> and a beautiful diadem from the hand of the Lord,
> because with his right hand he will cover them,
> and with his arm he will shield them.
> [17]The Lord will take his zeal as his whole armor,
> and will arm all creation to repel his enemies;
> [18]he will put on righteousness as a breastplate,
> and wear impartial justice as a helmet;
> [19]he will take holiness as an invincible shield,
> [20]and sharpen stern wrath for a sword,
> and creation will join with him to fight against the madmen.
> [21]Shafts of lightning will fly with true aim,
> and will leap to the target as from a well-drawn bow of clouds,

²²**and hailstones full of wrath will be hurled as from a catapult;**
the water of the sea will rage against them,
and rivers will relentlessly overwhelm them;
²³**a mighty wind will rise against them,**
and like a tempest it will winnow them away.
Lawlessness will lay waste the whole earth,
and evil-doing will overturn the thrones of rulers.

OT: Deut 32:40–42; Pss 7:10–13; 91:4; Isa 28:5; 59:16–17; 62:3
NT: Luke 1:52; 1 Cor 9:25; Eph 6:13–17; 2 Tim 4:8
Catechism: our vocation to beatitude, 1716–29

5:15–16   While the hope of the wicked will come to nothing, **the righteous** will **live for ever**. Here the author affirms that the †immortality of righteousness (Wis 1:15) pertains to the actual lives of righteous persons. Before, he described humanity as created "in the image" of God and his eternity (2:23), but now immortality is characterized as a **reward** (Greek *misthos*), to be with God forever. The Greek *misthos* could even be translated as "pay" or "wages." God's concern for the righteous is emphasized as he **takes care of them**. Their eternal reward is represented by **a glorious crown** or **beautiful diadem**, imagery common to biblical kingship (Isa 28:5; 62:3), as well as †Hellenistic kingship. Just as the author addresses his audience as "rulers" (Wis 1:1), "kings," and "judges" (6:1), so here he paints a picture of eternity where the righteous are elevated to royal status to reign with God (see 3:8). This divine crown is the opposite of the "crown [or dominion] of †Hades" in 1:14—one will be crowned either with †death or with divine radiance.[1] Before, being "in the hand of God" was highlighted (3:1); now the righteous receive their crowns **from the hand of the Lord**, and they are covered **with his right hand** and shielded with **his arm**. God's hand symbolizes his power, which here protects the righteous from persecution by the wicked and from divine judgment. This consoling depiction of the joyful destiny of the righteous interrupts Wisdom's doleful meditation on the fate of the ungodly (5:1–14), which will now be developed with a poetic description of God's †wrath.

5:17–23   Building on the imagery of Isa 59:16–17, the author describes the Lord putting on battle armor to mete out punishment on the ungodly. Each piece of armor is given a metaphorical meaning: the **armor** is **zeal**; the **breastplate** is **righteousness**; the **helmet** is **justice** (Greek *krisis*, "judgment"); the **shield** is **holiness**; and the **sword** is **wrath**. While these metaphors may feel distant and antiquated to us, they reflect a time when kings like Alexander the Great (356–323 BC) really did put on battle armor and lead their troops in the field. God's purpose here is **to repel**, or to punish, **his enemies**. **Creation** itself plays a role in the execution of divine justice here. It is "armed" by the Lord (Wis 5:17)

---

1. The Greek word *basileion* appears in both Wis 1:14 ("dominion") and 5:16 ("crown").

Immortality in the Old Testament

BIBLICAL BACKGROUND

The doctrine of immortality, which Wisdom fully embraces, developed slowly over time in the Old Testament. The earliest hints of immortality in the Bible are indirect. In the garden of Eden, God warns that eating of the tree will bring †death (Gen 2:17), indicating that human death has not yet entered the world, and the serpent tempts Eve with the false promise, "You will not die" (3:4). Though Adam and Eve did die, Enoch mysteriously "walked with God; and he was not" (5:24). While Genesis is tantalizingly reticent on the meaning of this episode, Wisdom takes it up with enthusiasm as indicating that Enoch's life continued with God (Wis 4:10–14). Later, Elijah is taken up to heaven in a whirlwind, another hint of immortal life with God (2 Kings 2:11). Other passages in the Old Testament emphasize the resurrection of the dead, who are reunited with their bodies in a transformed state (Ps 16:10; Isa 26:19; Dan 12:2–3; 2 Macc 7:14). In the time that Wisdom was written, Greek philosophy in general viewed immortality as an innate characteristic of the human soul. While avoiding the topic of bodily resurrection, Wisdom upholds the immortality of the soul, at least for the righteous (Wis 2:23; 3:1–4; 5:15), and teaches that immortality is "the result of a positive divine judgment over one's decisions and actions."[a] The Catholic Church teaches both that the soul is immortal and that it will be reunited with the body in the general resurrection of the dead (Catechism 366, 997, 1005).

a. Michael Kolarcik, "The Book of Wisdom," in *The New Interpreter's Bible*, ed. Leander E. Keck, 12 vols. (Nashville: Abingdon, 1997), 5:447.

and joins **with him to fight against the madmen**. This cooperation of creation demonstrates God's sovereignty, recalling the plagues against Egypt and foreshadowing the topics of chapters 11–19. God's "enemies" are "madmen" who have rejected the sanity of wisdom and have opted for the lunacy of evildoing.

The author continues using the divine warrior imagery to show God taking up his complete power as creator, weaponizing **lightning** as his arrows (as in Pss 18:14; 77:17; 144:6) and the **clouds** as his **bow**. He will use **hailstones, the water of the sea,** and the **rivers** to overwhelm his opponents. The **catapult** (Greek *petrobolos*) here likely denotes a ballista, a siege engine like a giant bow used to hurl stones and other projectiles. Water's destructive power was feared in biblical times (Song 8:7; Matt 7:25–27), and here God wields its full force against his foes. The final image of this panoply of divine weapons is the weather: **a mighty wind** and **a tempest**. Like the other elements of creation that the divine warrior has used to upend his enemies, here the weather itself is turned against them.

The final two lines of this section could easily be misread: **Lawlessness will lay waste the whole earth, and evil-doing will overturn the thrones of rulers**. Yet these two lines contain the message of the book of Wisdom in miniature. The "lawlessness" and "evil-doing" they indicate do not refer to God's activity of punishing his enemies. Rather, they refer to the very sins of the wicked, which bring calamity upon them. When people practice lawless deeds (Wis 1:9; 3:14; 4:20; 5:7) and do evil, they "bring on destruction by the works of [their] hands" (1:12). This warning about the dire consequences of sin sets the stage for the author's next appeal to seek wisdom.

Reflection and Application (5:1–23)

The biblical authors struggled with a problem that is close to home: life is not fair. Sometimes the bad guys win, and the good guys lose. Or, in biblical terms, the righteous suffer while the wicked prosper. Yet we have hope. As Christians, we hope in God and his justice, that in the end he will vindicate the righteous and punish the wicked. All the injustices we have experienced will be reversed by his awesome power. His justice does not only punish, but it redeems.

The despairing regret of the ungodly (Wis 5:4–13) is a reminder of what not to do. We do not want to look back on our life from our deathbed with such miserable disappointment. While the bitter taste of guilt is familiar, our guilt can be canceled by the mercy of God in Christ as we turn from sin, believe in Jesus, receive the grace of baptism, and regularly confess our sins in the Sacrament of Reconciliation. With his grace, we can come to conquer sin and truly live for God so that we do not find the regret piling up in our hearts.

Lastly, the vision of God as a mighty warrior conquering his foes should encourage our hearts. In times when injustice prevails and the strong trample the weak, we can remember that God's power is greater than any other, that he is master of all creation, and that in the end "every knee [will] bow . . . and every tongue confess that Jesus Christ is Lord" (Phil 2:10–11). His enemies will eventually be defeated. Even now, we are called to unite ourselves to him in spiritual battle and "put on the whole armor of God" (Eph 6:11) so that we too can wage war against sin, temptation, and the demonic forces that oppose God and his people.

Honor Wisdom

Wisdom 6:1–21

This last chapter of the first part of Wisdom on Life and Death (1:1–6:21) returns to the theme of the opening exhortation, advising kings and judges to seek wisdom. While at first the author warns of the "strict inquiry" awaiting rulers and the terror of divine justice (vv. 1–11), he closes by expressing the desirability of wisdom and showing how desire for her "leads to a kingdom" (vv. 12–21). This balanced approach both warns and welcomes potential readers. Only by seeking wisdom can rulers truly establish and strengthen their rule.

O Monarchs, Learn Wisdom (6:1–11)

¹Listen therefore, O kings, and understand;
learn, O judges of the ends of the earth.
²Give ear, you that rule over multitudes,
and boast of many nations.
³For your dominion was given you from the Lord,
and your sovereignty from the Most High,
who will search out your works and inquire into your plans.
⁴Because as servants of his kingdom you did not rule rightly,
nor keep the law,
nor walk according to the purpose of God,
⁵he will come upon you terribly and swiftly,
because severe judgment falls on those in high places.
⁶For the lowliest man may be pardoned in mercy,
but mighty men will be mightily tested.
⁷For the Lord of all will not stand in awe of any one,
nor show deference to greatness;
because he himself made both small and great,

and he takes thought for all alike.
⁸But a strict inquiry is in store for the mighty.
⁹To you then, O monarchs, my words are directed,
that you may learn wisdom and not transgress.
¹⁰For they will be made holy who observe holy things in holiness,
and those who have been taught them will find a defense.
¹¹Therefore set your desire on my words;
long for them, and you will be instructed.

OT: Wis 1:1; Lev 20:26; Deut 1:17; Ps 2:10; Prov 8:15–16; 22:2
NT: Luke 12:48; John 19:11; Rom 13:1; James 2:1; 3:1; 1 Pet 3:15
Catechism: governing well, 2213; political authority, 2234–37
Lectionary: 6:1–11: Ordinary Time, Week 32, Wednesday (Year I)

6:1–3   This new section begins with three exhortations to **listen**, **learn**, and **give ear**. Like other biblical invitations to listen to wisdom or to the word of a prophet, this triple command enjoins the audience to obey. But who is the audience? The author addresses his speech to **kings** and **judges**, but it is unlikely that actual Gentile kings and judges would be reading the philosophical writings of an Alexandrian Jewish sage. Rather, the author is addressing all people, and in particular, the people most likely to read his writing: young, literate Jewish men in Alexandria who are tempted to give up their religion and wholly assimilate to the wider †Hellenistic culture. He uses the literary device of addressing his audience as "kings" for two reasons. First, this rhetorical technique flatters his audience—much more than the paternal "my son" of Proverbs or Sirach—making them more receptive to his message by recognizing their "kingship" over their own lives and moral choices. Second, the author embraces a vision of Hellenistic kingship as an office won by moral achievement rather than received by inheritance, and then he expands that concept to include all people. Everyone, by virtue of their moral lives, can obtain kingship in this sense.[1] These "kings" **rule over multitudes**, but again, this is a literary device, a way of indirectly speaking to the actual audience.

Their **dominion** and **sovereignty** point us toward the nature of political power in ancient times. While modern people tend to think of power as coming from the consent of citizens, the Bible and other ancient sources emphasize that power comes from God. Here, that teaching is on display: **your dominion was given you from the Lord**. The universality of this power, which in part justifies the rhetoric of "kings," rests on the "dominion" over creation which God grants to Adam and Eve in Gen 1:26, 28. Thus all human beings have been granted power, and that power ultimately comes from God. Jesus says as much to Pontius Pilate: "You would have no power over me unless it had

---

1. See Judith H. Newman, "The Democratization of Kingship in Wisdom of Solomon," in *The Idea of Biblical Interpretation: Essays in Honor of James L. Kugel* (Leiden: Brill, 2004), 309–28.

Philo of Alexandria

BIBLICAL BACKGROUND

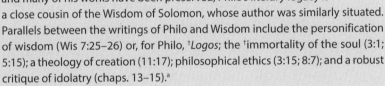

Philo (ca. 20 BC–AD 50) was an important Jewish philosopher in the city of Alexandria, born into a wealthy family. He became involved in the city's politics and famously led a Jewish delegation from Alexandria to an audience with the emperor Caligula at Rome (ca. AD 40). Philo was a prolific writer. His works include philosophical treatises, biblical commentaries that emphasize allegorical interpretation, expositions of biblical law, and historical writings. Since his own life and career straddled the Greek and Jewish communities of Alexandria and many of his works have been preserved, Philo's literary legacy is a close cousin of the Wisdom of Solomon, whose author was similarly situated. Parallels between the writings of Philo and Wisdom include the personification of wisdom (Wis 7:25–26) or, for Philo, †*Logos*; the †immortality of the soul (3:1; 5:15); a theology of creation (11:17); philosophical ethics (3:15; 8:7); and a robust critique of idolatry (chaps. 13–15).[a]

a. For more on this topic, see David Winston, *The Wisdom of Solomon*, AB 43 (Garden City, NY: Doubleday, 1979), 59–63.

been given you from above" (John 19:11). St. Paul likewise asserts that "there is no authority except from God" (Rom 13:1). Yet with power comes responsibility, so the Lord **will search out your works and inquire into your plans**. The rest of this section focuses on the heightened moral accountability of the powerful to God.

The author judges the rulers of the world as lacking. They **did not rule** **6:4–5** **rightly, nor keep the law**. This negative evaluation of their moral performance sadly could be applied universally to all rulers and all persons, since "there is none that does good" (Ps 14:3). "Keeping the law" typically refers to observing the law of Moses (Deut 17:19; Ps 119:34), but here, since Gentile kings are the ostensible audience, we must consider a wider definition of "law." Likely, the Wisdom author shares a concept of law with †Philo of Alexandria, who viewed the law of Moses as a copy of the natural law.[2] The Gentile kings, like the pre-Mosaic patriarchs, could observe the law even with no knowledge of the Sinai code (Rom 2:14–16). Their violation of the law will receive an especially harsh response from God **because severe judgment falls on those in high places**. Increased responsibility means increased accountability. The New Testament also emphasizes this principle: "To whom much is given, of him will much be required" (Luke 12:48; see also James 3:1).

2. See John W. Martens, *One God, One Law: Philo of Alexandria on the Mosaic and Greco-Roman Law* (Leiden: Brill, 2003), 103–30.

6:6   Wisdom adopts a complementary view—that **the lowliest man may be pardoned in mercy**. J. A. F. Gregg explains: "The thought is not that the poor man is compensated for his low estate by a corresponding laxity on God's part, but that necessity presses on the humble with an insistence special to their case."[3] This sentiment is similar to that expressed in Prov 6:30, where "men do not despise a thief if he steals to satisfy his appetite when he is hungry." Thus, the weak and lowly may experience additional mercy from God because of the exigencies of their situations, while **mighty men will be mightily tested** because of their grave responsibilities. Wisdom here explains the final judgment as a trial in which a person and his works are "tested" or examined by God, a metaphor that alludes to the refining of precious metals (1 Cor 3:13–15; 1 Pet 1:7).

6:7–8   The author pivots from the comparison of small and great to emphasize the Lord's impartiality in judgment. He does not **stand in awe of any one, nor show deference to greatness**. His impartiality is meant to be embodied by the leaders of Israel (Lev 19:15; Deut 1:17) and by all leaders. While we instinctively detest unfair judgments, we are also prone to make them for our own advantage. But God is free from the social situations which incline us toward partiality and away from justice. His judgments are always true. Lest anyone think that the Lord's impartiality will make him soft on the kings and judges, Wisdom reminds us that **a strict inquiry is in store for the mighty**. The Lord's impartiality will lead him to be "strict," but not unfairly so.

6:9   The author addresses his audience directly yet again: **To you then, O monarchs, my words are directed**. The Greek word for "monarch" is *tyrannos*, which is a technical term for "an absolute ruler who has no hereditary rights to his throne."[4] Many kings in the Hellenistic period did not inherit their thrones but won them on the battlefield. While these kings could be viewed as upstarts of doubtful legitimacy, they do allow for the universalizing of the kingship ideal that Wisdom embraces. If anyone can be a king, then maybe everyone is a "king" in a certain sense. Words of wisdom are meant for learning, and learning has a moral purpose: that the hearers may **not transgress**. The Greek concept of education as philosophy—literally, "love of wisdom"—is a moral ideal, not just an intellectual one. When people learn, they should become good, not just clever.

6:10–11   The next verse doubles down on this theme: **they will be made holy who observe holy things in holiness**. Wisdom is quietly marrying the Greek educational ideal (*paideia*) with observance of the law of Moses as prescribed in Leviticus: "You shall be holy to me; for I the Lord am holy" (Lev 20:26). While much of the biblical discussion of holiness centers on ritual purity rules,

---

3. J. A. F. Gregg, *The Wisdom of Solomon in the Revised Version with Introduction and Notes*, Cambridge Bible for Schools and Colleges (Cambridge: Cambridge University Press, 1922), 56.

4. James M. Reese, *The Book of Wisdom, Song of Songs*, Old Testament Message 20 (Wilmington, DE: Michael Glazier, 1983), 62.

St. Cyril of Jerusalem on the *Sancta sanctis*

The *Sancta sanctis* ("holy things to the holy"), a phrase present in Eastern liturgies when the priest invites the communicants forward (Catechism 948, 1331), shares some key words with Wis 6:10: "For they will be made holy who observe holy things in holiness." St. Cyril of Jerusalem (ca. 315–87) explains the phrase in describing the order of the liturgy following the Lord's Prayer:

> Next the priest says: "Holy things to the holy." Holy are the offerings after they have received the visitation of the Holy Spirit; and you are holy after you have been privileged to receive the Holy Spirit. So things and persons correspond: both are holy. Next you say: "One is holy, one is the Lord, Jesus Christ." For truly One only is holy—holy, that is, by nature; yet we also are holy, not, indeed, by nature, but by participation, training, and prayer.
>
> After this you hear the chanter inviting you with a sacred melody to communion in the holy mysteries, in the words: "O taste and see that the Lord is good." Entrust not the judgment to your bodily palate, but to unwavering faith. For in tasting you taste, not bread and wine, but the . . . Body and Blood of Christ.[a]

a. "Foreword to Catecheses 13–18," in *The Works of Saint Cyril of Jerusalem*, ed. Bernard M. Peebles, trans. Leo P. McCauley and Anthony A. Stephenson, FC 64 (Washington, DC: Catholic University of America Press, 1970), 202.

here Wisdom emphasizes the moral dimension of holiness as encompassing justice. When the author continues with **those who have been taught them will find a defense**, we must ask what "them" refers to. It refers to the "holy things" mentioned in the first part of the verse, which could be defined as "the unassailable proofs of grace which Yahweh will give in faithfulness to His promises,"[5] but perhaps they refer to the laws of God (compare Isa 55:3). It is of no little importance that Wisdom holds out to ostensibly Gentile kings the possibility of their becoming holy, a status previously reserved for Israel alone. This notion illustrates Wisdom's universal interest in all of humanity's relation to God.

The last verse of this section highlights the necessity of **desire** and longing for wise **words** in order to obtain true understanding. Desire is often a negative notion in the Bible, associated with temptation to sin, but here, the positive potential of desire is taught. The author explains desire as a necessary first step in the acquisition of wisdom. In order to obtain wisdom, people must first realize that they do not possess it, and then they must desire it.

5. Friedrich Hauck, "ὅσιος, ὁσίως, ἀνόσις, ὁσιότης," in *Theological Dictionary of the New Testament*, ed. Gerhard Kittel, Geoffrey W. Bromiley, and Gerhard Friedrich, 10 vols. (Grand Rapids: Eerdmans, 1964), 5:491.

Desire for Wisdom Leads to a Kingdom (6:12–21)

[12]Wisdom is radiant and unfading,
and she is easily discerned by those who love her,
and is found by those who seek her.
[13]She hastens to make herself known to those who desire her.
[14]He who rises early to seek her will have no difficulty,
for he will find her sitting at his gates.
[15]To fix one's thought on her is perfect understanding,
and he who is vigilant on her account will soon be free from care,
[16]because she goes about seeking those worthy of her,
and she graciously appears to them in their paths,
and meets them in every thought.

[17]The beginning of wisdom is the most sincere desire for
instruction,
and concern for instruction is love of her,
[18]and love of her is the keeping of her laws,
and giving heed to her laws is assurance of immortality,
[19]and immortality brings one near to God;
[20]so the desire for wisdom leads to a kingdom.

[21]Therefore if you delight in thrones and scepters, O monarchs
over the peoples,
honor wisdom, that you may reign for ever.

OT: Wis 1:1; Prov 1:20–33; 8:1–21; Sir 6:18–31
NT: Matt 7:7–8
Lectionary: 6:12–16: 32nd Sunday in Ordinary Time (Year A)

6:12–13   While verses 1–11 served as a warning of divine judgment to rulers, verses 12–21 present an appealing invitation to seek Lady Wisdom. In the Bible, wisdom is personified as a woman (Prov 1; 8; Sir 6:18–31), in part because of the feminine gender of the Hebrew and Greek words for wisdom, *hokhmah* and *sophia*. Desire for her, mentioned briefly in verse 11, now becomes the dominant theme (Wis 6:13, 17, 20). **Wisdom is radiant and unfading**, resplendent with divine glory. Verse 12 uses the same verbs for pursuing wisdom as Wis 1:1–2: to **love, seek,** and find. Loving and seeking precede finding her. She is not an unattainable goal but is in fact **easily discerned by those who love her**. Turning one's heart and mind toward wisdom requires only an interior movement of thought. That desire, once made manifest, will receive an enthusiastic response from Lady Wisdom, who **hastens to make herself known**. Her effort here is reminiscent of Proverbs' depiction of Lady Wisdom crying aloud in the streets and welcoming those who want understanding (Prov 1:20; 8:1–7).

Wisdom, Moses, and the Natural Law

BIBLICAL BACKGROUND

Philosophically minded †Hellenistic Jewish writers tended to equate wisdom with keeping the law of Moses (a Jewish ideal) and the law of Moses with the natural law (a Greek ideal). These examples show the fusion of the Greek and Jewish ideals that was a unique feature of this time period:

4 Maccabees

Reason, I suggest, is the mind making a deliberate choice of the life of wisdom. Wisdom, I submit, is knowledge of things divine and human, and of their causes. And this wisdom, I assume, is the culture [*paideia*] we acquire from the Law, through which we learn the things of God reverently and the things of men to our worldly advantage. The forms of wisdom consist of prudence, justice, courage, and temperance.[a]

Philo, *On the Life of Moses*

But Moses is alone in this, that his laws, firm, unshaken, immovable, stamped, as it were, with the seals of nature herself, remain secure from the day when they were first enacted to now, and we may hope that they will remain for all future ages as though immortal, so long as the sun and moon and the whole heaven and universe exist.[b]

a. *4 Maccabees* 1.14–17 (trans. H. Anderson, *OTP* 2:545).
b. Philo, *On the Life of Moses* 2.13–14 (Colson, Whitaker, and Earp, LCL 6:457).

The author depicts an eager student of wisdom, **who rises early to seek her,** finding her **sitting at his gates,** the place of local judgments by elders in biblical times (Deut 21:19; Ruth 4:1; Zech 8:16). Seeking the advice of the elders would be practically the same as seeking her. Again, the author emphasizes how effortless the turn toward wisdom can be: one need only **fix one's thought on her.** That alone constitutes **perfect understanding.** This conversion, which begins in the mind, leads to being **free from care,** though perhaps "free from anxiety" would be a better translation. Wisdom does not make one cavalier and carefree, but free from the common interior conflict that afflicts the minds of those trapped in sin (see Rom 2:15).   6:14–15

The next verse repeats the idea that wisdom eagerly seeks her seekers, appearing to them and meeting them **in every thought.** That she appears **in their paths** indicates her nearness, as in Proverbs' description of Lady Wisdom—"In the paths she takes her stand" (Prov 8:2)—or in Solomon's prayer for wisdom, which will soon be the focus of attention (1 Kings 3:9). **Those worthy of her** are people of good will who are willing to learn, who desire instruction.   6:16

Verses 17–20 form a special chain syllogism called a †sorites, where each predicate serves as the subject of the next clause. The logic appears to be strict   6:17–20

Desire to Rule

BIBLICAL
BACKGROUND

The author of Wisdom teaches that "desire for wisdom leads to a kingdom" (Wis 6:20), indicating that those who seek wisdom would make good rulers. Early in the Bible, God entrusts "dominion" (Gen 1:26, 28) over the earth to Adam and Eve. When Joseph interprets Pharaoh's dream, he recognizes God's wisdom in Joseph and grants him high office (Gen 41:38–40). Daniel and his companions similarly display great wisdom in the court of a foreign king and are appointed to powerful roles (Dan 1:17–20). It is good for rulers to be wise and for the wise to become rulers, "for the throne is established by righteousness" (Prov 16:12). In the New Testament, Jesus promises "twelve thrones" to his disciples (Matt 19:28). St. Paul teaches that believers will "reign in life through the one man Jesus Christ" (Rom 5:17) and that they "sit with him in the heavenly places" (Eph 2:6). Revelation promises that the redeemed will be "a kingdom and priests to our God, and they shall reign on earth" (Rev 5:10). The Bible thus consistently depicts salvation in terms of participating in God's righteous rule. The Wisdom of Solomon does not encourage the powerless to seek to dominate others, but to humble themselves to seek wisdom and so come to share in God's reign.

---

but is in fact poetic and playful. **Desire for instruction** leads to **love**. The lines could read "concern for instruction is love, and love is the keeping of her laws."[6] Observance of her laws leads to †**immortality**, which **brings one near to God**. Finally, this sequence highlights desire for wisdom as leading inevitably to the "kingdom" that would-be rulers desire. Yet it is not desire for a kingdom that leads to wisdom, but rather **desire for wisdom leads to a kingdom**. The author is piling up ideas in an impressive array, where wisdom, wisdom's laws (a summation of natural law and its embodiment in Mosaic law), immortality, and communion with God are all held together at once.

6:21   The last verse of this section summarizes the point of the sorites sequence: that **if you delight in thrones and scepters**—that is, if you want power—then seek wisdom first **that you may reign for ever**. The author is deliberately tricking his audience by equivocating on the meaning of power. Earthly rulers desire earthly power, but what Wisdom holds out to wisdom seekers is far more enduring and valuable: an eternal reign with God in his kingdom (3:8; Dan 7:27).

---

6. In the RSV-2CE, "of her" is added twice for clarity.

Part 2

Solomon's Pursuit of Wisdom

Wisdom 6:22–9:18

Solomon's Quest for Wisdom

Wisdom 6:22–8:1

The first major part of the Wisdom of Solomon (1:1–6:21) focused on the just and the unjust, the final judgment, and the need for wisdom for all kings and rulers. This new section begins the second major part: "Solomon's Pursuit of Wisdom" (6:22–9:18). Solomon has not been mentioned in the book until this point, but his fictive voice will become dominant for chapters 6–9 as the author impersonates the greatest of all wise men to describe Lady Wisdom's grandeur and to invite the reader to join Solomon's great quest for her.[1]

How Wisdom Came to Be (6:22–25)

> [22]I will tell you what wisdom is and how she came to be,
> and I will hide no secrets from you,
> but I will trace her course from the beginning of creation,
> and make knowledge of her clear,
> and I will not pass by the truth;
> [23]neither will I travel in the company of sickly envy,
> for envy does not associate with wisdom.
> [24]A multitude of wise men is the salvation of the world,
> and a sensible king is the stability of his people.
> [25]Therefore be instructed by my words,
> and you will profit.

OT: Wis 7:13; Tob 12:11; Job 28:20–28; Prov 8:23–31; 11:14; 29:4; Sir 10:1–3
NT: James 3:14–16

---

1. I will refer to this fictive Solomon simply as "Solomon," without circumlocutions like "Pseudo-Solomon."

This brief passage turns from admonitions to rulers (in particular, 1:1–15; 6:1–21) to explain how wisdom forms the foundation for the life of the righteous. It introduces Solomon's speech, which will occupy the next few chapters. The "I" is King Solomon.

6:22   The author, in Solomon's voice, describes what he is setting out to do: **tell you what wisdom is and how she came to be**. Here, he follows Proverbs in personifying divine wisdom as a female character, Lady Wisdom. The origins of wisdom are explored in Prov 8:23–31 and in Job 28:20–28. She participates in the event of creation. Wisdom 6:22 presents wisdom as not mere practical knowledge but a cosmic power, a spiritual entity close to God. The author entices his audience by professing to **hide no secrets** and get at the heart of the matter. His insistence on transparency is a technique to secure the attention of his audience, yet it may also represent a response to esoteric philosophies or mystery cults of the time, which regarded knowledge of spiritual things as best kept reserved only for initiates.

6:23–25   After promising to tell the truth, Solomon goes on to reject **the company of sickly envy**, a personified antithesis of Lady Wisdom. Envy is no minor fault but rather the entry point of the devil and †death into human history (Wis 2:24). It **does not associate with wisdom** because it is a vice of self-seeking, the greedy "evil eye," the opposite of wisdom's beneficent and generous nature (James 3:14–16). Wisdom is of practical value, since **a multitude of wise men is the salvation of the world**, in that wise leaders prevent disaster and preserve peace. Wisdom, again, is not merely technical knowledge or shrewdness but involves an interior transformation of the individual. The one who is wise is not simply smart but just. Wise rulers produce good outcomes. The statement that **a sensible king is the stability of his people** serves as an introduction to the words of Solomon, known in the Bible as the wisest of all kings and resembling †Plato's "philosopher-king."[2] Here again, Wisdom is bringing together the Hebrew biblical tradition with Greek philosophy, proposing Solomon as the ideal of both systems. The final verse repeats the invitation to listen, promising **profit** to the attentive.

Solomon's Mortality (7:1–6)

---

¹I also am mortal, like all men,
a descendant of the first-formed child of earth;
and in the womb of a mother I was molded into flesh,
²within the period of ten months, compacted with blood,

---

2. *Republic* 473c. Plato (ca. 427–347 BC) believed that philosophers, those who love wisdom, would be the best kind of rulers.

from the seed of a man and the pleasure of marriage.
³And when I was born, I began to breathe the common air,
and fell upon the kindred earth,
and my first sound was a cry, like that of all.
⁴I was nursed with care in swaddling cloths.
⁵For no king has had a different beginning of existence;
⁶there is for all mankind one entrance into life, and a common
    departure.

OT: Wis 10:1; Gen 2:7; Job 10:9–12; Ps 139:13–16; Sir 17:1
NT: Luke 2:12; Acts 14:15; 1 Cor 15:47–49; 1 Tim 6:7

Solomon has already introduced his main character, Lady Wisdom, but now   7:1-2
he will introduce himself, revealing that the words directed to kings and rulers (Wis 1:1; 6:1), the whole book thus far, were coming from a genuine king.
Yet this king is not self-important but adopts a humble attitude. To begin his
autobiography, this Solomon freely acknowledges, **I also am mortal, like all
men**. While Lady Wisdom may be a cosmic power that worked with God at the
beginning of the universe (Prov 8:30), Solomon is a mere mortal. He goes into
detail about his gestation, birth, and babyhood to make a simple point: that he
was great and wise not by nature but only because wisdom made him so. He
affirms his brotherhood with all men as **a descendant of the first-formed child
of earth**—that is, Adam. The author is inviting all the readers to put themselves
in Solomon's shoes, to become kings, so to speak, by obtaining wisdom like the
original Solomon did.

He goes on to describe his gestation **in the womb of a mother**, drawing
on a widely held ancient view of embryology, in which the woman's blood is
coagulated by addition of **the seed of a man**. The liquid is then **molded** and
compacted into a baby like the way cheese is formed from liquid milk and
rennet (Job 10:10). This act of creation is regarded as a marvel of divine power
(see Ps 139:13–16). The Greek words translated **pleasure of marriage** are more
literally rendered "the pleasure that accompanies sleep." The author names
ten lunar **months** as the gestation period, which is roughly equivalent to nine
solar months.

Finally, when Solomon is born, he begins **to breathe the common air**, show-   7:3
ing again his identification with all of humanity. He uses a very unusual word
to describe **earth** as being **kindred**: *homoiopathē*, meaning "having similar
feelings or passions." This word reappears in Acts 14:15, where Paul and Barna-
bas protest being worshiped, telling their audience, "We also are men, of like
nature [*homoiopathē*] with you." While the earth does not share human nature,
it is the source of the "dust" out of which Adam was formed (Gen 2:7) and the
destination of the "dust" to which all human beings will return (3:19). **Like that
of all**, Solomon's first utterance was a **cry**. While it is easy for us to dismiss a

newborn's cry as a routine aspect of birth, the ancients were apt to ascribe deep significance to this fact. For example, Seneca asks, "Do you not see what sort of life Nature has promised us—she who has decreed that the first act of man at birth should be to weep?"[3] This concept is enshrined in the *Salve Regina* prayer, which regards earthly life as "mourning and weeping in this valley of tears."

7:4–6   Solomon emphasizes his dependence in infancy, being **nursed with care in swaddling cloths**. As the source of his nourishment and care, his mother would come to symbolize Lady Wisdom (see Wis 7:11–12). The "swaddling cloths" here are perhaps referred to in Luke 2:12, where the baby Jesus is famously depicted as wrapped in such. In the final verses of this section, Solomon insists again that **no king** has a better beginning, but **all mankind** shares the same origin story and will share the same **departure** story. Both birth and †death are universal. Solomon's admission of his own mortality prepares the reader to understand his love affair with wisdom as a pattern to be imitated. Solomon was not unique in nature. Everyone can follow his example since it was not some innate status that made him great but his embrace of Lady Wisdom.

Solomon's Love for Wisdom (7:7–14)

> [7]Therefore I prayed, and understanding was given me;
> I called upon God, and the spirit of wisdom came to me.
> [8]I preferred her to scepters and thrones,
> and I accounted wealth as nothing in comparison with her.
> [9]Neither did I liken to her any priceless gem,
> because all gold is but a little sand in her sight,
> and silver will be accounted as clay before her.
> [10]I loved her more than health and beauty,
> and I chose to have her rather than light,
> because her radiance never ceases.
> [11]All good things came to me along with her,
> and in her hands uncounted wealth.
> [12]I rejoiced in them all, because wisdom leads them;
> but I did not know that she was their mother.
> [13]I learned without guile and I impart without grudging;
> I do not hide her wealth,
> [14]for it is an unfailing treasure for men;
> those who get it obtain friendship with God,
> commended for the gifts that come from instruction.

OT: Wis 8:5; 1 Kings 3:5–15; 2 Chron 1:6–12; Job 28:15–19; Prov 3:13–15; Sir 47:12–17

---

3. *Ad Polybium de consolatione* 4.3, quoted in David Winston, *The Wisdom of Solomon*, AB 43 (Garden City, NY: Doubleday, 1979), 166.

NT: Matt 6:33; 13:45–46; Luke 12:33
Lectionary: 7:7–11: 28th Sunday in Ordinary Time (Year B); 7:7–10, 15–16: Common of Doctors of the Church

Solomon now recalls his famous prayer for wisdom early in his reign as king of   7:7
Israel. He sought the Lord for "an understanding mind to govern your people"
(1 Kings 3:9). The Lord honored Solomon for his prayer and promised to give
him not only wisdom but also "riches and honor" (3:13). Here, the author,
speaking in Solomon's name, recalls this famous episode to demonstrate that
Solomon's wisdom had a divine origin. God gave him wisdom as a gift. Solomon
was an ordinary person, but he was given an extraordinary gift by God. This gift
was **the spirit of wisdom**—not merely intelligence but a supernatural insight,
a spiritual gift (see Isa 11:2).

Solomon **preferred her to scepters and thrones**, meaning that he loved   7:8–10
wisdom more than power. For him, great wealth was **as nothing in comparison
with her**. People have always been motivated by money and power, but Solomon
was motivated by wisdom. The author has already shown us how those who
seek after mere power are on a fool's quest (Wis 4:20–5:14), but those who are
on the quest for wisdom will receive true power in the end (6:21). Solomon is
an example for all. Since he is a human being like us, we can make his prayer
for wisdom our own.

Solomon compares wisdom to power, riches, gems, health, light—all good
things. Yet they all pale in comparison with her. Wisdom is the key that unlocks
every other good. Jesus teaches a similar lesson: "Seek first the kingdom of God
and his righteousness, and all these things will be added to you" (Matt 6:33
ESV-CE). In comparison with wisdom, **gold is but a little sand**, and **silver
will be accounted as clay**. Wisdom surpasses physical **health and beauty**,
which are so highly prized by the world. The divine **radiance** of wisdom is
always shining.

Solomon received **all good things** from wisdom, and wisdom herself was   7:11–14
the source: she **leads them** and **was their mother**. Solomon's riches, power,
and enjoyment of life all derived from wisdom. Our author could not be more
emphatic regarding wisdom's outsized and singular role at unleashing all the
good things of life.

As in Wis 6:22, he pledges to hold nothing back. Wisdom is not a secret
knowledge for the elite or esoteric few but available to all, so he says, **I do not
hide her wealth**. Wisdom's wealth is productive and manifold, **an unfailing
treasure for men**. Unlike gold, which diminishes as it is spent, wisdom ac-
cumulates the more it is sought and employed. Finally, he reveals the destiny
of the wisdom seeker: **friendship with God**. Wisdom *is* friendship with God.
And "friendship with God" is a classic definition of the foremost Christian
virtue of charity.[4]

---

4. See Thomas Aquinas, *Summa Theologica* I-II, q. 23, a. 1.

Reflection and Application (7:7–14)

This Solomonic praise of wisdom as the good above all other goods, as the source of all good things, as the only thing to be sought, prompts us to reflect on our own motivations. Wealth, power, reputation, and health are good things, yet if we make them our primary aim, we err. Scripture constantly reminds us that earthly wealth is temporary and perishable (Matt 6:19–20), and that we cannot take it with us after †death (1 Tim 6:7). On the contrary, giving money to the poor in this life will be rewarded (Tob 12:9; Prov 28:27), and what awaits us is an "inheritance that is imperishable, undefiled, and unfading" (1 Pet 1:4). Wisdom, charity, and friendship with God are the enduring goods we should pursue.

Solomon Taught by Divine Wisdom (7:15–22a)

---

¹⁵May God grant that I speak with judgment
and have thoughts worthy of what I have received,
for he is the guide even of wisdom
and the corrector of the wise.
¹⁶For both we and our words are in his hand,
as are all understanding and skill in crafts.
¹⁷For it is he who gave me unerring knowledge of what exists,
to know the structure of the world and the activity of the
    elements;
¹⁸the beginning and end and middle of times,
the alternations of the solstices and the changes of the seasons,
¹⁹the cycles of the year and the constellations of the stars,
²⁰the natures of animals and the tempers of wild beasts,
the powers of spirits and the reasonings of men,
the varieties of plants and the virtues of roots;
²¹I learned both what is secret and what is manifest,
^{22a}for wisdom, the fashioner of all things, taught me.

OT: Wis 3:1; Exod 35:31; 1 Kings 4:29–34; Job 12:10; Prov 8:30
NT: Eph 6:19–20
Catechism: God teaches us about creation, 216; God and scientific research, 283; Creator of seen and unseen, 325; art as practical wisdom, 2501

7:15   Now that he has outlined his great love for wisdom, Solomon asks God for eloquence to speak about her. Solomon's speech about wisdom will arrive at its climax beginning in Wis 7:22b. In the first verse of this section, Solomon explains that God is **the guide even of wisdom**, though wisdom is the mother of all good things (vv. 11–12). As when he admitted his mortality to illustrate that wisdom was God's gift (v. 6), now again he explains that wisdom and God are closely linked. He prays to **have thoughts worthy of what I have received**, acknowledging his dependence on God for the gift of wisdom.

Earlier in the book the righteous were "in the hand of God" (Wis 3:1), but **7:16** here Solomon and his words **are in his hand**. Both the human person and his knowledge—**we and our words**—are in God's hand. Solomon regards wisdom not as a one-time gift but as an ongoing divine enlightenment of his intellect, foreshadowing a Christian view of faith as a cooperation between the grace of God and human intellect and will (Catechism 155).

The author will develop the idea of Solomon's wisdom into a multifaceted description of intellectual enlightenment. When it came to knowledge, the ancients did not prize expertise in a narrow subject area but rather a plenitude of knowledge across all areas. The great philosopher Aristotle (384–322 BC), for example, wrote on the soul, physics, rhetoric, animals, dreams, and many other topics. Solomon will thus expound his own wisdom by describing the wide variety of topics that he understood. However, he constantly acknowledges God as the source of **all understanding and skill in crafts**.

The discussion now turns to the **structure of the world** and calendrical **7:17–20** matters, **the beginning and end and middle of times** as well as **the cycles of the year**. In contemporary times, the calendar has been fixed and perfected for centuries, universally agreed upon, and so people rarely think about it. Yet in the ancient world, the calendar was a matter of constant dispute, research, and discussion. The length of the solar year, which is about 365 and one-quarter days, can be fixed only through painstaking astronomical observations and detailed calculation over extended periods of time. The winter and summer **solstices** were especially important occasions for precise observation and were even incorporated into the architecture of many ancient temples.[5] Solomon's knowledge of astronomy is thus very fitting. He is portrayed as receiving from God knowledge of the structure of the universe, insight into what modern people might call the very fabric of space-time. This kind of knowledge is no pedestrian know-how but reaches to the heights of the mysteries of physics, time, and the whole created order.

Solomon is familiar with everything from the lofty heights of cosmology down to the commonplace affairs of **animals**, **spirits**, humans, **plants**, and folk medicines. What we would divide into disciplines like zoology, demonology, botany, and psychology are all united in Solomon's wisdom.

Solomon now summarizes his knowledge of all things as encompassing **7:21–22a** **what is secret and what is manifest**. Solomon's gift of divine knowledge and wisdom is all-encompassing. As the highest prize to be sought, as the means to

---

5. For example, the Egyptian temple of Ramesses II at Abu Simbel is aligned so that the light of dawn on the winter solstice penetrates to the inner sanctum.

Josephus on Solomon

BIBLICAL
BACKGROUND

The ancient Jewish historian Josephus (AD 37–ca. 100) explains Solomon's wisdom as follows:

> Now the sagacity and wisdom which God had bestowed upon Solomon was so great, that he exceeded the ancients, insomuch that he was no way inferior to the Egyptians, who are said to have been beyond all men in understanding; indeed, it is evident that their sagacity was very much inferior to that of the king's. He also excelled and distinguished himself in wisdom above those who were most eminent among the Hebrews at that time for shrewdness: those I mean were Ethan, and Heman, and Chalcol, and Darda, the sons of Mahol. He also composed books of odes and songs, a thousand and five; of parables and similitudes, three thousand; for he spoke a parable upon every sort of tree, from the hyssop to the cedar; and in like manner also about beasts, about all sorts of living creatures, whether upon the earth, or in the seas, or in the air; for he was not unacquainted with any of their natures, nor omitted inquiries about them, but described them all like a philosopher, and demonstrated his exquisite knowledge of their several properties. God also enabled him to learn that skill which expels demons, which is a science useful and curative to men.[a]

a. Josephus, *Jewish Antiquities* 8.42–45. Translation modified and taken from *The Works of Josephus: Complete and Unabridged*, trans. William Whiston (Peabody, MA: Hendrickson, 1987), 214.

friendship with God, wisdom includes all types of knowledge and insight, even into secret and hidden matters. Later, Jesus will assure his hearers that "nothing is hidden that shall not be made manifest" (Luke 8:17). In the last line, Wis 7:22a, Solomon attributes all his knowledge to the teaching he received from **wisdom** herself. This line will serve as a springboard into the most elaborate description of wisdom yet.

The Nature of Wisdom (7:22b–8:1)

> [22b]For in her there is a spirit that is intelligent, holy,
> unique, manifold, subtle,
> mobile, clear, unpolluted,
> distinct, invulnerable, loving the good, keen,
> irresistible, [23]beneficent, humane,
> steadfast, sure, free from anxiety,
> all-powerful, overseeing all,
> and penetrating through all spirits
> that are intelligent and pure and most subtle.

²⁴For wisdom is more mobile than any motion;
because of her pureness she pervades and penetrates all things.
²⁵For she is a breath of the power of God,
and a pure emanation of the glory of the Almighty;
therefore nothing defiled gains entrance into her.
²⁶For she is a reflection of eternal light,
a spotless mirror of the working of God,
and an image of his goodness.
²⁷Though she is but one, she can do all things,
and while remaining in herself, she renews all things;
in every generation she passes into holy souls
and makes them friends of God, and prophets;
²⁸for God loves nothing so much as the man who lives with
wisdom.
²⁹For she is more beautiful than the sun,
and excels every constellation of the stars.
Compared with the light she is found to be superior,
³⁰for it is succeeded by the night,
but against wisdom evil does not prevail.
^{8:1}She reaches mightily from one end of the earth to the other,
and she orders all things well.

OT: Exod 24:16–17; Song 6:10; Sir 24:3–8
NT: John 1:5; Col 1:15; Heb 1:2–3; 4:12–13; James 3:17
Catechism: the order of creation, 302; the beauty of truth, 2500
Lectionary: 7:22b–8:1: Ordinary Time, Week 32, Thursday (Year I)

Starting in 7:22b, the spirit of wisdom is described exhaustively with twenty-   7:22b–23
one attributes in three sets of seven. The numeric symbolism here involves
multiplying two important numbers—seven (signifying perfection) times three
(signifying wholeness) to make twenty-one—but it also likely relates to the
alphabet. The Hebrew alphabet contains twenty-two letters. The twenty-one
descriptive terms lead up to the crowning twenty-second term: "wisdom"
(v. 24). A similar pattern is found in Deut 32:1–3, where the name of the
Lord is preceded by twenty-one Hebrew words.[6] In Greek, the first twenty
descriptors are single words, and only the twenty-first is longer: **penetrating
through all spirits that are intelligent and pure and most subtle**. The first
terms describe the spirit of wisdom as **intelligent**—that is, possessing a rational
nature—and **holy**, like God. The author here describes the spirit of wisdom as
penetrating all things, using similar terms as earlier, thus identifying the spirit
of wisdom with the "Spirit of the Lord [that] has filled the world" (Wis 1:7;
see also Isa 11:2). This long litany of adjectives is reminiscent of inscriptions
that honor the goddess Isis with long aretalogies, lists of her attributes, titles,

---

6. See *Sifre Deuteronomy* 306.

and accomplishments (see the sidebar "Wisdom and the Egyptian Goddess Isis," p. 97).[7]

The extensive list of wisdom's qualities applies terms often used by the popular †Hellenistic philosophical school of †Stoicism to describe the †*Logos*, or divine world-spirit from which all things emanate. What unbelievers attributed to a pagan goddess, Solomon ascribes to the wisdom of God. Wisdom's spiritual nature is difficult to explain. Indeed, the notion of the immateriality of spiritual beings was still being developed in the Hellenistic period. Stoic philosophers described spirit as a very fine, subtle substance, invisible to the naked eye yet still material in some way. Wisdom's ability to "penetrate" and its **subtle** nature allude to this Stoic tradition and teach the principle of divine omnipresence. The Letter to the Hebrews will speak of the "word [*logos*] of God" in similar terms as discerning thoughts and intentions (Heb 4:12–13). Not only is wisdom subtle, but it is **all-powerful, overseeing all**. These traits of omnipotence and omniscience are typically attributed to God alone (Catechism 268), but here they are attributed to wisdom, showing how closely God and wisdom are linked in the author's mind, being essentially identical.

7:24–26   The author illustrates the mobility or "agility" of **wisdom**, reflecting the common Greek philosophical observation that human thought is faster than physical **motion**. Wisdom's ability to penetrate **all things** is due not to her fineness of substance but to **her pureness**, which indicates her moral integrity or cleanness.

Verse 25, like the preceding verse, shifts away from wisdom's attributes toward her role in the divine realm. She comes forth from God like **breath**, light, or water, **a pure emanation** flowing out from his eternal being. In keeping with the notion of purity, **nothing defiled gains entrance into her**, as if she were a holy temple. Wisdom is also a **reflection**, **mirror**, and **image** of God's **light**, activity, and **goodness**. Her qualities all come from God and spread knowledge of him. Here the notion of God's image unites Greek concepts of the *Logos* being the image of God with the Hebrew idea of man created in God's image (Gen 1:26–27) and prefigures the New Testament's portrayal of Christ as God's image (Col 1:15).

7:27–28   Wisdom is portrayed in her unity and diversity, her oneness and universality. On the one hand, wisdom is a singular entity, but on the other hand, she **renews all things**. Wisdom, though **one** in herself, can enter **into holy souls**, enlightening their minds with truth and making **them friends of God** (mentioned in 7:14) **and prophets**, that they might speak for God. A more literal translation of verse 28 says, "God loves nothing except the person who lives with wisdom" (NETS). God's love for us is unearned and undeserved, yet his delight in us increases as we allow his wisdom to renew our souls and draw us

---

7. See James M. Reese, *Hellenistic Influence on the Book of Wisdom and Its Consequences*, Analecta Biblica 41 (Rome: Biblical Institute Press, 1970), 36–50.

closer to him. To reject wisdom is to make God's love inaccessible to us. The idea of "living with" wisdom is a marital metaphor: the wise man pursues Lady Wisdom and makes her his bride.

While wisdom has been described as a breath, an emanation, a reflection, a mirror, and an image, now she is described in astral terms, as **more beautiful than the sun** and **every constellation of the stars**. In ancient times, heavenly bodies were often associated with divinities—as if the sun, moon, planets, and stars were actually gods, angels, or other quasi-divine beings that traversed the heavens each night. †Philo says that "Wisdom is God's archetypal luminary and the sun is a copy and image of it."[8] Elsewhere, Scripture teaches that to become like God is to be "like the stars" (Dan 12:3) or "like the sun" (Matt 13:43). Here wisdom is eulogized in the most glowing, divine terms, as greater than the sun or stars and even **superior** to **light** itself. The author's argument for this superlative claim is that day gives way to **night** (Wis 7:30). Light ends at sunset each day, but wisdom remains even in the dark: **against wisdom evil does not prevail**. While light and darkness follow an astronomical cycle, wisdom is always superior to folly. The power of wisdom reaches, literally, "from one end to the other." Translations of Wis 8:1 add "of the earth" (e.g., RSV, ESV-CE) or "of the world" (e.g., NETS; compare NABRE) to make sense of this common biblical expression (Gen 47:21; Deut 4:32; Matt 24:31), which here indicates that wisdom's reach is utterly comprehensive. More importantly, Lady Wisdom **orders all things well**. Creation is not random but ordered by the good governance of God in his wisdom.

7:29–8:1

In the Light of Christ (7:22b–8:1)

Jesus came as wisdom incarnate (1 Cor 1:24), the divine Word (†*Logos*) himself, to restore the image of God in man (see Catechism 474, 1701). Since he is the perfect "image" of God (Col 1:15), he can restore the image of God in man. Wisdom 7:29–30, which declares wisdom to be better than light since "evil does not prevail" against it, recalls the prologue to the Gospel of John, where Jesus is portrayed as the *Logos* and as light: "The light shines in the darkness, and the darkness has not overcome it" (John 1:5).

Reflection and Application (6:22–8:1)

Solomon's autobiography here prompts us to think about our own lives and the meaning that we can find in them. It is always tempting to think that success

---

8. Philo, *On the Migration of Abraham* 8 (Colson, Whitaker, and Earp, LCL 4:155).

in life is about money, fame, power, and even family—important things, yes, but the vision of Solomon ranges far higher. For him, life is about God, about wisdom. His love of wisdom motivates his lifelong pursuit of her. Though Solomon admits that he has no superpowers, that he is a mortal like the rest of us, he is driven by something much deeper than a pursuit of selfish advantage. He wants access to God's wisdom: to think like God, to know God, and thus in the end, to become like God. It is an elevated and idealistic vision of human life. All our material gains, our social success, amount to nothing in the end. Only wisdom garners for us the ultimate prize: friendship with God. Jesus, as wisdom incarnate, gives us access through the gospel to what Solomon sought. In Christ, the path of wisdom is open to everyone willing to repent and believe.

Solomon's Love for Wisdom

Wisdom 8:2–21

After expounding the nature of wisdom and all her wonders, our literary Solomon tells his own story, recounting his courtship of Lady Wisdom, the effects she had in his life, and the benefits that she brought to his reign.

I Loved Her (8:2–8)

²I loved her and sought her from my youth,
and I desired to take her for my bride,
and I became enamored of her beauty.
³She glorifies her noble birth by living with God,
and the Lord of all loves her.
⁴For she is an initiate in the knowledge of God,
and an associate in his works.
⁵If riches are a desirable possession in life,
what is richer than wisdom who effects all things?
⁶And if understanding is effective,
who more than she is fashioner of what exists?
⁷And if any one loves righteousness,
her labors are virtues;
for she teaches self-control and prudence,
justice and courage;
nothing in life is more profitable for men than these.
⁸And if any one longs for wide experience,
she knows the things of old, and infers the things to come;
she understands turns of speech and the solutions of riddles;
she has foreknowledge of signs and wonders
and of the outcome of seasons and times.

OT: 1 Kings 3:7–9; Prov 8:27–30; Sir 15:2; 39:1–3
Catechism: four cardinal virtues, 1805–9; the beauty of truth, 2500

8:2–4   The author, speaking as Solomon, describes his courtship of Lady Wisdom, his love and seeking after her. Here love and desire are essential motivating factors in the quest for wisdom. An apathetic or complacent attitude will not suffice, but only an ardent pursuit. He describes his passion for wisdom in romantic terms: **I became enamored of her beauty**. His attraction to her leads to an active seeking and then a lifelong relationship, a "marriage" with wisdom herself.

To describe her incomparable beauty, Solomon turns to her origins at the dawn of creation. Her worthiness as a companion for the king comes from her prior role as a companion of God. By associating with her, Solomon draws near to God. Wisdom's **noble birth** is her preexistence, a nobility above all human nobility, her origin from God before the creation of the world (Prov 8:22), which foreshadows the profession that the Son is "eternally begotten of the Father" in the Nicene Creed. Her **living with God** is her loving union with him, described in the language of marriage. Using the same word to describe how she lives with God in eternity, Solomon will take her to live with him in verse 9 (and v. 16).

To describe Lady Wisdom's access to divine **knowledge**, the author uses an unusual word, **initiate** (Greek *mystis*), a term normally used to indicate persons initiated into the secrets of Greek mystery religions. This term hints that Solomon has access to secret matters through her, and he has professed to hide nothing of what he knows of wisdom. The last phrase of verse 4, **an associate in his works**, is often translated "chooses his works" (NETS, NABRE). Wisdom shares in God's creation of the world and in his governance of it as a kind of coworker with him, as Prov 8:27–30 describes. This plurality that the book of Wisdom sees in God foreshadows the development of Christian trinitarian theology.

8:5–6   Now Solomon switches from praising wisdom directly to asking rhetorical questions in order to praise her indirectly. Desire for wealth is common, but the value of wisdom far outweighs that of worldly wealth, a comparison presented earlier (5:8; 7:8). The second comparison is harder to catch: **if understanding is effective**—literally, "if prudence works"—then how much more practical is wisdom herself, since she was God's agent at creation?

8:7   Loving **righteousness** allows one to benefit from wisdom's **labors**, which are **virtues**, habits of doing good (see also 4:1; 5:13). These qualities do not belong exclusively to wisdom herself but are granted to those who pursue her: **she teaches self-control and prudence, justice and courage**. These are the four cardinal virtues of Greek philosophy,[1] which will be recognized by the Church (Catechism 1805–9). The purpose of this section (8:2–8) is that the virtues taught by wisdom are **profitable**. Speaking as Solomon, the author seeks to convince readers that the virtues of wisdom make it easier to do the right thing and live a happy life.

1. Plato, *Phaedo* 69c; *Laws* 631c.

St. Gregory the Great on the Cardinal Virtues

LIVING TRADITION

St. Gregory the Great (540–604) was a monk and abbot who eventually became pope. His comments on the book of Job describe the human mind as a "house" upheld by virtue:

> But this house stands by four corners for this reason, that the firm fabric of our mind is upheld by Prudence, Temperance, Fortitude, Justice. This house is grounded on four corners, in that the whole structure of good practice is raised in these four virtues. And hence do four rivers of Paradise water the earth. For while the heart is watered with these four virtues, it is cooled from all the heat of carnal desires.[a]

a. Saint Gregory the Great, *Morals on the Book of Job*, vol. 1 (Oxford; London: John Henry Parker; J. G. F. and J. Rivington, 1844), 118–19.

Normally, we gain knowledge by experience, which takes a great deal of time **8:8** and effort. But Solomon judges the path of wisdom to be a shortcut. By associating with her through loving righteousness and practicing virtue, one gains from her extensive experience, even if still young (see 4:9). Wisdom **knows the things of old, and infers the things to come**. She knows all the things people want to know: past, future, eloquence, riddles, calendrical matters, even **foreknowledge of signs and wonders**. This last phrase is a biblical term for God's miraculous deeds[2] but could also refer to natural disasters like earthquakes and floods, which wisdom would know about in advance. Wisdom's knowledge is comprehensive, so coming to know her gives one access to her **wide experience**.

Companionship with Wisdom (8:9–21)

> [9]**Therefore I determined to take her to live with me,**
> **knowing that she would give me good counsel**
> **and encouragement in cares and grief.**
> [10]**Because of her I shall have glory among the multitudes**
> **and honor in the presence of the elders, though I am young.**
> [11]**I shall be found keen in judgment,**
> **and in the sight of rulers I shall be admired.**
> [12]**When I am silent they will wait for me,**
> **and when I speak they will give heed;**
> **and when I speak at greater length**
> **they will put their hands on their mouths.**

2. Deut 29:3; Ps 135:9; Dan 6:27; John 4:48; see the sidebar "'Wonders and Signs,'" p. 115.

¹³Because of her I shall have immortality,
and leave an everlasting remembrance to those who come
    after me.
¹⁴I shall govern peoples,
and nations will be subject to me;
¹⁵dread monarchs will be afraid of me when they hear of me;
among the people I shall show myself capable, and courageous
    in war.
¹⁶When I enter my house, I shall find rest with her,
for companionship with her has no bitterness,
and life with her has no pain, but gladness and joy.
¹⁷When I considered these things inwardly,
and thought upon them in my mind,
that in kinship with wisdom there is immortality,
¹⁸and in friendship with her, pure delight,
and in the labors of her hands, unfailing wealth,
and in the experience of her company, understanding,
and renown in sharing her words,
I went about seeking how to get her for myself.
¹⁹As a child I was by nature well endowed,
and a good soul fell to my lot;
²⁰or rather, being good, I entered an undefiled body.
²¹But I perceived that I would not possess wisdom unless God
    gave her to me—
and it was a mark of insight to know whose gift she was—
so I appealed to the Lord and implored him,
and with my whole heart I said:

OT: 1 Kings 3:9, 28; Job 29:8–10, 21–22; Prov 3:17–18; Sir 15:6
NT: James 1:5
Catechism: human soul, 362–68

8:9–12 After lauding wisdom's desirability and her loving union with God, Solomon explains that he **determined to take her to live with me**. She lives with God and now with Solomon. Wisdom is here the source of **good counsel**, which is advice on practical matters, but she is also the source of **encouragement** when one is tempted to despair in the face of **cares and grief**.

In the same way that "the desire for wisdom leads to a kingdom" (6:20), wisdom leads to **honor** and **glory among the multitudes**. Like the young Daniel (Dan 13) or the young Jeremiah (Jer 1:6–7), the young Solomon is wise despite his age. Jesus, too, as a boy will be found to be wise beyond his years (Luke 2:46–47). The author illustrates how Solomon's wisdom will be acknowledged in his time: people will admire him for his sound **judgment**, hanging on his every word with fervent expectation and reverent silence, just as they did to Job in the time of his prosperity (Job 29:8–10).

Wisdom and the Egyptian Goddess Isis

BIBLICAL BACKGROUND

Scholars have frequently noticed that the book of Wisdom's portrayal of Lady Wisdom bears some similarity to descriptions of the Egyptian goddess Isis, whose cult was popular in Hellenistic times. The era was an age of cultural and religious †syncretism. While Greek culture overtook the Mediterranean world, it has been argued that the age was also characterized by "Egyptomania," where everything Egyptian was celebrated as exotic and fascinating. During this time, the worship of Isis was widespread and is attested by inscriptions of long lists of first-person statements about herself. These so-called aretalogies or virtue lists, reminiscent of Wis 7:22b–8:1, are found in their fullest form at Kyme (in Turkey) but are also in evidence at Thessaloniki, Ios, and even in the writings of the ancient Greek historian Diodorus Siculus. Though obviously the result of pagan syncretism, a few lines illustrate some similarities and differences with biblical wisdom:

> I gave and ordained laws for men, which no one is able to change.
> I am eldest daughter of Kronus.
> I am wife and sister of King Osiris.
> I am she who findeth fruit for men.
> I am mother of King Horus.
> I am she that riseth in the Dog Star.
> I am she that is called goddess by women.
> For me was the city of Bubastis built.
> I divided the earth from the heaven.
> I showed the paths of the stars.
> I ordered the course of the sun and the moon.
> I devised business in the sea.
> I made strong the right.
> I brought together woman and man.
> I appointed to women to bring their infants to birth in the tenth month.[a]

The book of Wisdom was likely written, at least in part, to attract Jewish young people away from the popular worship of Isis. They lived in a pluralistic culture, similar to our own, in which values, philosophies, and religions competed for followers. Using the genre of an aretalogy, the author seeks to show that whatever virtues were attributed to the pagan goddess are far surpassed by the wisdom of the one true God.

a. Excerpt from Frederick C. Grant, *Hellenistic Religions: The Age of Syncretism*, Library of the Liberal Arts (Indianapolis/New York: Bobbs-Merrill, 1953), 132.

8:13–15 Wisdom will grant Solomon not only virtue or honor but two kinds of †**immortality**—a personal immortality of the soul, as presented earlier (1:15; 3:1, 4; 4:1), and **an everlasting remembrance**, in which his memory will be held in honor by those who come after him (compare Sir 39:9–11). The context indicates that an immortality beyond mere reputation is in view (Wis 6:19; 8:17).

Again, as earlier, gaining wisdom leads to governance for Solomon (3:8; 6:20). His rule over **peoples and nations** will lead foreign **monarchs** to respect him, and he will win still greater respect on the battlefield. This addition of military prowess to Solomon's reign is consistent both with †Hellenistic ideals that saw kingship as an honor attained through military success and personal virtue, and with biblical ideals of kingship as involving battlefield achievements (1 Sam 18:7; Ps 45:5) and religious devotion (2 Kings 18:5; Ps 21:7).

Figure 5. This figure of Isis-Aphrodite from about AD 150 incorporates aspects of both Isis and Aphrodite and illustrates how Egyptian religion was freely combined with Greco-Roman religion.

8:16–18   Taking up the theme of marriage to Lady Wisdom again (v. 16), the author depicts Solomon as enjoying marital bliss with her: no strife or argument, only tranquility and **rest**. His enjoyment of rest is reminiscent of God's rest after creation (Gen 2:2–3) and the promised rest of the Holy Land (Deut 25:19). In his **life with her**, he **has no pain, but gladness and joy**. Instead of finding fleeting satisfaction among the death-conscious revelers (Wis 2:5–6), Solomon is looking forward to enjoying the fruits of his pursuit of wisdom, the durable happiness of virtue.

The book of Wisdom describes Solomon's thinking, his interior process of reflection that leads to the next development, where he summarizes the results of his reflection on wisdom and her benefits. These include **immortality, delight, wealth, understanding**, and **renown**. Friendship with wisdom brings great rewards. In this plentiful description of all of wisdom's abundant blessings, Solomon finds motivation to seek her out and **get her for myself**.

8:19–21   Solomon considers that **a good soul fell to my lot**, an apparent reference to the †Platonic doctrine of the preexistence of souls (the view that human souls exist before they are infused into human bodies), which has rendered these verses among the most disputed in the book of Wisdom. Did the author subscribe to the preexistence of souls? The ensoulment of Adam depicted in 15:11 seems to indicate that the author views the soul, or at least Adam's soul, as directly created by God at the moment of his ensoulment. He never discusses the soul's existence before entering the body. Also, he seems to have a relatively positive view of the body (see 8:20). While the Hebrew tradition emphasizes the unity of the human person and the Greek tradition emphasizes the soul (often downplaying the body), we could regard this passage as reflecting some of the contemporary Hellenistic vision of the human person but without a wholesale adoption of Platonic principles. Later Christian theological development will complete our understanding of the human person as a union of soul and body (Catechism 362–68) and emphasize that each human soul is "created from nothing."[3]

In the final verse of this chapter, Solomon winds up for the prayer he is about to utter, reminding us of his desire for wisdom and of the fact that wisdom is God's gift, not a mere natural talent nor a goal to be attained by hard work. Rather than relying on his own inner resources for insight, Solomon **appealed to the Lord** with his **whole heart**.

---

3. Pope St. Leo IX, "Symbol of Faith" (DS 685).

Solomon's Prayer for Wisdom

Wisdom 9:1–18

Now that Solomon has described his quest for wisdom and his love for her, he finally makes his solemn prayer for wisdom here. This prayer, often regarded as the climax of the entire book, expands on the prayer that Solomon prayed to the Lord in 1 Kings 3:6–9.

Humble Address to the Lord of Mercy (9:1–6)

> ¹"O God of my fathers and Lord of mercy,
> who have made all things by your word,
> ²and by your wisdom have formed man,
> to have dominion over the creatures you have made,
> ³and rule the world in holiness and righteousness,
> and pronounce judgment in uprightness of soul,
> ⁴give me the wisdom that sits by your throne,
> and do not reject me from among your servants.
> ⁵For I am your slave and the son of your maidservant,
> a man who is weak and short-lived,
> with little understanding of judgment and laws;
> ⁶for even if one is perfect among the sons of men,
> yet without the wisdom that comes from you he will be regarded
> as nothing."

OT: Gen 1:28; 1 Kings 3:6–9; 2 Chron 1:8–10; Ps 116:16; Prov 8:22–31
NT: Luke 1:38

9:1–3   Solomon's prayer addresses the Lord as **God of my fathers**, in the same way that God identifies himself to Moses as "the God of Abraham, the God of Isaac, and the God of Jacob" (Exod 3:6). Solomon adds another title, unique in all of

St. Thomas Aquinas on Wisdom as the Greatest of Intellectual Virtues

LIVING TRADITION

The great Doctor of the Church St. Thomas Aquinas (1225–74) listed the intellectual virtues as wisdom, science, understanding, prudence, and art. He regarded wisdom as the greatest of all of them:

> The greatness of a virtue . . . is taken from its object. Now the object of wisdom surpasses the objects of all the intellectual virtues: because wisdom considers the Supreme Cause, which is God. . . . And since it is by the cause that we judge of an effect, and by the higher cause that we judge of the lower effects; hence it is that wisdom exercises judgment over all the other intellectual virtues, directs them all, and is the architect of them all.[a]

a. Thomas Aquinas, *Summa Theologica* I-II, q. 66, a. 5, trans. Fathers of the English Dominican Province (New York: Benziger Brothers, 1947–48), 1:869–70.

Scripture, calling God the **Lord of mercy**. Mercy is at the core of God's covenantal relationship with his people and essential to his explanation of himself (Exod 33:19; 34:5). Mercy is God's loving forbearance toward sinful people. Solomon also acknowledges God as creator of all things.

As Proverbs illustrates (Prov 8:22–31), God created the world **by his word and by** his **wisdom**. Only by his wisdom has God **formed man**. While people often think of God's act of creating humans with freedom to do good or evil as reckless, Solomon recognizes it as truly wise. Citing God's command to Adam and Eve in Gen 1:28, Solomon recalls their **dominion over the creatures** and even characterizes their role as "ruling the *kosmos*." Adam thus serves as a precursor of Solomon's own reign as king. While earlier the author taught that "desire for wisdom leads to a kingdom" (Wis 6:20), here Solomon sets the example himself as he prays for wisdom from God's heavenly kingdom in order that he might rule on earth.

The main petition appears here (v. 4): **give me the wisdom that sits by your throne**, and it will recur later (v. 10). Wisdom is no passive companion of God but shares in his rule, sitting beside him. As wisdom shares in God's reign, so Solomon needs her to help him reign well. We could think of her as God's closest adviser, and now she will become the same for Solomon. In conjunction with his request for wisdom, he pleads **do not reject me**, knowing that every petition to God is at the same time a moral test of the supplicant. God could reject his prayer and thus reject him (e.g., Gen 4:5; 1 Sam 16:1; Sir 4:4). **9:4–6**

To support his petition, Solomon professes his low estate before God. He calls himself merely a **slave, weak, short-lived**, and of **little understanding**. These protestations of humility might strike us as obsequious but are not out of place in prayer before the almighty God. In fact, they are commonplace in biblical prayer (Pss 22:6; 40:17; 109:23). Solomon's weakness indeed strengthens his argument for his request to be granted. Using the language of Ps 116:16, he recalls his mother, Bathsheba (see 2 Sam 12:24), as **your maidservant**, which perhaps is a reflection on her lowly origins—a commoner made royal consort—and thus on his (see Wis 7:1–2). Lastly, Solomon recalls that even if a man were **perfect** in every other regard, he could still not obtain wisdom for himself since it is exclusively a divine gift. Only the wisdom that comes from God has true value.

Solomon's prayer thus begins by recalling creation, Adam, the patriarchs, God's reign, his humble origins, and his own dependence on God's provision.

Solomon's Vocation and Petition (9:7–12)

[7]"You have chosen me to be king of your people
and to be judge over your sons and daughters.
[8]You have given command to build a temple on your holy mountain,
and an altar in the city of your habitation,
a copy of the holy tent which you prepared from the beginning.
[9]With you is wisdom, who knows your works
and was present when you made the world,
and who understands what is pleasing in your sight
and what is right according to your commandments.
[10]Send her forth from the holy heavens,
and from the throne of your glory send her,
that she may be with me and toil,
and that I may learn what is pleasing to you.
[11]For she knows and understands all things,
and she will guide me wisely in my actions
and guard me with her glory.
[12]Then my works will be acceptable,
and I shall judge your people justly,
and shall be worthy of the throne of my father."

OT: 2 Sam 7:12–13; 1 Kings 1:13; 1 Chron 28:11–19
NT: Rom 12:1–2
Catechism: God creates by wisdom, 295

9:7–8   Solomon moves from extolling God's power to reflecting on his calling from God. Solomon identifies his threefold vocation as **king**, **judge**, and temple builder. From before he was born, he was called by God to "build a house for my name" (2 Sam 7:13). Solomon embraces this mission for his life **to build a temple on your holy mountain**. The mountain referred to here is Mount Moriah,

Aristobulus

**BIBLICAL
BACKGROUND**

Aristobulus was a Jewish philosopher who lived in Alexandria in the †Hellenistic period during the second century BC. Sadly, little is known about his life, and only fragments of his writing survive. Yet these fragments reveal that his outlook was like that of the Wisdom of Solomon in that he attempts to weave together the Jewish biblical tradition and the Greek philosophical tradition. Some scholars have even proposed that Aristobulus might be the author of Wisdom of Solomon. This quote illustrates his perspective:

Fragment 2.3–4

For what our lawgiver Moses wishes to say, he does so at many levels, using words that appear to have other referents. . . . Those who have keen intellectual powers are amazed at his wisdom and inspired spirit, in virtue of which he has also been proclaimed a prophet. Included among these are the philosophers mentioned above, and many others as well as poets, who have taken from him significant seeds of inspiration, so that they too are admired.[a]

a. Carl R. Holladay, *Fragments from Hellenistic Jewish Authors: Volume III*, Texts and Translations 39, Pseudepigrapha Series 13 (Atlanta: Scholars Press, 1995), 137.

the location where Abraham offered up Isaac (Gen 22:2; 2 Chron 3:1), which becomes synonymous with Mount Zion in the biblical tradition (Pss 2:6; 74:2; 78:68–69). The temple will be a place for God to dwell with his people, but Solomon also highlights the **altar** of sacrifice, which is the link between heaven and earth, between God and his people. Even though the temple will be the greatest architectural accomplishment of ancient Israel, Solomon acknowledges that it is merely **a copy of the holy tent which you prepared from the beginning**. That the earthly temple was merely a "copy" of the heavenly one is well established in biblical theology. Moses himself designed the tabernacle "after the pattern" which God revealed to him at Mount Sinai (Exod 25:40). This theological concept will be a point of special emphasis in the New Testament (Acts 7:44; Heb 8:5). It also corresponds both to the rabbinic idea of a preexistent heavenly temple and to the †Platonic doctrine of the heavenly ideal forms being instantiated in earthly material.[1] Solomon's temple will be a place of communion with God, but it cannot contain him (1 Kings 8:27).

9:9–10   Solomon returns from reflecting on his royal vocation to the theme of **wisdom** here (v. 9) to prepare for his final appeal (v. 10). In verse 9, he emphasizes wisdom's knowledge, her closeness to God, her role in creation, and her intimate knowledge of God's law. The author carefully unites the various components of

1. See David Winston, *The Wisdom of Solomon*, AB 43 (Garden City, NY: Doubleday, 1979), 203–5.

biblical history and literature under the auspices of wisdom. For him, biblical narrative, law, prophecy, and wisdom teaching belong under one heading—namely, wisdom. Wisdom also encompasses both the elements of divine revelation and human reasoning. To obtain her is to obtain the key to all knowledge. Solomon therefore begs God to **send her forth from the holy heavens**. Wisdom is no human achievement, but the gift of God. Solomon desires wisdom's authentic divine counsel but also her companionship in his challenging reign: **that she may be with me and toil**. His desire is to please God, and he knows that he can do that only with her at his side.

9:11-12   Solomon describes how wisdom will aid him in his reign. Because of her all-encompassing knowledge, she will **guide** and **guard** him. Wisdom emerges here almost like a guardian angel for Solomon. He is concerned that his **actions** and his **works** be acceptable to God. While his intellectual acumen may be heightened by the gift of divine wisdom, ultimately it is in action that his integrity will be tested. He longs to be a just **judge** like God and to be worthy of his **father** David's **throne**. We hear the voice of Solomon here as profoundly conscious of his heritage—of lowliness from his mother, of royalty from his father—aware of his own human weaknesses and truly in need of God's gift of wisdom.

Human Frailty and Saving Wisdom (9:13–18)

> [13]"For what man can learn the counsel of God?
> Or who can discern what the Lord wills?
> [14]For the reasoning of mortals is worthless,
> and our designs are likely to fail,
> [15]for a perishable body weighs down the soul,
> and this earthy tent burdens the thoughtful mind.
> [16]We can hardly guess at what is on earth,
> and what is at hand we find with labor;
> but who has traced out what is in the heavens?
> [17]Who has learned your counsel, unless you have given wisdom
> and sent your holy Spirit from on high?
> [18]And thus the paths of those on earth were set right,
> and men were taught what pleases you,
> and were saved by wisdom."

OT: Job 4:18–19; Isa 40:13; 55:8
NT: John 14:26; Rom 11:33–34; 1 Cor 2:10–11; 6:19; 2 Cor 5:1–4
Catechism: tension between body and spirit, 2516
Lectionary: 9:13–18b: 23rd Sunday in Ordinary Time (Year C)

9:13–14   This eloquent conclusion of Solomon's prayer for wisdom emphasizes the contrast between the frailty of the human intellect and the greatness of God's mind.

The author insists on the inscrutability of God's thoughts (Rom 11:33–34), like Isaiah, who proclaims, "My thoughts are not your thoughts, neither are your ways my ways, declares the LORD" (Isa 55:8). The rhetorical question he poses, **who can discern what the Lord wills?**, does not regard God's thoughts as unintelligible or illogical, but rather far above normal human thinking, far greater than what we can grasp. To continue explaining the concept, he argues that our **reasoning** is simply **worthless**, a word which could also be translated as "cowardly." Humanity's intellectual weakness is not merely a limited capacity for processing information but a lack of courage.

The author offers an explanation for the limitations of human reasoning that **9:15** reflects a common †Platonic view of the **body** as hindering the activity of the **soul**, weighing it down.[2] While not fully appropriating Plato's (ca. 427–347 BC) body-soul dualism, the author takes up a biblical line of thinking that views the body as a source of sinful desires (Gen 3:6; see Rom 8:13; 1 John 2:16). The rabbinic tradition identifies this desire as "inclination toward evil" (Hebrew *yetzer hara'*), similar to what the Catholic theological tradition names "concupiscence."

Though the body is described as the burdensome source of sinful desire, the fact that it is described as a **tent** links back to Wis 9:8, which described the temple as "a copy of the holy tent." Like the earthly temple that corresponds to the greater heavenly temple, the body is a lesser reality that corresponds to the greater reality of the soul. The body also houses the soul like the temple houses God's presence. In the New Testament, St. Paul will speak of the body of a Christian as a temple of the Holy Spirit (1 Cor 6:19).

Returning to the weakness of human thinking, the author bewails the diffi- **9:16–18** culty of achieving knowledge even of what is close **at hand**, to emphasize how dramatically God's knowledge of heavenly things surpasses what human beings are capable of. It is reminiscent of Job 38–41, where the vast domain of divine knowledge is contrasted with human understanding. The rhetorical question, **Who has learned . . . ?**, repeats themes from the earlier petitions for wisdom— "Give me" (Wis 9:4); "Send her" (v. 10). This time, wisdom is identified as **your holy Spirit**, using language similar to his previous description of wisdom as "a holy and disciplined spirit" (1:5). Indeed, wisdom is one of the seven gifts of the Holy Spirit (Isa 11:2–3) and is thus appropriately labeled as God's "holy Spirit" even though the third person of the Holy Trinity was not fully revealed until after the resurrection of Jesus (John 20:22; Acts 2:4).

The final verse of the prayer highlights the powerful effects of wisdom: (1) setting right one's path—giving humans a sure route to living for God; (2) teaching humanity—likely a reference to the law of Moses; and (3) saving humanity. James Reese explains that "Lady Wisdom is a personification of God's saving

---

2. Plato, *Phaedo* 81c. Plato saw the soul as longing for escape from the confines of the body.

grace at work in the world."[3] The theme of wisdom saving God's people points forward to the historical reflections of chapters 10–19 and wisdom's starring role in salvation history (especially 10:4; 16:7).

Reflection and Application (9:1–18)

Solomon's prayer here, like his great prayer of dedication for the temple in 1 Kings 8:22–61, provides us with a model for our own prayer. While we might not spontaneously string together rhetorical questions in prayer, we can follow his pattern of reflecting on what God has done, on his greatness, and on our own weakness and limitation. So often we rush to press our petitions into God's hand without thinking. But Solomon's example teaches us to be patient, to firmly ground our prayers in God's goodness toward us, and to remember our dependence on him for all things. St. James teaches us how to pray: "If any of you lacks wisdom, let him ask God, who gives to all men generously and without reproaching, and it will be given him" (James 1:5). In the end, our hope and expectation is that God will "send his holy Spirit from on high" and save us too by his great wisdom.

---

3. James M. Reese, *The Book of Wisdom, Song of Songs*, Old Testament Message 20 (Wilmington, DE: Michael Glazier, 1983), 106.

Part 3

Book of History

Wisdom 10:1–19:22

Prologue: Wisdom from Adam to Moses

Wisdom 10:1–21

This chapter marks the transition from Solomon's Pursuit of Wisdom (6:22–9:18) to the Book of History (chaps. 10–19). The king's voice fades to the background as the glorious interventions of wisdom in salvation history are recounted from the lives of seven biblical heroes: Adam, Noah, Abraham, Lot, Jacob, Joseph, and the people of Israel. Each hero will be contrasted with an antihero or group of opponents. Again, the author omits all names so that the reader must identify each character (see the sidebar "Why Omit Names?," p. 61). The retelling of biblical history in chapters 10–19 is part of a wider Jewish tradition of teaching about God through renarrating the events of sacred history, often with embellishments and explanatory comments (see Sir 44:1–49:16; 1 Macc 2:49–68).

Adam, Cain, Noah, Abraham, and Lot (10:1–8)

[1]Wisdom[1] protected the first-formed father of the world,
when he alone had been created;
she delivered him from his transgression,
[2]and gave him strength to rule all things.
[3]But when an unrighteous man departed from her in his anger,
he perished because in rage he slew his brother.
[4]When the earth was flooded because of him, wisdom again
saved it,
steering the righteous man by a paltry piece of wood.

---

1. The Greek text uses "she" to denote wisdom in these verses, but the RSV-2CE and other translations insert "Wisdom" a few times for clarity (10:1, 5, 6).

> ⁵Wisdom also, when the nations in wicked agreement had been
>   confounded,
> recognized the righteous man and preserved him blameless
>   before God,
> and kept him strong in the face of his compassion for his child.
> ⁶Wisdom rescued a righteous man when the ungodly were
>   perishing;
> he escaped the fire that descended on the Five Cities.
> ⁷Evidence of their wickedness still remains:
> a continually smoking wasteland,
> plants bearing fruit that does not ripen,
> and a pillar of salt standing as a monument to an unbelieving
>   soul.
> ⁸For because they passed wisdom by,
> they not only were hindered from recognizing the good,
> but also left for mankind a reminder of their folly,
> so that their failures could never go unnoticed.

OT: Gen 1:28; 4:8–16; 6:5–8:5; 11:7–9; 19:12–29; 22:6–14; Sir 44:17–21
NT: Luke 17:26–33; 1 Tim 2:14; 2 Pet 2:5–8; James 2:21
Catechism: human ambition at Babel, 57

10:1–2 Starting with **the first-formed father of the world**, Adam, the author describes how wisdom intervened in the stories of major biblical characters. He refers to a time when Adam **alone had been created**. During this time before Eve, wisdom **protected** him from sin. But later, after the fall, wisdom **delivered him from his transgression**. While this statement does not mean that wisdom completely reversed the effects of Adam's sin, it alludes to the Jewish tradition that Adam felt profound remorse for his sin and even did penance in hope of restoration.[2] Wisdom prompted his repentance and led to his ultimate salvation in Christ.[3] Wisdom also led to Adam's restoration as ruler of the earth because his ability to reason enabled him to govern (see 1 Kings 3:9). God had promised Adam dominion (Gen 1:28), and our author here again reiterates his teaching that "desire for wisdom leads to a kingdom" (Wis 6:20). Adam is his very first case in point.

10:3–5 Now the chapter will proceed to compare **the righteous man** (vv. 4, 5, 6, 10, 13) with the **unrighteous man** (v. 3). These descriptive labels show that the biblical characters being discussed are object lessons for us. They are not merely historical figures but moral archetypes. Each of the seven heroes is compared with an antihero or antihero group: Adam versus Cain, Noah versus the wicked descendants of Cain, Abraham versus the builders of the Tower of Babel, Lot

---

2. See *Life of Adam and Eve* 1–8, where Adam is depicted as fasting for forty days while standing in the chilly water of the Jordan River.
3. See Irenaeus, *Against Heresies* 3.23.

St. Irenaeus on Adam's Salvation

St. Irenaeus (ca. AD 140–98) is the first Church Father to explicitly quote Wisdom. Reflecting on †immortality and the glorification of the saints, he quotes Wis 6:19, "Immortality brings one near to God."[a] Here he explains how Christ brings salvation to Adam himself:

> Now Adam had been conquered, all life having been taken away from him. For that reason, when the foe was conquered in his turn, Adam received new life. And the last enemy, death, is destroyed, which at the first had taken possession of man. Therefore, when man has been liberated, "what is written shall come to pass, Death is swallowed up in victory. O death, where is thy victory? O death, where is thy sting?" (1 Cor 15:54–55). This could not be said with justice, if that man, over whom death first obtained dominion, were not set free. For his salvation is death's destruction. When therefore the Lord vivifies man, that is, Adam, death is at the same time destroyed.[b]

a. See Irenaeus, *Against Heresies* 4.38.3.
b. Irenaeus, *Against Heresies* 3.23 (*ANF* 1:457; translation modified).

versus the men of Sodom, Jacob versus Esau, Joseph versus his accusers, Israel versus ungodly Egyptians.[4]

Cain is the "unrighteous man" who murdered his brother, Abel. Cain's downfall came about by his own action; as †Philo says, "Cain rose up and slew himself."[5] His sin brought about his own "perishing," but it also had harmful effects on all of humanity. The author of Wisdom blames the flood of Noah's time on the violence of Cain and his descendants (as in Gen 6:11–13) and later will refer to the "arrogant giants" who were punished by it (Wis 14:6). During the destructive flood, **wisdom again saved** the earth through Noah's obedience. Wisdom keeps appearing as though it were the hand of God, helping Adam, punishing Cain, now rescuing humanity through Noah, "the righteous man," and his ark, **a paltry piece of wood**. After Noah, **the nations in wicked agreement** began to build the Tower of Babel, but they were **confounded** by the Lord, who confused their languages (Gen 11:7–9). This judgment against the tower builders led to God's recognition of "the righteous man" Abraham. God had told Abraham, "Walk before me, and be blameless" (Gen 17:1). This key word, **blameless**, reappears here, where wisdom is depicted as protecting Abraham's blamelessness. Even when God tested Abraham by commanding him to sacrifice **his child**, Isaac, wisdom led Abraham to obey.

4. David Winston, *The Wisdom of Solomon*, AB 43 (Garden City, NY: Doubleday, 1979), 211.
5. Philo, *That the Worse Attacks the Better* 47 (Colson, Whitaker, and Earp, LCL 2:235).

10:6–8   While readers of Genesis may not remember Lot as especially righteous (although 2 Pet 2:7 does), angels do come to rescue him and his family from Sodom before destruction falls upon it (Gen 19). Here the angels' efforts are attributed to wisdom. Lot **escaped the fire that descended on the Five Cities**. The Greek word here, *Pentapolis*, is used to indicate a group of five cities destroyed by God's †wrath: Sodom, Gomorrah, Admah, Zeboiim, and Zoar (Gen 14:2)—though Genesis reports that Zoar was spared for Lot's sake (19:20–30). The **evidence of their wickedness**—a **smoking wasteland** that cannot bring forth ripe fruit and **a pillar of salt**—refers to the area around the Dead Sea. Philo (ca. 20 BC–50 AD) and Josephus (AD 37–ca. 100) also refer to the constant smoking of the desolate land, the inedible fruit, and the evidence of fiery judgment.[6] The "pillar of salt" refers to Lot's wife, who disobediently looked back on Sodom and so was turned into a pillar of salt (Gen 19:26), a pillar that Josephus claimed to have witnessed personally.[7] The final verses summarize the importance of the "continually smoking wasteland" and "pillar of salt"—namely, that they might serve as warnings to future generations, **a reminder of their folly**. This introduction to the Book of History signals the author's understanding of salvation history as a set of moral lessons that amount to a divine curriculum, a view that he will flesh out in his presentation of the exodus story in the remaining chapters of the book.

Wisdom Guided Jacob and Delivered Joseph (10:9–14)

⁹Wisdom rescued from troubles those who served her.
¹⁰When a righteous man fled from his brother's wrath,
she guided him on straight paths;
she showed him the kingdom of God,
and gave him knowledge of angels;
she prospered him in his labors,
and increased the fruit of his toil.
¹¹When his oppressors were covetous,
she stood by him and made him rich.
¹²She protected him from his enemies,
and kept him safe from those who lay in wait for him;
in his arduous contest she gave him the victory,
so that he might learn that godliness is more powerful than
    anything.

¹³When a righteous man was sold, wisdom did not desert him,
but delivered him from sin.
She descended with him into the dungeon,

---

6. Philo, *On the Life of Abraham* 27.140–41; *On the Life of Moses* 2.56; Josephus, *Jewish War* 4.8.4 (§484).
7. Josephus, *Jewish Antiquities* 1.11.4 (§203).

> ¹⁴and when he was in prison she did not leave him,
> until she brought him the scepter of a kingdom
> and authority over his masters.
> Those who accused him she showed to be false,
> and she gave him everlasting honor.

OT: Gen 27:43–45; 28:10–17; 31:5–16, 23–29; 37:1–45:28
NT: 1 Tim 4:8

The lesson of this section is that serving wisdom leads to being rescued by wisdom.   **10:9–10**
The author offers yet another example from Genesis: the life of Jacob. In six lines,
he recounts five episodes from Jacob's life. First, he recalls his flight from Esau,
his brother, who sought to kill him for stealing his father's blessing. Second, he
mentions how Jacob's mother, Rebekah, offered him a life-saving warning and
advice (Gen 27:43–45). Third, he mentions the revelation Jacob received of the
kingdom of God and the **angels** ascending and descending from heaven at Bethel
(28:10–17). Fourth, he recalls Jacob's fourteen years of **labors**, which he pledged
to his father-in-law for his two wives (29:20, 30). Fifth, he retells how wisdom
guided Jacob's wealth to increase in the form of goats (31:5–16). Laban had at-
tempted to deprive Jacob of an inheritance by a clever division of his flocks, but
Jacob outsmarted him by even more clever tricks of animal husbandry, which led
to his enrichment. In every episode, Jacob is depicted as constantly guided by the
hand of wisdom, who leads him, teaches him, and brings him prosperity. Jacob
plays the role of the "righteous man," exemplifying docility to wisdom. In the Book
of History (Wis 10–19), the author characterizes the nation of Israel and famous
biblical figures as "righteous" and their opponents, especially the Egyptians, as
"ungodly." This is not a judgment on every individual Israelite or Egyptian but a
convenient way to teach lessons from biblical history by way of example.

Here Laban is classified as an unrighteous "oppressor," while Jacob is depicted   **10:11–12**
as the persecuted righteous man, a scene that resembles the machinations of the
wicked against the righteous in Wis 2:12–20. Yet in the midst of persecution,
wisdom upheld Jacob **and made him rich**. The author downplays the moral
ambiguity of Jacob's biography to accommodate his story to the two representative roles he is working with: the righteous and the unrighteous. In 2:12, the
wicked plan to "lie in wait for the righteous man," and here Jacob's **enemies** are
Laban and Esau, **those who lay in wait for him**. The author likely has in mind
the scene in which Jacob fears for his life as he is about to confront Esau (Gen
32:6–8), a scene which ends in a reconciling embrace rather than a conflict
(33:4). The **arduous contest** refers to Jacob's mysterious wrestling match with
God (32:24–32). The lesson the author draws from this scene, **that godliness is
more powerful than anything**, returns to his teaching that "desire for wisdom
leads to a kingdom" (Wis 6:20), which was already reiterated in his emphasis
on Adam's dominion (10:2).

10:13–14   This lesson will be furthered by yet another example: Joseph. Joseph was
sold into slavery (Gen 37:28), then he fled from the temptations of his master
Potiphar's wife (39:12), and then was imprisoned in a **dungeon** (39:20). Our
author shows that wisdom helped him flee from temptation (see 1 Cor 6:18)
and constantly accompanied him, even in his most difficult moments. But Joseph's life did not conclude with his imprisonment; rather, wisdom raised him
up by giving him the ability to interpret dreams. Her accompaniment was not
just for his comfort, but **she brought him the scepter of a kingdom**. Joseph
was raised up to reign over his previous persecutors: the jailers, Potiphar, his
brothers. **Those who accused him** might refer to Potiphar's wife and household slaves mentioned in Genesis, but some nonbiblical traditions claim that
Joseph had been accused by multiple women, which could be in view here.[8]
Joseph's story forcefully exemplifies the principle that wisdom-seeking leads
to authority, despite temporary degradation or suffering. Joseph's redemption
and rise is the great reversal, which our author poses as the lesson of wisdom's
role in salvation history. Though persecuted for a time, in the end, Joseph the
wisdom seeker is redeemed from oppression by wisdom and comes to possess
everlasting honor or glory.

Wisdom Delivered Israel from Egypt (10:15–21)

> [15]**A holy people and blameless race
> wisdom delivered from a nation of oppressors.
> [16]She entered the soul of a servant of the Lord,
> and withstood dread kings with wonders and signs.
> [17]She gave to holy men the reward of their labors;
> she guided them along a marvelous way,
> and became a shelter to them by day,
> and a starry flame through the night.
> [18]She brought them over the Red Sea,
> and led them through deep waters;
> [19]but she drowned their enemies,
> and cast them up from the depth of the sea.
> [20]Therefore the righteous plundered the ungodly;
> they sang hymns, O Lord, to your holy name,
> and praised with one accord your defending hand,
> [21]because wisdom opened the mouth of the mute,
> and made the tongues of infants speak clearly.**

OT: Exod 3:9; 14:21–29; 15:1–21; 19:6; Deut 7:6; Pss 8:2; 135:8–10
NT: Matt 21:16

8. Philo, *On the Life of Joseph* 51.

"Wonders and Signs"

BIBLICAL BACKGROUND

Wisdom 10:16 uses a key phrase to describe the miracles of the exodus generation: "wonders and signs." Elsewhere in the Old Testament, as in Wis 8:8, the order of the words is reversed as "signs and wonders," and typically refers to the exodus (Exod 7:3; Deut 26:8; Neh 9:10; Ps 135:9). This phrase reappears in the New Testament. Jesus warns against false prophets who perform "signs and wonders" (Matt 24:24; Mark 13:22; see also 2 Thess 2:9) and reproves those who refuse to believe in him without such signs (John 4:48). His miraculous deeds are referred to as "signs" in the Gospel of John (e.g., 2:11), and they confirm his messianic identity (Heb 2:4). The book of Acts uses the phrase "wonders and signs" to describe not only the great works of God during the exodus (7:36) but also the miracles worked by Jesus (2:22) and by the apostles (2:43; 6:8). St. Paul explains that his own apostolic authority in Christ was confirmed by "signs and wonders" (Rom 15:19; 2 Cor 12:12). While "wonders and signs" showed that God's wisdom was at work for the deliverance of the exodus generation, they reemerge in the ministry of Christ and his Church to indicate the arrival of the new exodus that Jesus brings.

The comparison of the righteous and unrighteous continues in the exodus story. The author holds up Israel as **a holy people and blameless race** (Exod 19:6; Deut 7:6), as opposed to the "accursed race" of Canaanites (Wis 12:11). Again, he downplays the moral problems in Israel's history to focus solely on the nation's holiness before God, chosen by him to fulfill his purposes. Wisdom is still the protagonist of the story, the one who rescues Israel from Egypt, **a nation of oppressors**. **10:15–16**

Wisdom **entered the soul of a servant of the Lord**—namely, Moses. While Moses had been inarticulate and fearful, God empowered him to lead the people and confront Pharaoh. The concept of wisdom "entering a soul" appeared at the beginning of the book (1:4), and it is now a fitting way to describe Moses's empowerment. **Kings** here is the so-called allusive plural, which refers to a single entity—namely, Pharaoh.[9] The **wonders and signs** denote the miraculous deeds granted to Moses: turning water to blood, turning his staff into a serpent, and making his hand leprous and healthy in turn (Exod 4:2–9), as well as the ten plagues that the Lord brought against Egypt.

Wisdom then guides the Israelites out of Egypt. The **reward of their labors** would be the silver and gold that the Israelites obtained from their Egyptian masters on their way out of the land, a paltry payment for years of slavery (Exod **10:17–19**

9. Herbert Weir Smyth, *Greek Grammar* (Cambridge, MA: Harvard University Press, 1920), §1007.

12:35–36). The **marvelous way** is the dry path through the Red Sea (14:22). The pillar of cloud and fire is alluded to as a **shelter** from the sun and **a starry flame** to light up the **night** (13:21–22). This visible manifestation of God is now attributed to wisdom.

By God's power working through Moses, wisdom leads Israel through the sea to victory over the Egyptians. Wisdom brings the victory by drowning the Egyptian army and then causing the sea to spew out their bodies (Exod 14:30).[10] Thus the Israelites doubly profit from the Egyptians: by collecting their silver and gold, then by despoiling the dead of their weapons and other possessions.

10:20–21   The final two verses of this section recount the Israelites' victory celebration on the shores of the Red Sea, where they sing a triumphant victory song (Exod 15). Our author switches from speaking of wisdom to describing praise of the Lord: **they sang hymns, O Lord, to your holy name**. The opening of **the mouth of the mute** likely alludes to Moses's confession to being "slow of speech" (Exod 4:10). In Greek, the word for **infant** etymologically means "not yet speaking."[11] Perhaps on the basis of Ps 8:2, Jewish literature contains a tradition that all the babies who had not yet learned to speak were enabled to praise God in song at the Red Sea.[12] The book of Wisdom alludes to this same tradition, which fits a wider biblical pattern of mute persons, animals, and objects speaking by divine power (Num 22:28; Isa 35:6; Luke 19:40). In the end, wisdom not only empowers Moses and leads the Israelites to victory but enables those incapable of speech to praise the Lord.

Reflection and Application (10:1–21)

In comparing Genesis and Exodus with Wis 10, it might seem that our author is putting on rose-colored glasses when looking at Israel's history, ignoring important problems. On the other hand, his view of salvation history as the divine curriculum of wisdom coheres with St. Paul's principle that such things "were written down for our instruction" (1 Cor 10:11). For the author of Wisdom, the biblical story is not merely a rehearsal of the tragedy of sin but a glorious recounting of the victories of wisdom. In the face of challenge, persecution, and pressure, wisdom consistently delivers the righteous. Seeking wisdom is the route to a power greater than the world offers, since "godliness is more powerful than anything" (Wis 10:12). If we seek the Lord and his will for us—that is, if we seek wisdom—then we too will enjoy the deliverance that wisdom offers in Christ. When that happens, our mute tongues will be loosed in praise as well.

10. A tradition referred to by Josephus, *Jewish Antiquities* 2.16.6.

11. H. G. Liddell, *A Lexicon: Abridged from Liddell and Scott's Greek-English Lexicon* (Oak Harbor, WA: Logos Research Systems, Inc., 1996), 532.

12. See *t. Sotah* 6.4.

Water from the Rock versus River of Blood

Wisdom 11:1-14

Chapter 11 is a major turning point in the book. It begins the formal structural development of the Book of History (chaps. 10–19), which will take up the remainder of the Wisdom of Solomon with a series of seven major antitheses. This short beginning passage announces the essential principle of God's guidance of history—that God uses the very same things to punish the ungodly and to bless his people (11:5)—and explains the first example of it: the unsatisfied thirst of the Egyptians in contrast to the miraculous quenching of the Israelites' thirst. While most of the material in Wisdom up to this point is written in the third person, from now until the end of the book the author addresses God as "you," writing his reflections in the form of a prayer.

Punishment and Benefit (11:1-5)

> ¹Wisdom prospered their works by the hand of a holy prophet.
> ²They journeyed through an uninhabited wilderness,
> and pitched their tents in untrodden places.
> ³They withstood their enemies and fought off their foes.
> ⁴When they thirsted they called upon you,
> and water was given them out of flinty rock,
> and slaking of thirst from hard stone.
> ⁵For through the very things by which their enemies were
>   punished,
> they themselves received benefit in their need.

OT: Exod 17:1–16; Num 20:1–13; Deut 2:7; 18:15–18; Sir 39:27; Hosea 12:13
NT: John 4:14; 1 Cor 10:4
Catechism: divine pedagogy, 53, 1950

11:1–5   Now that wisdom's involvement in salvation history has been explored up through the events of Genesis and Exodus from Adam to the Red Sea (chap. 10), our author is ready to move on to the events that follow Israel's departure from Egypt, which will constitute his major focus for the rest of the book. In a series of seven antitheses or †*synkrises* (see the sidebar "Structure of the Book of History," p. 119), the author will draw out the major lesson of the †divine pedagogy: that God uses the same means to punish the wicked and bless the righteous (11:5). He will compare the miraculous plagues that God sent against Egypt with the miraculous blessings he provided for the Israelites in the wilderness. Not every Israelite was a perfect saint, nor was every Egyptian a wicked person. Rather, the author uses these two groups, the Israelites and Egyptians, as teaching examples. These generalizations are meant not to praise or blame individuals but to serve as helpful lessons for readers.

Wisdom is still the main character, guiding the course of history as the loving presence of divine providence.[1] After emphasizing "wisdom" in chapter 10, the author will mostly omit the name of this key figure and "move almost imperceptibly from the attribution of certain historical events to the instrumentality of Wisdom (or the prophet she inspires) to their attribution directly to God."[2] The people of Israel are guided **by the hand of a holy prophet**— namely, Moses (Deut 18:15, 18). The overlap between God and wisdom now becomes an overlap between wisdom and Moses, who is inhabited by divine wisdom (Wis 10:16) and functions as mediator between God and the people. Our author simply summarizes the events of Exodus 16 and 17: the people march their way through the **wilderness**, camping as they go. They become severely thirsty, and God gives them to drink from the **rock** (Exod 17:1–7). Then they have a battle with the Amalekites, who oppose their march through the wilderness (17:8–16). The author interprets the Israelites' complaint to Moses in the best possible light as a devout prayer: **When they thirsted they called upon you**.

The thesis statement of Wisdom's meditation on the exodus deserves careful attention: **For through the very things by which their enemies were punished, they themselves received benefit in their need**. This principle is the biblical philosophy of history. It defines how "God revealed himself progressively to man, through the prophets and through salvific events,"[3] what Christian tradition names the "divine pedagogy." Essentially, it affirms that God teaches through cause and effect, where "he transforms events in the life of his people

---

1. At 11:1 the Greek omits the keyword "wisdom," which is inserted here by the RSV-2CE for clarity. From this point on, the author uses "wisdom" only twice (14:2, 5).

2. David Winston, *The Wisdom of Solomon*, AB 43 (Garden City, NY: Doubleday, 1979), 226.

3. Sacred Congregation for the Clergy, *General Directory for Catechesis*, §40, https://www.vatican.va/roman_curia/congregations/cclergy/documents/rc_con_ccatheduc_doc_17041998_directory-for-catechesis_en.html.

Structure of the Book of History

BIBLICAL BACKGROUND

The third major section of the Wisdom of Solomon, the Book of History, has a relatively complex structure of seven antitheses or *synkrises* and two excurses (digressions from the main structure). A *synkrisis* is an evaluative comparison common in †Hellenistic rhetoric.[a] The comparisons here show how the same elements of creation serve as means to punish the Egyptians and bless the Israelites. The following outline explains the plan of these chapters:

Prologue: Wisdom from Adam to Moses (10:1–21)
Antithesis 1: Water from the Rock versus River of Blood (11:1–14)
  †Excursus 1—God's Mercy toward Egyptians and Canaanites (11:15–12:27)
  Excursus 2—Against Idol Worship (13:1–15:19)
Antithesis 2: Unappetizing Animals versus Delicious Quail (16:1–4)
Antithesis 3: Lethal Creatures versus Saving Bronze Serpent (16:5–14)
Antithesis 4: Storms of Wrath versus Manna from Heaven (16:15–29)
Antithesis 5: Plague of Darkness versus Pillar of Light (17:1–18:4)
Antithesis 6: Death of the Firstborn versus Israel's Deliverance from Death (18:5–25)
Antithesis 7: Drowning in the Sea versus Being Saved by the Sea (19:1–9)
Epilogue: Summary and Doxology (19:10–22)

a. Friedrich Focke, "Synkrisis," *Hermes* 58 (1923): 327–68.

into lessons of wisdom."[4] Every created reality can serve God's will by blessing or punishing, depending on the moral disposition of those who encounter it. The same things are the instruments of divine punishment and blessing (see the sidebar "Structure of the Book of History," above).

Disciplined in Mercy (11:6–14)

> [6]Instead of the fountain of an ever-flowing river,
> stirred up and defiled with blood
> [7]in rebuke for the decree to slay the infants,
> you gave them abundant water unexpectedly,
> [8]showing by their thirst at that time
> how you punished their enemies.
> [9]For when they were tried, though they were being disciplined
> in mercy,

4. Sacred Congregation for the Clergy, *General Directory for Catechesis*, §139.

they learned how the ungodly were tormented when judged
   in wrath.
¹⁰For you tested them as a father does in warning,
but you examined the ungodly as a stern king does in
   condemnation.
¹¹Whether absent or present, they were equally distressed,
¹²for a twofold grief possessed them,
and a groaning at the memory of what had occurred.
¹³For when they heard that through their own punishments
the righteous had received benefit, they perceived it was the
   Lord's doing.
¹⁴For though they had mockingly rejected him who long before
   had been cast out and exposed,
at the end of the events they marveled at him,
for their thirst was not like that of the righteous.

OT: Wis 12:22; 16:3–4; Exod 1:22; 7:17–24; Deut 8:2–5; Prov 3:12
NT: Heb 12:5–9

11:6–10 The first plague of the exodus was the Nile turning to **blood** (Exod 7:17–24). It struck at the heart of Egyptian commerce and transportation, threatening the nation's very survival. Wisdom sees this plague as proper divine retribution for the Egyptian pharaoh's command to kill the Hebrew baby boys by casting them into the Nile (Exod 1:22). The drinking water that later poured forth from the rock at Horeb for the Israelites (17:6) stands in stark contrast to the Egyptians digging at the banks of the Nile looking for water to slake their thirst (7:24). The Israelites' thirst, which God mercifully quenched, helped them learn the lesson he was teaching. It gave them a taste of divine †wrath, from which they were delivered by divine mercy (see also 16:4). The Israelites **were tried, disciplined in mercy**, and **tested**. In verse 10, our author draws a contrast between fatherly kindness in discipline and the royal strictness of **a stern king**. This distinction draws on a larger biblical principle—that "the LORD reproves him whom he loves, as a father the son in whom he delights" (Prov 3:12). God's discipline tests hearts—on the one hand, it teaches, converts, and purifies those who are his own, but in the end, it brings condemnation on those who persist in rebellion against him.

11:11–14   The plagues afflicted the Egyptians indiscriminately, whether they were **absent or present**, an idea found in other statements in the Bible about God's universal authority (Ps 86:9; Matt 5:45). The plague of the firstborn affected everyone "from the first-born of Pharaoh who sat on his throne to the first-born of the captive who was in the dungeon" (Exod 12:29).

The Egyptians endured a **twofold grief** in that they experienced the pain of punishment on the one hand and the pain of envy at the Israelites' good fortune

St. Irenaeus on the Divine Pedagogy

In one of the earliest descriptions of the †divine pedagogy, St. Irenaeus explains how God teaches us through experience, delivers us by grace, and brings us to live in constant thankfulness for what God has done for us:

> Such, therefore, was the long-suffering of God, that humans might pass through all things and might experience the knowledge of †death and arrive at the resurrection from the dead, and learn by experience from what they were freed. Thus humankind might always continue to be grateful to God, since it was from God that the human race received the gift of imperishability, in order that it might love Him the more. Surely those love more to whom more has been forgiven. Moreover, as a result humans would know themselves, that they are mortal and weak; they would understand God, too, that He is immortal and powerful to such an extent that He grants †immortality to the mortal, and eternity to the temporal. They would understand the rest of God's powers that were shown toward themselves, and, having been taught through these, they would understand about God, how great God is.
>
> In truth, God is the glory of humanity, but humanity is the vessel of God's working, of all His wisdom and power. Just as a physician proves himself among the sick, so God is manifested among human persons.[a]

a. Irenaeus, *Against Heresies* 3.23, in *St. Irenaeus of Lyons: Against the Heresies, Book 3*, ed. Matthew C. Steenberg, trans. Dominic J. Unger, Ancient Christian Writers 64 (New York: Newman, 2012), 95–96.

on the other. Their sadness concerned the past—**what had occurred**—but also the present divine blessing of the Israelites. They saw how **through their own punishments the righteous had received benefit**, thus experiencing the negative side of the principle of just deserts enunciated earlier, that "through the very things by which [Israel's] enemies were punished, they themselves received benefit" (Wis 11:5). When the Egyptians saw that their punishment benefited the Israelites, they realized **it was the Lord's doing**. The last verse of this section describes the Egyptians' change of mind regarding Moses. They progress from driving him out of the country to marveling at all the works God did through him. **Their thirst** was different from the thirst of the Israelites, since God used thirst to judge the Egyptians in his wrath and to correct the Israelites in his mercy.

Excursus: God's Mercy toward Egyptians and Canaanites

Wisdom 11:15–12:27

This new section interrupts the series of seven comparisons that the author uses to structure chapters 11–19. In fact, it is the first of two excurses (the second follows immediately after it in 13:1–15:19). This first †excursus reflects on God's kindness and restraint toward the pagan Egyptians, a divine trait also seen in his treatment of the Canaanites and his chosen people. The Lord teaches human beings through the consequences of their actions in order that their hearts may be converted.

Learning by Punishment (11:15–20)

> ¹⁵In return for their foolish and wicked thoughts,
> which led them astray to worship irrational serpents and
>   worthless animals,
> you sent upon them a multitude of irrational creatures to punish
>   them,
> ¹⁶that they might learn that one is punished by the very things by
>   which he sins.
> ¹⁷For your all-powerful hand,
> which created the world out of formless matter,
> did not lack the means to send upon them a multitude of bears,
>   or bold lions,
> ¹⁸or newly created unknown beasts full of rage,
> or such as breathe out fiery breath,
> or belch forth a thick pall of smoke,
> or flash terrible sparks from their eyes;

[19]**not only could their damage exterminate men,**
but the mere sight of them could kill by fright.
[20]**Even apart from these, men could fall at a single breath**
when pursued by justice
and scattered by the breath of your power.
But you have arranged all things by measure and number and
weight.

OT: Exod 8:1–32; 10:12–16; Deut 32:24; 2 Kings 17:25–26; Job 4:8–9; 41:18–21
NT: Rom 1:18–32
Catechism: creation out of nothing, 296; God's order in creation, 299

Although the author here interrupts the series of comparisons he has just begun, **11:15–20** he continues to reflect on the fate of the Egyptians in the time of the exodus. He explains how appropriate the plagues of Egypt were. The punishment of animal plagues fits the crime of animal worship. The Egyptians begin with an error in thinking, a false theology: **their foolish and wicked thoughts**. This intellectual error leads to a [†]cultic one: **to worship irrational serpents and worthless animals**. In order to correct their error, God sends **a multitude of irrational creatures**—namely, the gnats, flies, and locusts of the plagues. "Irrational" here not only means without the powers of reasoning but also likely means "without speech"—that is, animals that do not make sounds. The author formulates this recollection as a prayer to God: **you sent**. The pain of punishment is not purposeless, but through it God teaches the Egyptians **that one is punished by the very things by which he sins**. As one scholar put it, punishment "is implicit in the very structure of sin."[1] The idea corresponds to the wider biblical theology of retribution, that "those who plow iniquity and sow trouble reap the same" (Job 4:8). Wisdom's view of retribution also corresponds to the legal version of this concept, the so-called *lex talionis*, the "eye for eye, tooth for tooth" (Exod 21:24), wherein legal penalties are designed to be proportionate and befitting. Wisdom sees this principle at work throughout the world, in which God enforces a just correspondence between sin and its consequences.

Now that the essential argument has been presented, the author will develop the theme through a series of colorful examples. First, however, he cites God's almighty power to create and explains that God **created the world out of formless matter**. This idea in some ways matches Gen 1:1–2 but is in contrast with other biblical depictions of *creatio ex nihilo*, creation out of nothing (2 Macc 7:28). It does correspond to Greek notions of the eternity of primordial matter (the concept that matter has existed for all eternity), yet the author makes no clear claims in this direction. St. Augustine resolves the discrepancy by positing a two-stage creation: "First there was made confused and formless matter

---

1. Michael Kolarcik, "The Book of Wisdom," in *The New Interpreter's Bible*, ed. Leander E. Keck, 12 vols. (Nashville: Abingdon, 1997), 5:540–41.

Philo on the Animal Plagues

Philo (ca. 20 BC–AD 50) explains why God would punish the Egyptians with powerless animals who could not do serious harm. God aims to teach them, not destroy them:

> Someone perhaps may ask why He punished the land through such petty and insignificant creatures, and refrained from using bears and lions and panthers and the other kinds of savage beasts which feed on human flesh; and, if not these, at any rate the asps of Egypt, whose bites are such as to cause immediate death. If such a person really does not know the answer, let him learn it: first, God wished to admonish the inhabitants of the land rather than to destroy them, for had He wished to annihilate them altogether He would not have taken animals to co-operate in His visitation, but calamities sent direct from heaven—pestilence and famine. And after this the inquirer should be taught a further lesson, and one that is needed throughout life. What is this? When men make war, they look round to find the most powerful auxiliaries to fight beside them, and so compensate for their own weakness; but God, the highest and greatest power, needs no one. But if, at any time, He wills to use any as instruments for His vengeance, He does not choose the strongest and the greatest, of whose might He takes no account, but provides the slightest and the smallest with irresistible and invincible powers, and through them wreaks vengeance on the evil-doers. So it was in this case. For what is slighter than a gnat? Yet so great was its power that all Egypt lost heart, and was forced to cry aloud: "This is the finger of God"; for as for His hand not all the habitable world from end to end could stand against it, or rather not even the whole universe.[a]

a. Philo, *On the Life of Moses* 1.109–12 (Colson, Whitaker, and Earp, LCL 6:331–33).

so that out of it there might be made all the things that God distinguished and formed."[2]

Since God is the creator of all things, the author suggests that instead of sending harmless insects and frogs upon the Egyptians, God could have sent deadly **bears or bold lions**. Here †Philo is helpful since he makes the same argument at greater length (see the sidebar "Philo on the Animal Plagues," above). The Egyptians do eventually recognize that "this is the finger of God" (Exod 8:19). The weak and benign nature of the animals God sent gives the Egyptians the opportunity to learn the right lesson.

To extend the idea, the author suggests that God could have even specially **created unknown beasts** to torment them with **fiery breath** and **terrible sparks from their eyes**. This fantastical description of dragon-like creatures is like other

2. Augustine of Hippo, *On Genesis: Two Books on Genesis against the Manichees; And, on the Literal Interpretation of Genesis: An Unfinished Book*, ed. Thomas P. Halton, trans. Roland J. Teske, FC 84 (Washington, DC: Catholic University of America Press, 1991), 57.

biblical reflections on divine power enacted through terrifying creatures (Job 41:18–21) or on such creatures posing as deities (Dan 14:23–27). To bring this imaginary speculation to its logical conclusion, the author visualizes how such spectral brutes could **exterminate men** and even **kill by fright**. Yet God chose less-frightening animals to punish the Egyptians in order that they might not die but learn the lesson he was seeking to teach them.

The last verse in this passage illustrates how even **apart from** monsters like **these** God could easily destroy the Egyptians **at a single breath . . . by the breath of** his **power** (see Isa 11:4). God willingly restrains his power in a measured dispensation of mercy. In prayerful assent to God's order, the author says, **you have arranged all things by measure and number and weight**. This statement about God's government refers to a widespread †Platonic tradition of recognizing measure, number, and weight as inherent in the divine design.[3] The proportionality of God's punishment of human sin reflects his rational ordering of all things. The point is that the animals used to punish and teach the Egyptians were playing a role in God's larger designs for the universe, where he has arranged all things according to his wisdom.

Power, Mercy, Love, and Freedom (11:21–12:2)

> [21]**For it is always in your power to show great strength,**
> **and who can withstand the might of your arm?**
> [22]**Because the whole world before you is like a speck that tips**
>   **the scales,**
> **and like a drop of morning dew that falls upon the ground.**
> [23]**But you are merciful to all, for you can do all things,**
> **and you overlook men's sins, that they may repent.**
> [24]**For you love all things that exist,**
> **and you loathe none of the things which you have made,**
> **for you would not have made anything if you had hated it.**
> [25]**How would anything have endured if you had not willed it?**
> **Or how would anything not called forth by you have been**
>   **preserved?**
> [26]**You spare all things, for they are yours, O Lord who love**
>   **the living.**
> [12:1]**For your immortal spirit is in all things.**
> [2]**Therefore you correct little by little those who trespass,**
> **and remind and warn them of the things wherein they sin,**
> **that they may be freed from wickedness and put their trust in**
>   **you, O Lord.**

---

3. E.g., Plato, *Laws* 757b; see also *Testament of Naphtali* 2.3.

OT: 2 Chron 20:6; Ps 145:9; Sir 18:12; 44:16; Isa 40:15; Hosea 13:3
NT: Acts 17:30; Rom 2:4; 2 Pet 3:9
Catechism: the universal power of God, 269; the infinite mercy of God, 270; God sustains creation, 301
Lectionary: 11:22–12:2: 31st Sunday in Ordinary Time (Year C)

This passage pivots from considering God's terrifying power to destroy (11:17–20) toward contemplating what God's **great strength** reveals about his mercy. It would be tempting to think of God's patience and clemency as a form of weakness, as if he were unable to punish wrongdoers. Yet the author argues the opposite, that God's mercy is evidence of his power. God has the power to create everything and to destroy everything, yet he holds his destructive power in check in order that people have time to repent and amend their ways.

11:21–23   The author highlights God's sheer power by asking, **who can withstand the might of your arm?** God's might is so immense that no one can resist or oppose him. Yet God does not use his great power to pummel his creatures but holds it back for mercy's sake. In the next verse, the author alludes to Isaiah's memorable image ("as the dust on the scales," Isa 40:15) to compare the vastness of the Almighty to the world, which is **like a speck that tips the scales**. This way of describing God's transcendence—that God is bigger than everything else—appeals to the imagination and is easy to understand.

It is God's very immensity that makes his mercy possible and available to all: **you are merciful to all, for you can do all things**. The Lord's clemency is universal, aimed at all people for all time. And again, it is not a sign of his weakness but evidence of his strength and his strategy. In his goodness, he overlooks **men's sins, that they may repent** (Greek *metanoia*). St. Paul will repeat this theme as a rhetorical question: "Or do you presume on the riches of his kindness and forbearance and patience, not knowing that God's kindness is meant to lead you to repentance?" (Rom 2:4 ESV-CE). God's mercy is an invitation to conversion.

11:24–26   God's mercy arises from his love: **for you love all things that exist**. This reaffirms the positive view of creation established in Genesis: "And God saw everything that he had made, and behold, it was very good" (Gen 1:31). Wisdom points out the obvious—God would not have **made anything if** he **had hated it**. God did not create beings just to destroy them. The author highlights how God's creative activity not only brings creatures into existence but "upholds and sustains them in being" (Catechism 301).

To review the logic of verses 21–25: God's power leads to mercy, and his mercy is rooted in love, and his love holds things in existence. Now the author returns to the theme of mercy. As God loves all things, he also will **spare all things**. All his interventions in human history must be interpreted through his love, goodness, and mercy. God is not capricious but predictable. Every divine intervention is meant to instruct, invite, and convert, and the author seeks to

Catechism of the Council of Trent on God's Sustaining Creation in Existence

The *Catechism of the Council of Trent* quotes Wisdom when it teaches that created things are held in being by God's power:

> We must not . . . think that God was the creator and accomplisher of all things in such a way, as to suppose that, when once the work was completed and perfected, those things which he had made could continue to exist unsupported by his infinite power. For as they obtain their existence from the supreme power, wisdom, and goodness of the Creator, so also, unless his continual providence were ever present unto the things created, and by the same power by which they were first produced, they would instantly return to their original nothing. This the Scripture declares, when it says: *How could anything have endured, if it had not been thy will? or been preserved, if not called by thee?* (Wis 11:25).[a]

St. Thomas Aquinas similarly explains that God not only creates all things but sustains them "by continually pouring out existence into them."[b]

a. *The Catechism of the Council of Trent*, trans. Theodore Alois Buckley (London: George Routledge and Co., 1852), 29 (translation modified).
b. *Summa Theologica* I, q. 104, a. 3, trans. Fathers of the English Dominican Province (New York: Benziger Brothers, 1947–48), 1:514.

interpret salvation history in this light. The Lord's **love** for **the living** is a common biblical theme.[4]

Though Wisdom teaches that God's **immortal spirit is in all things**, it does **12:1–2** not teach †pantheism (that concept that the universe is God), but rather it reasserts the biblical teaching that the "breath of life" that sustains all creatures comes from God (Gen 2:7; Job 27:3; Ps 104:29–30; Eccles 12:7).[5] The final verse in this section explains God's motives for punishing people. Namely, his goal is to correct, admonish, and instruct people **little by little**. This gradual correction of mind and heart is meant to lead **those who trespass** to conversion. Like the purpose of the plagues discussed above (Wis 11:15–16), God is at work in all things to **remind and warn** people to repent and turn to him. Those who respond will be **freed from wickedness** as they come to **trust** (Greek *pisteuō*) in the Lord, a striking parallel to St. Paul's explanation of Christian freedom (see Rom 6:16–23).

Using the same Greek vocabulary as New Testament authors, Wisdom invites its readers to repent (*metanoia*, 11:23), to believe (*pisteuō*, 12:2),[6] and to

4. See Isa 63:9; Ezek 18:23; John 3:16.
5. See Paul Heinisch, *Das Buch der Weisheit*, Exegetisches Handbuch zum Alten Testament 24 (Münster in Westalen: Aschendorff, 1912), 231–32.
6. Matt 21:35; Mark 1:15; Acts 19:4; 20:21; Heb 6:1.

experience freedom from sin.[7] The teaching of the New Testament regarding the response that God desires of human beings is never more clearly prefigured in the Old Testament than here.

The Canaanites' Chance to Repent (12:3–11)

³Those who dwelt of old in your holy land
⁴you hated for their detestable practices,
their works of sorcery and unholy rites,
⁵their merciless slaughter of children,
and their sacrificial feasting on human flesh and blood.
These initiates from the midst of a heathen cult,
⁶these parents who murder helpless lives,
you wanted to destroy by the hands of our fathers,
⁷that the land most precious of all to you
might receive a worthy colony of the servants of God.
⁸But even these you spared, since they were but men,
and sent wasps as forerunners of your army,
to destroy them little by little,
⁹though you were not unable to give the ungodly into the hands
    of the righteous in battle,
or to destroy them at one blow by dread wild beasts or your stern
    word.
¹⁰But judging them little by little you gave them a chance
    to repent,
though you were not unaware that their origin was evil
and their wickedness inborn,
and that their way of thinking would never change.
¹¹For they were an accursed race from the beginning,
and it was not through fear of any one that you left them unpun-
    ished for their sins.

OT: Wis 14:23; Exod 23:28–30; Lev 18:21–30; Deut 7:17–26; 18:9–12; Ps 106:34–39
NT: Gal 5:20; Heb 12:17

12:3 The †excursus on God's clemency (11:15–12:27) began with the example of his dealings with the Egyptians, and now it turns to another case from biblical history, the Canaanites. "Canaanites" is a catchall term for all the nations who lived in the land of Canaan before Joshua's conquest (Deut 20:17). In keeping with the author's practice of omitting names, he simply calls them **those who dwelt of old in your holy land**. Like other Jewish authors of the period, Wisdom's

7. See, for example, Acts 3:19; Rom 6:18, 22.

author feels the need to offer an apologetic defense of the Israelites' conquest of Canaan.[8] The Israelites could be accused of illegally and violently taking land from people who had not harmed them. The author argues that the biblical history demonstrates God's mildness, not harshness, toward the Canaanites.

The author justifies God's condemnation of the Canaanites on the basis of their **detestable practices** (see Lev 18:21–30), which serves as a headline for what follows. The **works of sorcery** (*pharmakeia*) refer to magical arts that employ potions or drugs (see Gal 5:20; Rev 9:21; 21:8), while their **unholy rites** denote their worship of false gods. In biblical descriptions of the Canaanites and their practices, the supreme example of their moral degradation is their sacrifice of children to the god Molech (a practice that some Israelites adopted as well; see Lev 18:21; 2 Kings 23:10; Jer 7:31). Wisdom recounts and emphasizes the Canaanites' sacrifice of children to establish the legality of their execution according to biblical law (Gen 9:6; Lev 20:2–5). Wisdom 12:5, which is notoriously difficult to translate, takes the sacrifice of children to yet another horrific level, as the author claims that the Canaanites would actually eat the entrails of the children being sacrificed. While it was customary for worshipers to partake of the animals offered on the altar, this is the only biblical mention of cannibalism in the worship of Molech. 12:4–5

Here the Canaanite **parents who murder helpless lives** are contrasted with the Israelite settlers who come to carry out God's justice and inhabit the Holy Land as **a worthy colony of the servants of God**. The Canaanites had defiled the land by their wicked practices (Lev 18:24–30), and the Israelites arrive on the scene as the agents of God's justice, bringing an end to the horrifying wickedness of Canaanite religion. 12:6–9

The author next highlights the mercy of God that teaches people gradually through punishments that begin gently, yet steadily increase in severity over time. He cites the biblical tradition that God would send wasps or hornets ahead of his people to drive out the inhabitants of the land (Exod 23:28; Deut 7:20; Josh 24:12). Like the plagues of Egypt, these insects would be the vanguard of God's conquering army, bringing his punishment against the Canaanites **little by little**. Again, recalling God's universal power and his ability to command **dread wild beasts** (Wis 11:15–20), the author argues that the mild punishments God sends are evidence of his moderation, not harshness.

The purpose of gradual punishment is made perfectly clear: **But judging them little by little you gave them a chance to repent**. The theme of repentance, which was introduced in 11:23, now returns as the solution to the problem of disobedience and sin. Even though in his divine foreknowledge, God knew that the Canaanites would not change their ways, in his mercy he gave them time to repent (hinted at in Gen 15:16). Yet they proved their **inborn** sinfulness and their obstinacy, that **their way of thinking would never change**. These descriptions of 12:10–11

---

8. *Jubilees* 8–10; Philo, *Hypothetica* 6.5–8.

the Canaanites' extraordinary sinfulness do not fall into †determinism (the idea that humans have no free will), but they correspond to similar pessimistic biblical statements about humanity's tendency to sin (Gen 6:5; Eccles 9:3; Jer 17:9; Matt 7:21). In the final verse of this section, the author doubles down on the terrible fate of the Canaanites by calling them **an accursed race from the beginning**. This claim is rooted in Noah's curse of Canaan in Gen 9:25. With the words **it was not through fear of any one that you left them unpunished**, the author defends God's clemency against the charge of lenience, perhaps to explain to the author's questioning Jewish audience why God would permit contemporaneous Greeks and Egyptians to sin without being punished when the Canaanites were punished.

The Mildness of God's Judgment (12:12–18)

¹²For who will say, "What have you done?"
Or who will resist your judgment?
Who will accuse you for the destruction of nations which
    you made?
Or who will come before you to plead as an advocate for
    unrighteous men?
¹³For neither is there any god besides you, whose care is for
    all men,
to whom you should prove that you have not judged unjustly;
¹⁴nor can any king or monarch confront you about those whom
    you have punished.
¹⁵You are righteous and rule all things righteously,
deeming it alien to your power
to condemn him who does not deserve to be punished.
¹⁶For your strength is the source of righteousness,
and your sovereignty over all causes you to spare all.
¹⁷For you show your strength when men doubt the completeness
    of your power,
and rebuke any insolence among those who know it.
¹⁸You who are sovereign in strength judge with mildness,
and with great forbearance you govern us;
for you have power to act whenever you choose.

OT: Gen 18:23–32; Job 9:2–12; Isa 45:9; Dan 4:35
NT: Rom 9:14–21
Catechism: God's power revealed through mercy, 277
Lectionary: 12:13, 16–19: 16th Sunday in Ordinary Time (Year A)

The author shifts his focus from explaining God's mercy (11:21–12:11) to defending God's justice (12:12–18). He steps back from specific examples and considers the question philosophically.

The author begins by posing four rhetorical questions about God's justice   12:12–15
that all inquire whether anyone is in a position to call God to account. They
all focus on the incommensurability of human beings with God, like earlier
biblical defenses of God's justice (Job 9:2–12; 38:4–40:2; Isa 45:9). We cannot
justly accuse God of injustice since he is the source of justice itself (Wis 12:16).
No higher authority can be appealed to since God is the ultimate authority and
by implication, the source of all other authority. The human temptation is to
question God's goodness when experiencing his punishments and accuse him of
being unjust (Rom 3:4–5), but Wisdom points out the absurdity of such a view.
God's righteousness and his power go hand in hand. He invariably exercises
his power in accord with his justice, never condemning a person **who does not
deserve to be punished**.

To resolve the seeming conflict between God's punishments and his goodness,   12:16–18
the author declares God's power to be **the source of righteousness**. This is not
a mere "might makes right" principle. Instead, he argues that God's complete
power over the world **causes** him **to spare all** (see 11:26). It is a practical argument: Why would God destroy what is under his jurisdiction (his **sovereignty**)?
People take care of what belongs to them, and the fact that the world belongs to
God means that he cares for it. When necessary, he will on occasion "show [his]
strength"—for instance, **when men doubt the completeness of** his **power**. The
author here likely has Pharaoh in mind (Exod 7:22–23). Among the people who
know God's power but disregard it, he will **rebuke any insolence**. The author
is probably thinking of the biblical evaluation of the exodus generation, who
tested God "though they had seen my work" (Ps 95:9) and were punished for
their defiance (Num 14:23; Ps 95:11; 1 Cor 10:9). To polish off the argument
with one more point, the final verse compares God's power with his **mildness**.
Rather than being evidence of God's weakness, the kindness and **forbearance**
of God flow from his righteousness, which flows from his **strength**.

Good Hope and Good Promises (12:19–27)

> [19]Through such works you have taught your people
> that the righteous man must be kind,
> and you have filled your sons with good hope,
> because you give repentance for sins.
> [20]For if you punished with such great care and indulgence
> the enemies of your servants and those deserving of death,
> granting them time and opportunity to give up their wickedness,
> [21]with what strictness you have judged your sons,
> to whose fathers you gave oaths and covenants full of good
> promises!

> [22]So while chastening us you scourge our enemies ten thousand
> times more,
> so that we may meditate upon your goodness when we judge,
> and when we are judged we may expect mercy.
> [23]Therefore those who in folly of life lived unrighteously
> you tormented through their own abominations.
> [24]For they went far astray on the paths of error,
> accepting as gods those animals which even their enemies
> despised;
> they were deceived like foolish infants.
> [25]Therefore, as to thoughtless children,
> you sent your judgment to mock them.
> [26]But those who have not heeded the warning of light rebukes
> will experience the deserved judgment of God.
> [27]For when in their suffering they became incensed
> at those creatures which they had thought to be gods, being
> punished by means of them,
> they saw and recognized as the true God him whom they had
> before refused to know.
> Therefore the utmost condemnation came upon them.

OT: Wis 11:15–16, 23; 16:1, 16; Deut 7:6–14; 2 Macc 6:12–16
NT: Matt 7:2; Rom 1:21–23; 1 Cor 10:13

This closing section of this first †excursus, on God's mercy toward Israel's en-emies (Wis 11–12), sums up the argument to this point and transitions to the second excursus, against idol worship (chaps. 13–15). The summary, presented in the first half of this passage (12:19–22), applies to Israel the principle that all of God's judgments reveal his clemency and his desire for people to repent. The transition in the second half (vv. 23–27) recalls the animal worship of the Egyptians, which had been discussed earlier (11:15–16), and invites the reader into the much longer evaluation of idolatry in chapters 13–15.

12:19–22   The **works** through which God **taught** his **people** likely refer to the peda-gogical rebukes mentioned earlier (vv. 2, 17). God teaches through punishment. **The righteous man** possibly refers to "a strict observer of the ceremonial law."[9] Wisdom does not view this kind of righteousness as sufficient, but such a person must also be **kind** (*philanthrōpos*)—this keyword means "loving of human-ity" and appears as a characteristic of wisdom herself (1:6 and 7:23).[10] Thus in order to respond to the divine lesson, one must be not only law observant but

---

9. A. T. S. Goodrick, *The Book of Wisdom with Introduction and Notes* (London: Rivingtons, 1913; repr., New York: Cambridge University Press, 2012), 269.

10. The virtue of *philanthrōpia* was a favorite theme of †Philo. See David Winston, *The Wisdom of Solomon*, AB 43 (Garden City, NY: Doubleday, 1979), 43–44; Winston, "Philo's Ethical Theory," *ANRW* II.21.1 (1984): 372–416, here 391–99.

Egyptian Animal Worship

BIBLICAL
BACKGROUND

The Egyptians worshiped hundreds of deities, major and minor, who took many forms: human, astral, and zoomorphic. Wisdom's author aims his critique of Egyptian religion primarily at the worship of animals, which even their pagan critics "despised" (12:24). While Egyptian polytheism had been practiced for millennia, the †Hellenistic period witnessed the blending of Greek and Egyptian religion with popular †syncretistic deities like Isis and Serapis.

Wisdom's critique of Egyptian religion and culture was not unique. The Greek historian Herodotus (484–425 BC), for example, describes Egyptian "customs and laws of a kind contrary for the most part to those of all other men."[a] The Greek playwright Anaxandrides places this mocking speech in the mouth of the Athenian representative who is replying to Egyptian ambassadors requesting an alliance:

> I could not have allied with you;
> for neither our ways agree nor our laws,
> but they differ greatly from one another.
> You grovel before a cow, but I sacrifice it to the gods;
> you consider the eel the greatest divinity,
> but we by far the greatest of delicacies.
> You do not eat pork, but I enjoy
> it especially; you worship a dog, but I beat it,
> whenever I catch it gulping down my food.
> It is law that priests here be whole [uncastrated],
> but among you, as it seems, that they have been dedicated as firstfruits.
>   [i.e., have been made eunuchs]
> If you see a cat doing poorly,
> you weep, while I gladly kill and skin it.
> Among you the mouse is powerful, but to me it is not.[b]

a. Herodotus, *Histories* 2.34.2, in *Herodotus: Books I–II*, ed. G. P. Goold, trans. A. D. Godley, vol. 1, LCL (Cambridge, MA: Harvard University Press, 1975), 317.

b. Benjamin Millis, *Anaxandrides: Introduction, Translation, Commentary* (Heidelberg: Verlag Antike, 2015), 187–88, fr. 40 K.-A. (translation slightly modified).

humane. This verse holds out a cheerful vision for life with God, whose children are filled **with good hope** because of the opportunity for **repentance** that God grants. The author reflects again on **the enemies of your servants**—namely, the Egyptians and Canaanites—arguing that God gave them **time and opportunity to give up their wickedness**. God's generous forbearance with these Gentiles gives his covenant people additional reason for hope that he will be kind toward them, whom he judges with great **strictness**. Since his people have been given **covenants**, laws, and **promises**, they will be held to a higher standard. And yet the purpose of punishment is pedagogical: it leads God's people to **meditate upon** God's **goodness when we judge**. God's kind and merciful judgment is the "philanthropic" example that we should follow when we evaluate other people. Jesus teaches the same concept from a different direction when warning against judging others: "With the judgment you pronounce you will be judged" (Matt 7:2). The idea is that by reflecting on God's mercy, we will be merciful in our own judgments, and if we are, then **when we are judged we may expect mercy**. Likewise, Jesus also teaches, "Blessed are the merciful, for they shall obtain mercy" (Matt 5:7).

12:23–27   The transitional section that prepares for the author's criticism of idol worship (vv. 23–27) takes us back to the idea of divine retribution presented earlier. The Egyptians were **tormented through their own abominations** when God used animals as the very means by which to punish them "that they might learn that one is punished by the very things by which he sins" (11:16). The author will develop the observation that the Egyptians' behavior was **folly**, unrighteous, abominable, in **error**, and made them **like foolish infants**. Animal worship is so obviously foolish, yet the Egyptians did not limit themselves to adoring noble animals but even worshiped animals **despised** by their fellow Gentiles. To correct their error, God "mocks" them **as thoughtless children** by sending **light rebukes**—namely, the first nine plagues. These divine "mockeries" are meant to teach the Egyptians a theological lesson: that animals are not gods. When they do not heed the "light rebukes," they receive **deserved judgment**, probably a reference to the plague of the firstborn and the destruction of the Egyptian army in the Red Sea. Yet in some way, the Egyptians learn the lesson God is teaching: **they saw and recognized as the true God him whom they had before refused to know**, a reference to the magicians' profession that "this is the finger of God" (Exod 8:19). Their continued obstinance despite their recognition of God resulted in the **utmost condemnation** coming upon them.

Reflection and Application (11:15–12:27)

Flying in a plane grants us a new perspective on the world in which we live. All the places important to us—our homes, our cars, our schools, our workplaces—shrink to amusingly tiny size, as if they were only toys on a wide expanse of land. This section of Wisdom similarly shifts our perspective to see things from God's vantage point.

When we witness the results of God's judgment in the Old Testament, whether the plagues and punishments or the harsh words of the prophets, we can be taken aback and even offended. Here, however, the author is drawing us into God's perspective: yes, God sent animals to punish the Egyptians, but not deadly ones—only pesky, "worthless" ones—that the Egyptians might not die but learn who God is and what he wants. Wisdom seeks to adjust our mentality, explaining that God's judgment gives his people hope in the possibility of repentance, even if all too often people reject the lessons God is teaching.

When we experience the sad consequences of our sins—guilt, disorder, and personal problems that arise from our choices against God—we can become discouraged. Yet Wisdom reminds us that these consequences can be a source of hope, hope that God is trying to get our attention, hope that he will overlook our sins if we repent (11:23), and that he desires to grant us the "time and opportunity" to do so (12:19–20). It explains the purpose of punishment: to convert our hearts to him and to help us let go of the lure of the world and our disordered desires. So, we can embrace his judgment as a reason for hope.

Excursus: Against Idol Worship

Wisdom 13:1–15:19

This second major digression attacks false worship. It begins by rejecting the understandable folly of nature worship (13:1–9), proceeds to describe and condemn the more egregious error of idol worship (13:10–15:13), and finally concludes in a crescendo of criticism by disparaging the worst form of false worship, the adoration of animals (15:14–19). In the context of this structured critique, the author speculates on the origins of false worship (14:12–31) and prays to God with a focus on the benefits of true worship (15:1–6).

The Folly of Nature Worship (13:1–9)

> ¹For all men who were ignorant of God were foolish by nature;
> and they were unable from the good things that are seen to know
>   him who exists,
> nor did they recognize the craftsman while paying heed to his
>   works;
> ²but they supposed that either fire or wind or swift air,
> or the circle of the stars, or turbulent water,
> or the luminaries of heaven were the gods that rule the world.
> ³If through delight in the beauty of these things men assumed
>   them to be gods,
> let them know how much better than these is their Lord,
> for the author of beauty created them.
> ⁴And if men were amazed at their power and working,
> let them perceive from them
> how much more powerful is he who formed them.
> ⁵For from the greatness and beauty of created things
> comes a corresponding perception of their Creator.

> ⁶Yet these men are little to be blamed,
> for perhaps they go astray
> while seeking God and desiring to find him.
> ⁷For as they live among his works they keep searching,
> and they trust in what they see, because the things that are seen
>   are beautiful.
> ⁸Yet again, not even they are to be excused;
> ⁹for if they had the power to know so much
> that they could investigate the world,
> how did they fail to find sooner the Lord of these things?

OT: Deut 4:19
NT: Acts 17:27; Rom 1:19–21; Heb 11:6
Catechism: knowledge of God from the order of the world, 32; correspondence of creatures to the Creator, 41; God as source of true knowledge, 216; traces of Creator in creation, 1147; prohibition of graven images of God, 2129; God reveals himself through creation, 2500
Lectionary: 13:1–9: Ordinary Time, Week 32, Friday (Year I)

This first segment of the long †excursus is a study of foolish thinking. The author considers the beauty of creation as elegant evidence for the existence of God, the source of creation, yet the wonder of creation has deceived other people into thinking that created things themselves are gods. He regards this as an understandable error, yet still an error. He argues for a kind of natural theology, a knowing of God through reason. Belief in God is not an irrational leap into the dark but the logical result of observing the world around us.

The author likens this logical process to coming to know **the craftsman** 13:1–5 (*technitēs*) by examining his **works**. This special term for the Creator was used for wisdom in Wis 7:22 and 8:6, again showing the overlap between God and his wisdom. God is he **who exists** (or "the one who is," NABRE), a philosophical term borrowed from †Platonism.[1] Since belief in God as the source of all things is a logical inference from observation of creation, to reject the Creator and worship creation instead is to be **ignorant** and **foolish**.

The gods of the nature worshipers include **fire**, **wind**, **air**, **stars**, **water**, and **the luminaries of heaven**—that is, the sun and moon. The author is painting a picture of †Stoic polytheism with broad brush strokes. These natural entities are beautiful, but not divine. They are evidence for **the author of beauty**—namely, God. The author of Wisdom is rejecting the Greek tendency to deify elements of creation, insisting instead that the creator of nature is far more

---

1. On the philosophical references in Wis 13:1–9, see James M. Reese, *Hellenistic Influence on the Book of Wisdom and Its Consequences*, Analecta Biblica 41 (Rome: Biblical Institute Press, 1970), 52–62. Reese states, "The Sage is aware of the difference in meaning that the expression ["he who is"] has in the Platonic tradition, as a technical term for the real or true Being, and in the †Septuagint, where it designates the personal God who revealed himself to the chosen people as the God of their fathers (Ex 3.14). In the former tradition the designation 'He who is' was applied to the 'super-intelligible principle,' and efforts to contemplate this deity motivated much of late †hellenistic mysticism" (53).

The Principle of Analogy

The Catholic theological tradition adopts the Greek principle of speaking about God "by analogy" (Wis 13:5 NABRE).[a] Our finite human terms always fall short of God's infinite greatness, so we cannot speak about him univocally—that is, with the same meaning we intend when we speak of created things. To call a man "wise" is different from calling God "wise" since God is the source of all wisdom and indeed is Wisdom Himself. Yet if our terms cannot describe God accurately, then we are left only with equivocation, where our words mean something completely different when applied to God so that we cannot say anything meaningful about him at all. The solution to the seeming impossibility of speaking about God is what theologians call "analogy," where the terms we use to describe God highlight the similarity between finite human perception and the infinite divine Being. We can say that God is "wise" by analogy with wise human persons we have encountered, recognizing both the similarity and the difference between the two.

a. St. Thomas Aquinas, *Summa contra Gentiles* 1.34.

worthy of adoration than the things he created. In this way he anticipates the cosmological argument for God's existence, which employs observations of the world to demonstrate the existence of God.[2] While the author accepts a simplified philosophical proof for God's existence—inferring the existence of the Creator from the reality of creation—he advocates for a view of God that is not merely intellectual but relational. God should be not just perceived but sought and desired (13:6). Indeed, he argues that the God whose existence is discovered intellectually by Greek philosophy is to be identified as the personal God of biblical revelation, the Lord of creation (vv. 3, 9).

While the natural order is indeed beautiful, powerful, and awe-inspiring, it should lead us to God, **he who formed them**. We can reason "by analogy" (v. 5 NABRE) from the beautiful things back to their source, **their Creator** (see the sidebar "The Principle of Analogy," above). When we encounter the goodness of creation, it should lead us back to the analogous, yet greater, goodness of the Creator.

13:6–9   Now the author introduces an objection to his own line of reasoning, suggesting that the pagan philosophers are not completely at fault. **While seeking God** they have been distracted by the beautiful things he has created, and **they trust**

2. The classic expression of the cosmological argument in the Catholic tradition is the proofs for the existence of God offered by St. Thomas Aquinas, commonly referred to as the "Five Ways"; see *Summa Theologica* I, q. 2, a. 3.

in what they see. These verses acknowledge the value of unbelievers honestly seeking after God. Yet, returning to his original conclusion (13:1), the author declares that **not even they are to be excused**. The seekers who do not find God are not without fault. While acknowledging the intrinsic value of pursuing God through reason, the author definitively rejects the possibility that such seeking justifies polytheism. The final verse of this section asks a rhetorical question about these seekers: If they **had the power . . . to investigate the world** (Greek *aiōn*) through their speculations, why could they not find the source of the *aiōn*—namely, the **Lord of these things**? *Aiōn* was indeed worshiped as a god by some Greeks as "maker of the divine nature,"[3] but Wisdom wants them to think more deeply, to reason one step further to recognize God himself.

In the Light of Christ (13:1–9)

St. Paul possibly has these chapters (Wis 13–14) in mind when he describes the Gentiles who reject the true God as "without excuse":

> For the †wrath of God is revealed from heaven against all ungodliness and wickedness of men who by their wickedness suppress the truth. For what can be known about God is plain to them, because God has shown it to them. Ever since the creation of the world his invisible nature, namely, his eternal power and deity, has been clearly perceived in the things that have been made. So they are without excuse; for although they knew God they did not honor him as God or give thanks to him, but they became futile in their thinking and their senseless minds were darkened. (Rom 1:18–21)

The beauty and grandeur of creation ought to bring us to faith in God, but sin can lead us astray into false thinking and unbelief. Both Wis 13:1 and Rom 1:21 describe the reasoning of the pagans as "futile" (Greek *mataios*), using the same root word. In both texts, unbelief arises from ethical failings that cause sinners to reject the truth of God's existence (Wis 13:8–9; Rom 1:18).

Reflection and Application (13:1–9)

This passage teaches us to honor "seekers" who are looking for God, searching for truth. Many churches have opened ministries primarily for those who seek God but have not yet found faith in him. Wisdom gives us hope that they will find the One Who Is, the God that they seek after. It acknowledges the authenticity and importance of this quest for God by use of human reasoning. Yet

---

3. See Reese, *Hellenistic Influence*, 60.

we are warned that philosophy alone is insufficient. Our use of solid reasoning should lead us to also embrace faith in God. Again, the Wisdom of Solomon portrays the search for wisdom as a union of faith and reason, of human intellectual striving (Wis 1–9) and divine revelation (Wis 10–19).

The Wretched Idol Worshipers (13:10–19)

[10]But miserable, with their hopes set on dead things, are the men
who give the name "gods" to the works of men's hands,
gold and silver fashioned with skill,
and likenesses of animals,
or a useless stone, the work of an ancient hand.
[11]A skilled woodcutter may saw down a tree easy to handle
and skilfully strip off all its bark,
and then with pleasing workmanship
make a useful vessel that serves life's needs,
[12]and burn the castoff pieces of his work
to prepare his food, and eat his fill.
[13]But a castoff piece from among them, useful for nothing,
a stick crooked and full of knots,
he takes and carves with care in his leisure,
and shapes it with skill gained in idleness;
he forms it like the image of a man,
[14]or makes it like some worthless animal,
giving it a coat of red paint and coloring its surface red
and covering every blemish in it with paint;
[15]then he makes for it a niche that befits it,
and sets it in the wall, and fastens it there with iron.
[16]So he takes thought for it, that it may not fall,
because he knows that it cannot help itself,
for it is only an image and has need of help.
[17]When he prays about possessions and his marriage and
children,
he is not ashamed to address a lifeless thing.
[18]For health he appeals to a thing that is weak;
for life he prays to a thing that is dead;
for aid he entreats a thing that is utterly inexperienced;
for a prosperous journey, a thing that cannot take a step;
[19]for money-making and work and success with his hands
he asks strength of a thing whose hands have no strength.

OT: Ps 115:3–8; Isa 44:9–20; Jer 10:1–16; Bar 6:4–73
NT: Acts 17:29
Catechism: condemnation of idolatry, 2112–14

Figure 6. A black, conical stone thought to represent Aphrodite at her temple in Paphos, Cyprus. It is described by Tacitus: "The representation of the goddess is not in human form, but it is a circular mass that is broader at the base and rises like a turning-post to a small circumference at the top. The reason for this is obscure" (Tacitus, *Histories* 2.3, trans. Clifford H. Moore, LCL [Cambridge, MA: Harvard University Press, 1937], 1:164–65).

CC BY-SA 3.0 Wojciech Biegun / Wikimedia Commons

The rhetorical crescendo builds. The nature worshipers were dismissed as "foolish" in 13:1. Here, the idolaters are even worse: they are **miserable** (or "wretched," 13:10 NABRE). But the author saves his vitriol for the animal worshipers, who are "most stupid of all" (15:14 NABRE).

The author's claim that the "miserable" place   **13:10** their hope in **dead things** echoes the general biblical critique of idolatry that contrasts the living God with the dead, inanimate objects with **the name "gods"** (Deut 5:26; Dan 6:26; Hosea 1:10). These images are explicitly forbidden by the first commandment (Exod 20:2–6). The denunciation of idols as **the works of men's hands** is another component of the common biblical condemnation of idolatry (Wis 14:8; Isa 2:8; Acts 19:26). With biting sarcasm, the author will develop this theme of how ridiculous it is that people would worship a thing that they themselves constructed. He lists three types of idols: those made of precious metals, those that portray **animals**, and those that are simply **useless stone**. This last reference likely alludes to meteorites and other unusual stones that were worshiped as deities, like the conical stone that represented the goddess Aphrodite at Paphos or "the sacred stone that fell from the sky" (Acts 19:35) and signified Artemis at Ephesus. The heavenly source of such stones could allow their defenders to claim that they were **the work of an ancient hand**, of superhuman origin, evidence for the existence of gods.[4]

The next few verses satirize a pagan **woodcutter** who uses the same wood to   **13:11–16** make both **a useful vessel that serves life's needs** and an idol. In fact, he uses the most useless **castoff piece** of the wood to carve his idol—wood that is not even fit for burning to prepare a meal. The author's presentation of the details of hewing, scraping, carving, and painting the idol repeatedly emphasizes the man-made nature of these so-called gods and the foolishness of worshiping such objects. To worship nature is to worship God's handiwork, but to worship an idol is to worship man's handiwork. Once the idol is made, it still needs human handicraft to attend to it—to set it up and nail it to the wall, so **that it may not fall**. The idol maker deceives himself, since **he knows that it cannot**

4. Cicero, *De natura deorum* 2.5.14.

Figure 7. A lararium, a shrine for household gods, at the House of Menander in Pompeii.

help itself. The everyday context of this idol-making montage likely indicates the author had in mind idols for household shrines rather than statues for major temples. Household gods were a feature of early biblical times (see Gen 31:19) and contemporary Greco-Roman culture, where many houses contained a lararium or shrine to household deities.

13:17–19   The final part of this passage underscores the ironies of idol worship: asking a helpless object for help, a soulless totem for aid in matters of soul, asking for power from **a thing that is weak**, for life from **a thing that is dead**, for help in travel from an idol **that cannot take a step**, for success from **a thing whose hands have no strength**. This recitation of the dramatic ironies of idol worship drives home the point: idol worship is irrational, undignified, degrading, and pointless. By praying to idols, people reveal how "miserable" (v. 10) they have become.

Wooden Gods and Wooden Ships (14:1–11)

> [1]Again, one preparing to sail and about to voyage over raging waves
> calls upon a piece of wood more fragile than the ship which carries him.
> [2]For it was desire for gain that planned that vessel,
> and wisdom was the craftsman who built it;
> [3]but it is your providence, O Father, that steers its course,
> because you have given it a path in the sea,
> and a safe way through the waves,

⁴showing that you can save from every danger,
so that even if a man lacks skill, he may put to sea.
⁵It is your will that works of your wisdom should not be without
effect;
therefore men trust their lives even to the smallest piece of wood,
and passing through the billows on a raft they come safely to land.
⁶For even in the beginning, when arrogant giants were perishing,
the hope of the world took refuge on a raft,
and guided by your hand left to the world the seed of a new
generation.
⁷For blessed is the wood by which righteousness comes.

⁸But the idol made with hands is accursed, and so is he who made it;
because he did the work, and the perishable thing was named a
god.
⁹For equally hateful to God are the ungodly man and his
ungodliness,
¹⁰for what was done will be punished together with him who did it.
¹¹Therefore there will be a visitation also upon the heathen idols,
because, though part of what God created, they became an
abomination,
and became traps for the souls of men
and a snare to the feet of the foolish.

OT: Gen 6:1–5; Ps 107:23–32; Bar 3:26–28
NT: Acts 28:11; Gal 3:13–14

Figure 8. Artist's depiction of the Lighthouse of Alexandria, one of the Seven Wonders of the Ancient World (Johann Bernhard Fischer von Erlach, 1721).

Extending his discussion of the problem of wooden idols, the author presents a second illustration. This time, instead of describing the wood-carving idol maker, he turns to another important use of wood—namely, its use in sailing ships. Since sailing was the primary means for unscrupulous merchants to transport goods for profit, some biblical texts are critical of those who sail (Isa 23; Ezek 26–27), but Wisdom presents a more positive view. One can imagine the author watching the merchant ships moving in and out of the famous harbor of Alexandria under the shadow of its great lighthouse.

14:1–3   On the one hand, the author offers high praise for the very feat of sailing, that human beings can make ships out of wood and float on the sea. He declares that **wisdom was the craftsman** of these ships and credits God's **providence** with guiding them on **a safe way through the waves**. On the other hand, he belittles that sailor who prays to a **fragile piece of wood** while sailing. As in the previous chapter's discussion, the author will show how worshiping an "idol made with hands" (Wis 14:8) is beneath human dignity and contradicts the skillful application of wisdom entailed in shipbuilding. How could a sailor who is guided by providence, sailing in a well-built craft, entrusting his life to the good wood of the ship, be so unreasonable as to worship a wooden god? The mention of praying to gods made of wood here concerns the Greek and Roman practice in which ships would carry idolatrous images on board to ward off calamity. This pagan custom is reflected in Acts 28:11, which depicts a ship with "the Twin Brothers"—that is, the Roman gods Castor and Pollux—carved in the wood of its prow.

14:4–7   The author pauses to contemplate the extent of divine providence, that God would provide "a path in the sea" (14:3), that he would **save from every danger**. The **works of your wisdom** likely refers to the goods that would be transported by Mediterranean ships (**not be without effect** could be translated "not be idle"—that is, undis-

Figure 9. Alexandrian ship on a coin of Commodus (Bibliothèque nationale de France. Used by permission).

tributed), but perhaps also it refers to the wisdom that God adds to the skill of shipbuilders and sailors to keep passengers safe. To illustrate the importance of ships, the author reaches back to the time of Noah **when arrogant giants were perishing**, a reference to the Nephilim of Gen 6:4. Noah and his family constituted **the hope of the world** when they boarded the ark on their perilous journey. Upon completion of their voyage, the Lord used them to leave behind **the seed of a new generation** for the human race. **Wood** is **blessed**, and sailing can be praised because it was the means **by which righteousness** came, and it made possible a future for the human race and for God's people through Noah and his descendants.

However, the blessing of wood (14:7) is followed by a curse upon the wooden   14:8–11 **idol** (v. 8). Three times, the author insists that divine judgment will fall upon "the thing made" along with "its maker" (NABRE). The idol and the idol maker share the same fate. They become **equally hateful to God**, meaning that God's judgment falls upon them for their sins of idolatry. As many other biblical passages emphasize, the **visitation** (or "judgment") of God will come upon **idols**. Trees, wood, and wooden things are good, but wooden idols, **though part of what God created**, become **an abomination**. These wooden objects are now accursed snares and **traps**, which seduce people into false worship.

In the Light of Christ (14:1–11)

"For blessed is the wood [Greek *xylon*] by which righteousness comes" (14:7). Since the same word is often used to refer to the cross in the New Testament,[5] St. Ambrose identifies the blessed wood mentioned here as the cross of Christ.[6] The blessed wood of the cross is the new means of salvation, the new ark, the "most frail wood" (14:5 NABRE) in which we must put our hope. Likewise, Christians have long understood the tree of life found at the beginning and end of the Bible to refer to the cross, in the garden of Eden (Gen 2:9) and in the New Jerusalem, where it yields "twelve kinds of fruit" (Rev 22:2).

This segment of Wisdom addresses God directly in the second person (Wis 14:3–6) as "O Father." God is rarely addressed as father in the Old Testament (Ps 89:26; Sir 23:1; Isa 63:16; 64:8), but Jesus prays to God as Father (Mark 14:36) and teaches us to do the same (Matt 6:9; Luke 11:2).

Origins and Ends of Idol Worship (14:12–31)

> [12]For the idea of making idols was the beginning of fornication,
> and the invention of them was the corruption of life,
> [13]for neither have they existed from the beginning
> nor will they exist for ever.
> [14]For through the vanity of men they entered the world,
> and therefore their speedy end has been planned.
> [15]For a father, consumed with grief at an untimely bereavement,
> made an image of his child, who had been suddenly taken from
>   him;

---

5. Acts 5:30; 10:39; 13:29; Gal 3:13; 1 Pet 2:24.
6. St. Ambrose, *Sermon* 8 on Ps 118 (CSEL 62:164).

and he now honored as a god what was once a dead human being,
and handed on to his dependents secret rites and initiations.
¹⁶Then the ungodly custom, grown strong with time, was kept as
     a law,
and at the command of monarchs graven images were
     worshiped.
¹⁷When men could not honor monarchs in their presence, since
     they lived at a distance,
they imagined their appearance far away,
and made a visible image of the king whom they honored,
so that by their zeal they might flatter the absent one as though
     present.
¹⁸Then the ambition of the craftsman impelled
even those who did not know the king to intensify their worship.
¹⁹For he, perhaps wishing to please his ruler,
skilfully forced the likeness to take more beautiful form,
²⁰and the multitude, attracted by the charm of his work,
now regarded as an object of worship the one whom shortly
     before they had honored as a man.
²¹And this became a hidden trap for mankind,
because men, in bondage to misfortune or to royal authority,
bestowed on objects of stone or wood the name that ought not to
     be shared.

²²Afterward it was not enough for them to err about the
     knowledge of God,
but they live in great strife due to ignorance,
and they call such great evils peace.
²³For whether they kill children in their initiations, or celebrate
     secret mysteries,
or hold frenzied revels with strange customs,
²⁴they no longer keep either their lives or their marriages pure,
but they either treacherously kill one another, or grieve one
     another by adultery,
²⁵and all is a raging riot of blood and murder, theft and deceit,
     corruption, faithlessness, tumult, perjury,
²⁶confusion over what is good, forgetfulness of favors,
pollution of souls, sex perversion,
disorder in marriage, adultery, and debauchery.
²⁷For the worship of idols not to be named
is the beginning and cause and end of every evil.
²⁸For their worshipers either rave in exultation, or prophesy lies,
or live unrighteously, or readily commit perjury;
²⁹for because they trust in lifeless idols
they swear wicked oaths and expect to suffer no harm.

³⁰**But just penalties will overtake them on two counts:**
because they thought wickedly of God in devoting themselves
     to idols,
and because in deceit they swore unrighteously through
     contempt for holiness.
³¹**For it is not the power of the things by which men swear,**
but the just penalty for those who sin,
     that always pursues the transgression of the unrighteous.

OT: Wis 12:5; Jer 3:1–25; Dan 3:1–7; 1 Macc 1:47–50
NT: Rom 1:23–32; Gal 5:19–21; 1 Tim 6:10
Catechism: unity of the Decalogue, 2069; commandment against coveting, 2534

After depicting the carpenter's construction of an idol and then meditating on wooden ships, the author now explains two of the ways in which idol worship originated and then outlines its moral consequences in detail.

The first verse of this passage proposes the idea that **the invention of them**,   14:12–14
idols, brought about **the corruption of life**, a notion that will be restated in verse 27. Idol worship was **the beginning of fornication**. This claim alludes to the broad biblical tradition of identifying false worship as spiritual adultery and also censures the literal sexual practices that sometimes accompanied idol worship. Two different concepts are hidden in such a short verse—first, that idols are mere human inventions, and second, that faults in worship logically progress to other faults. That is, the author sees pagan worship as the dark headwaters of sin. Idolatry is the opposite of the biblical principle that "the fear of the Lord is the beginning of knowledge" (Prov 1:7).

Next the author builds on the idea of idols as human inventions. Their very temporary nature argues against their validity. The true God is eternal, but idols have a beginning and will decay. They come from **the vanity**, the futile pride, **of men**. Their useless origin leads to a useless end. Wisdom's view of the beginning of idolatry is similar to what other Jewish authors of the time period think of its origin.[7]

Now the author will put forth the first of two explanations regarding the   14:15–16
origin of idolatry—namely, that a grieving **father** carved **an image of his child** who died. This image soon is **honored as a god** in the man's household, and he becomes an inventor of religious traditions, teaching **secret rites and initiations** to be performed in its honor. Again, viewing idolatry as a dynamic process, the author portrays this household worship developing into public worship and becoming **law** by **the command of monarchs**. What began as a mourning custom eventually becomes law; a private practice becomes public ritual.

---

7. *Jubilees* 11.4–5; *Letter of Aristeas* 134–37.

14:17–20   Then the author presents a second explanation for how idol worship arose: from the honoring of an absent ruler's image. He paints a picture of a ruler whose kingdom is so vast that many of his subjects live far from him and cannot honor him in person—a familiar problem in †Hellenistic and Roman times. For example, the emperor Caligula promoted worship of his visage in temples around the Roman Empire (AD 40). While the narrative begins with political fealty to an absent ruler and the skill of the **craftsman** who carves a **beautiful form** to represent him, it ends with **the multitude** of common people being seduced by the clever artistry of the statue to worship it as a deity instead of merely honor the artistic representation of **a man**.[8]

14:21   Like the wooden idols discussed earlier (14:11), these new idols, whether the child carving or the ruler statues, **became a hidden trap**. While the true God offers freedom, idolatry is a form of slavery to sin that has often seduced his people. Biblical history is full of examples such as the golden calf at Mount Sinai (Exod 32), the ephod of Gideon (Judg 8:27), the graven image of Micah (Judg 18:30–31), and the golden calves of Jeroboam (1 Kings 12:28). Biblical law warns against idols for precisely their tendency to ensnare people (Exod 23:33; Deut 7:16). Again, the author thinks of this as a predictable process: those who are **in bondage to misfortune** in grief (v. 15) **or to** the **royal authority** of an absent ruler (vv. 17–20) seek relief by praying to idols but become entrapped by the idols themselves. **The name that ought not to be shared** likely refers to Yʜᴡʜ, the unpronounceable name of the Lord that was on occasion fraudulently used to label idols (Exod 32:5; Judg 17:3). On the other hand, the phrase could refer to *theos*, the Greek term for God. Either way, by conferring God's name on a piece of wood or stone, a person profoundly misunderstands who God is, and this error predictably leads to slavery to sin.

14:22–26   Now the author pivots from analyzing idolatry's origins to contemplating its consequences. The misconception of God by the idolaters leads them not only to worship human artworks but to view themselves as at **peace** when in fact they are **in great strife due to ignorance**. Upside-down thinking about God obscures the idolaters' self-knowledge so that they cannot see how their false belief conflicts with reality, nor can they recognize the grievously sinful state they are truly in. The author proceeds to list twenty-two kinds of sins that idolators commit (vv. 23–27). This number of vices likely alludes to the twenty-two letters of the Hebrew alphabet, indicating an exhaustive list like the twenty-two-point catalog of wisdom's attributes in 7:22b–24.[9] This list of

---

8. The ruler-worship origin story for idolatry is shared by the Greek historian Euhemerus on the origins of Greek gods. He believed that Cronos, Zeus, Uranus, and others long ago were powerful kings who eventually came to be worshiped as gods. See Truesdell S. Brown, "Euhemerus and the Historians," *Harvard Theological Review* 39 (1946): 259–74.

9. James M. Reese, *The Book of Wisdom, Song of Songs*, Old Testament Message 20 (Wilmington, DE: Michael Glazier, 1983), 154.

sins begins with pagan rituals. Its depiction of child sacrifice likely refers to the Canaanites' practices (see 12:5), but **secret mysteries** and **frenzied revels** probably refer to the initiation rites of the mystery religions that were popular in Hellenistic times, especially in honor of the gods Demeter, Dionysius, Isis, Cybele, and Mithras. The whole twenty-two-point list illustrates the tendency of polytheistic worship to lead to dishonesty, sexual immorality, and violence. On the one hand, the author sees a strong link between respect for the purity of **marriages** and respect for human **lives**, while on the other hand, he sees an association between murder and **adultery**. The author's rejection of false religion relies on the teaching of the Ten Commandments. There is an intrinsic connection between worship of false gods (first commandment), disregard for life and property (fifth and seventh commandments), adultery (sixth commandment), and perjury (eighth commandment). He summarizes the ethical conduct of the idol worshipers: **all is a raging riot**. Idol worship opens the Pandora's box of immorality, doing untold harm to the those enslaved by it. **Sex perversion** (or "interchange of sex roles"[10]) likely refers to homosexual practices (Rom 1:26–27).[11]

The chaotic list ends with a restatement of the main principle at work, **14:27–31** that idol worship **is the beginning and cause and end of every evil**. While it might seem that he overstates the case here, this claim that idolatry is the root of every evil agrees with the Ten Commandments, which forbid idolatry first. Idolatry, worshiping anything that is not God, is indeed the core of all other sins (Catechism 2113). The author proceeds to show the implications. The pagans **rave** "in a state of euphoria" (14:28 NETS), a deliberate and sinful abandonment of reason and temperance (Catechism 2290–91). The idol worshipers are living a lie with false prophecy, false (unrighteous) living, and false testimony (**perjury**). On some level the pagans are aware that the idols are not really gods, so they feel no guilt when they break oaths sworn in their names. Their fake deities will not hold them to account, so they routinely perjure themselves without a pang of conscience. Yet they will not get off so easily. Rather, genuine divine justice from the true God will **overtake them** because of their false beliefs, false worship, and false oaths. The powerless idols will not do anything, but the idol worshipers will not escape **the just penalty for those who sin**.

This passage is meant to warn readers against the terrible dangers of idolatrous worship. Despite its trappings of religious celebration, idolatry is in fact a deadly serious snare for souls that seduces them into grave rebellion against God that will not go unpunished.

---

10. David Winston, *The Wisdom of Solomon*, AB 43 (Garden City, NY: Doubleday, 1979), 280.

11. See other contemporary Jewish texts that reject homosexual practices: *Testament of Naphtali* 3.4; Philo, *On the Cherubim* 92.

A Prayer to the True God (15:1–6)

---

¹But you, our God, are kind and true, patient, and ruling all
　　things in mercy.
²For even if we sin we are yours, knowing your power;
but we will not sin, because we know that we are considered
　　yours.
³For to know you is complete righteousness,
and to know your power is the root of immortality.
⁴For neither has the evil intent of human art misled us,
nor the fruitless toil of painters,
a figure stained with varied colors,
⁵whose appearance arouses yearning in fools,
so that they desire the lifeless form of a dead image.
⁶Lovers of evil things and fit for such objects of hope
are those who either make or desire or worship them.

OT: Exod 34:6–7; Job 10:14–15; Ps 85:6
NT: John 17:3; 1 John 3:6; 4:8
Catechism: 2520, purity of vision

After describing the moral and social chaos brought on by idol worship, the
author turns toward God in prayer. This short second-person address to God
switches away from the downward spiral of idolatry and refocuses the discussion on God himself. It is a positive expression of adoration, accompanied by
more critical statements about idolatry (vv. 4–6).

15:1–3　　While the pagans' false worship leads to false speaking and unfaithful living,
God is **kind and true**. The idol worshipers are thus transformed by false worship
to do false deeds, while true worshipers are transformed by true worship to live
truly: **to know you is complete righteousness**. Like "You are what you eat," the
profoundly transformative nature of worship could be expressed in an aphorism:
"You become what you worship" (see Ps 115:8). **Ruling all things** points back
to God's universal governance as before (Wis 6:3; 11:24) and his ordering of all
things (8:1–2). Yet the universal God is also the God of a particular people, **our
God**. Using the first-person plural here, the author clearly identifies himself as
a member of the chosen race and emphasizes the indissolubility of God's covenant bond with his people: **even if we sin we are yours**. Though the author is
surely aware of the many faults of God's people narrated in the Bible, here he
highlights the encouraging truth that even when they sin, they are still part of
his covenant family. However, he views their covenantal identity as grounds for
fidelity to God: **we will not sin, because we know that we are considered yours**.

Knowledge of God brings about "righteousness" and constitutes **the root
of ⁺immortality**. Previously, the author affirmed that righteousness (1:15) and

wisdom-seeking (6:18–19; 8:17–18) lead to immortality; now he says the same of the knowledge of God. Knowing God makes one like God—namely, righteous and immortal.

The second part of this passage (vv. 4–6) returns to the problem of idol wor- **15:4–6** ship, but from a slightly different vantage point. The author insists that these idols "did not deceive us" (NABRE), an enthusiastic endorsement of the fidelity and reasonability of the Jews. One could view this statement as a cheerful invitation to his audience to join him in faithfulness and rational thinking by rejecting †Hellenistic paganism. The **painters** of idols succeed in deceiving some, like the masses seduced by the beauty of a ruler's statue (14:20). The author satirizes those that **desire the lifeless form of a dead image** by likely comparing them to the legendary king Pygmalion, who made a beautiful statue of a woman and was seduced by its beauty.[12] The idolaters truly are **lovers of evil things**, like the wicked who made a covenant with †death (1:16). Their false and evil love leads them to **such objects of hope**—namely, the "dead images" of idols—while the love of wisdom and righteousness brings true enlightenment (1:1; 7:10).

The Potter's Meaningless Life (15:7–19)

> [7]For when a potter kneads the soft earth
> and laboriously molds each vessel for our service,
> he fashions out of the same clay
> both the vessels that serve clean uses
> and those for contrary uses, making all in like manner;
> but which shall be the use of each of these
> the worker in clay decides.
> [8]With misspent toil, he forms a futile god from the same clay—
> this man who was made of earth a short time before
> and after a little while goes to the earth from which he was taken,
> when he is required to return the soul that was lent him.
> [9]But he is not concerned that he is destined to die
> or that his life is brief,
> but he competes with workers in gold and silver,
> and imitates workers in copper;
> and he counts it his glory that he molds counterfeit gods.
> [10]His heart is ashes, his hope is cheaper than dirt,
> and his life is of less worth than clay,
> [11]because he failed to know the one who formed him
> and inspired him with an active soul
> and breathed into him a living spirit.

---

12. Ovid, *Metamorphoses* 10.243–97.

¹²But he considered our existence an idle game,
and life a festival held for profit,
for he says one must get money however one can, even by base
    means.
¹³For this man, more than all others, knows that he sins
when he makes from earthy matter fragile vessels and graven
    images.

¹⁴But most foolish, and more miserable than an infant,
are all the enemies who oppressed your people.
¹⁵For they thought that all their heathen idols were gods,
though these have neither the use of their eyes to see with,
nor nostrils with which to draw breath,
nor ears with which to hear,
nor fingers to feel with,
and their feet are of no use for walking.
¹⁶For a man made them,
and one whose spirit is borrowed formed them;
for no man can form a god which is like himself.
¹⁷He is mortal, and what he makes with lawless hands is dead,
for he is better than the objects he worships,
since he has life, but they never have.

¹⁸The enemies of your people worship even the most hateful
    animals,
which are worse than all others, when judged by their lack of
    intelligence;
¹⁹and even as animals they are not so beautiful in appearance that
    one would desire them,
but they have escaped both the praise of God and his blessing.

OT: Gen 2:7; Ps 115:4–7; Isa 44:20 LXX; Jer 18:3–4
NT: Luke 12:20; Rom 9:21–23; 2 Tim 2:20–21
Catechism: human dignity, 356

At this point, late in the long digression (13:1–15:19), after criticism of nature worship, idol worship, and the carving of wooden idols, the author now composes a new critique of the idol maker who works with clay (15:7–13). It parallels his critique of the idol-making carpenter (13:10–19) and leads up to his fiercest condemnation of all, the censure of animal worship (15:14–19).

15:7–9   The first part of this passage denounces the work of the idol-making **potter** with a series of arguments. First, the material he uses for making false gods is employed both for **clean uses** and **for contrary uses**. The same clay can produce a chamber pot and a deity. Paul makes a remarkably similar argument in his discussion of divine providence in Romans, where the potter asserts his right "to make out of the same lump one vessel for honorable use and another for dishonorable use" (Rom 9:21 ESV-CE). Second, the making of gods is left up to human judgment: **the worker in clay decides**.

Third, the potter uses **misspent toil** to make these items, as if they were the leftovers of a day's work making truly useful items. This assessment is like the author's critique of the carpenter using his spare time to make idols (Wis 13:13).

Fourth, the potter himself was recently created and will soon die, but he fails to reflect on his human condition. Just as Adam was shaped from the earth by God (Gen 2:7), the potter too is mortal and **made of earth**. Yet he reverses the proper roles: instead of God forming man out of clay, man is forming gods out of clay. The potter fails to consider the drama of his own impending †death **when he is required to return the soul** (or "life") **that was lent him** (see Luke 12:20).

Fifth, the potter is shortsighted, thinking only of market competition and profit, not his own mortality. **He is not concerned that he is destined to die**, but he should be! Laughably, **he competes with workers in gold and silver**, highly skilled artisans who work in precious metals that have some value. The making of small household idols that resembled the larger and more impressive temples and statues of the pagans was common in the Greco-Roman world, as exemplified by the silversmiths in Ephesus who made miniature "silver shrines of Artemis" (Acts 19:24). But the clay idols the potter makes are of the lowest substance imaginable: dirt.

The author condemns the potter, who failed to recognize God, rejecting **his heart** as **ashes**, echoing Isaiah's critique of idol worship (Isa 44:20 LXX). **His hope** and **his life** are as contemptible as the material with which he works: earth and **clay**. From this climactic verdict, the author will continue to enumerate the faults of the idolatrous potter.

15:10–13

As in the earlier allusion (Wis 15:8) to Adam's creation from the dust of the ground (Gen 2:7), the author now reflects on the willful ignorance of the potter who **failed to know the one who formed him**. He refuses to acknowledge God, who is the source of his **soul**. He is so obsessed with his craft of making gods, he has not paused to consider the God who made him.

The author characterizes the potter's mindset as like that of the ungodly in Wis 2:1–11, who regarded life as a meaningless excuse for enjoyment. The potter **considered our existence an idle game**, adopting a fundamentally unserious attitude toward the serious business of life and death, as was common in his time.[13] He thinks of life as **a festival held for profit**. This mentality impedes his potential relationship with God since his only concern is profit.

The final verse in the critique of the potter accuses him of duplicity: he is not truly ignorant but in fact **knows that he sins**. His sin as the maker of idols

---

13. †Plato (ca. 427–347 BC), for example, wonders whether we are mere puppets or toys of the gods. See Winston, *Wisdom of Solomon*, 288.

is greater than those who are deceived by his idols. The idol maker is deeply cynical, playing on the fears of the ignorant to **get money however one can, even by base means**. The one who makes gods and goblets from the same lump of clay knows better.

15:14–15   The second part of this passage returns to the problem of Egyptian worship of idols and animals,[14] bringing the long digression to a close. It picks up where 12:27 left off by describing the idolatrous Egyptians as **more miserable than an infant** (see 12:24). This evaluation reflects the ancients' belief that babies' lives were full of suffering, as indicated by their helplessness and crying. The crescendo of criticism now reaches full crest (see earlier comment at 13:10): while the nature worshipers were "foolish" and the wooden-idol worshipers were "wretched" (13:10 NABRE), the animal worshipers (15:18–19) are "most stupid of all" (15:14 NABRE). The fact that the Egyptians **oppressed** the Hebrews in ancient times is likely in view, although the word could allude to a contemporary persecution of the Jewish community in Alexandria as well. The fact that the Egyptians revere "all the idols of the nations" (15:15 NABRE) criticizes their religion as thoroughly debased, as if to say that the Egyptians never saw an idol that they were not eager to worship. In fact, Greco-Roman polytheism was †syncretistic in that the gods were combined and equated across cultural boundaries (the Egyptian goddess Isis, for example, was identified with the Greek goddess Demeter and worshiped widely).[15] The author proceeds to parody the idols' helplessness in their sense organs—**eyes, nostrils, ears, fingers, feet** (see Ps 115:4–7).

15:16–19   Now the discussion returns to the critique of the idol maker as in 13:10–19 and 15:7–13, pointing out the absurdity of a mortal being making an immortal god. A man can only make a **dead** god, not a living one. In his dignity as a living creature, **he is better than the objects he worships**, for God made man "in the image of his own eternity" (2:23).[16] Yet the Egyptians, blinded by their false worship, sought out **the most hateful animals** as objects of worship, proving **their lack of intelligence**. †Philo also censures the Egyptians for their choice of animals to worship: "The Egyptians have gone to a further excess and chosen the fiercest and most savage of wild animals, lions and crocodiles and among reptiles the venomous asp, all of which they dignify with temples, sacred precincts, sacrifices, assemblies, processions and the like."[17] They receive neither

14. Earlier references to Egyptian worship of animals include 11:15; 12:24; 13:10; 15:18.

15. See Jan Assmann, *Moses the Egyptian: The Memory of Egypt in Western Monotheism* (Cambridge, MA: Harvard University Press, 1997), 45–48.

16. Philo likewise argues, "In their general ignorance they have failed to perceive even that most obvious truth which even 'a witless infant knows,' that the craftsman is superior to the product of his craft both in time, since he is older than what he makes and in a sense its father, and in value, since the efficient element [the maker] is held in higher esteem than the passive effect [the thing made]" (*On the Decalogue* 69 [Colson, Whitaker, and Earp, LCL 7:41]).

17. Philo, *On the Decalogue* 78 (Colson, Whitaker, and Earp, LCL 7:45–47).

God's **praise** nor **his blessing**, which is likely a reference to God pronouncing created animals "good" (Gen 1:21, 25, 31) and cursing the serpent (Gen 3:14).

Reflection and Application (15:7–19)

The maker of clay idols is motivated by material gain, saying that "one must get money however one can, even by base means" (15:12). It shows that the idol maker worshiped not idols but wealth. Sadly, this way of thinking is common in business and investing, where profit for shareholders is often the only measure of success. Believers' choices must be different. St. John Paul II taught that investment "is always *a moral and cultural choice.*"[18] Not all business is ethical. Some profits are morally evil (Prov 1:19; 10:2; Catechism 2424)—for example, profits from in vitro fertilization, human cloning research, abortion, euthanasia, forced labor, and pornography.[19] When it comes to our investments and business activity, we must be on guard that we do not participate in evil, reaping a profit from sin.

---

18. John Paul II, *Centesimus Annus*, §36, May 1, 1991.
19. See United States Conference of Catholic Bishops, "Socially Responsible Investment Guidelines for the United States Conference of Catholic Bishops," November 2021, www.usccb.org, https://www.usccb.org/resources/socially-responsible-investment-guidelines-2021-united-states-conference-catholic-bishops.

Unappetizing Animals versus Delicious Quail

Wisdom 16:1–4

Now, finally, after two long excurses (11:15–12:27; 13:1–15:19), the author returns to his series of seven comparisons that began chapter 11. Wisdom 16 presents three antitheses between the plight of the Egyptians and the blessing of the Israelites in the exodus era. These examples illustrate the principle that God blesses his people with the same instruments that he uses to punish their enemies (11:5). This retelling of the exodus events is meant not to rehearse the entire story but to recount history with a view to the †divine pedagogy, seeking the lessons that God taught through the events.

Tormentors and Delicacies (16:1–4)

¹Therefore those men were deservedly punished through such
    creatures,
and were tormented by a multitude of animals.
²Instead of this punishment you showed kindness to your people,
and you prepared quails to eat,
a delicacy to satisfy the desire of appetite;
³in order that those men, when they desired food,
might lose the least remnant of appetite
because of the odious creatures sent to them,
while your people, after suffering want a short time,
might partake of delicacies.
⁴For it was necessary that upon those oppressors inexorable want
    should come,
while to these it was merely shown how their enemies were being
    tormented.

OT: Exod 8–10; 16:9–13; Num 11:18–33; Pss 78:26–31; 105:40

This second of the seven comparisons builds on the immediately preceding 16:1–4 critique of animal worship in Egypt. It was fitting that the Egyptians **were tormented by a multitude of animals**, or "vermin" (NETS)—the plagues of frogs, gnats, flies, and locusts—because they worshiped such animals. This demonstrates the principle that "one is punished by the very things by which he sins" (11:16).

The author juxtaposes the Egyptians' punishment by means of strange animals with the blessing of quail, **a delicacy**, which came to the Israelites in the desert when they wanted meat (Exod 16:9–13; Num 11:18–33). The Egyptians' ridiculous and blasphemous worship of animals backfired, bringing animal torments upon them, while the Israelites' devotion to God brought his blessings in the form of animals fit to eat.

The author omits negative aspects of the wilderness era in Israel's relationship with God—their grumbling at God and the facts that the quail would later become a punishment for complaining (Num 11:20) and were accompanied by a punishing plague (Num 11:33). At the same time, he adds details, depicting the Egyptians as being so disgusted at the vermin that invaded their homes that they lost **the least remnant of appetite**. The Israelites' **suffering want a short time** tacitly recalls their complaints about lacking meat to eat (Num 11:18). However, for the Egyptian **oppressors**, **inexorable want** was a **necessary** tool of the divine pedagogy, while the Israelites were able to learn merely by observing the Egyptians' plight.

This brief comparison, addressed to God in the second person, continues to illustrate the diverse means by which God teaches his enemies and his people. In this case, God punishes false worship of strange animals with appropriate and proportional punishment by strange animals, while providing those who worship the true God with strange animals to eat. The example demonstrates the reasonability and proportionality of God's justice, his punishments, and his blessings.

Lethal Creatures
versus Saving Bronze Serpent

Wisdom 16:5–14

This section offers the third antithesis of the seven-part structure (see the sidebar "Structure of the Book of History," p. 119), comparing the Egyptians' lethal animal encounters to the Israelites' experience of being healed by God from snakebites.

The Word Conquers the Serpents (16:5–14)

---

⁵For when the terrible rage of wild beasts came upon your people
and they were being destroyed by the bites of writhing serpents,
your wrath did not continue to the end;
⁶they were troubled for a little while as a warning,
and received a token of deliverance to remind them of your law's
command.
⁷For he who turned toward it was saved, not by what he saw,
but by you, the Savior of all.
⁸And by this also you convinced our enemies
that it is you who deliver from every evil.
⁹For they were killed by the bites of locusts and flies,
and no healing was found for them,
because they deserved to be punished by such things;
¹⁰but your sons were not conquered even by the teeth of
venomous serpents,
for your mercy came to their help and healed them.
¹¹To remind them of your oracles they were bitten,
and then were quickly delivered,
lest they should fall into deep forgetfulness

and become unresponsive to your kindness.
¹²For neither herb nor poultice cured them,
but it was your word, O Lord, which heals all men.
¹³For you have power over life and death;
you lead men down to the gates of Hades and back again.
¹⁴A man in his wickedness kills another,
but he cannot bring back the departed spirit,
nor set free the imprisoned soul.

OT: Exod 8:20–32; Num 21:4–9; 1 Sam 2:6; Tob 13:2
NT: Matt 16:18; John 3:14–17; 1 Tim 4:10
Catechism: symbolic images of salvation, 2130

This third comparison contrasts the animals that harmed the Egyptians with   **16:5–6**
the bronze serpent that saved the Israelites. The earlier discussions of animal
idolatry have led up to this comparison. The author needs to explain how an
apparently idolatrous item, the bronze serpent, could be part of God's plan to
save his people.

The first four verses discuss the wilderness episode when the Israelites were
attacked by fiery **serpents** (Num 21:4–9). In the overall sequence of comparisons, Wisdom portrays the Egyptians as wicked and the Israelites as righteous,
so this specific sequence is a challenge to explain. How could God's righteous
people be punished like this? Instead of explaining the people's sin that brought
on the serpents, he presupposes it and highlights God's merciful restraint and
teaching purpose. He recalls that **your †wrath did not continue to the end** to
show the limits of God's punishment and the goal of his anger, which was conversion of hearts. It relies on a broader biblical theme seen in other texts: "His
anger lasts but a moment; his favor a lifetime" (Ps 30:6 NABRE). The purpose
of the serpents sent by God was to warn and **remind** his people to observe his
law. This explanation of God's pedagogical purpose here refutes the Egyptians'
claim that God brought his people into the wilderness simply to destroy them
(Exod 32:12; Num 14:13–16; Deut 9:28). Wisdom counters that God did not
want to hurt them but wanted to save them. The bronze serpent then was *not*
an animal idol (although some Israelites later treated it as one, 2 Kings 18:4)
but a **token of deliverance** or "sign of salvation" (Wis 16:6 NABRE).

Lest anyone be confused, the author goes out of his way to explain that   **16:7–8**
the bronze serpent possessed no inherent, totemic power to heal people. The
bitten people who looked at it were **saved, not by what** they **saw, but by you,
the Savior of all**. The unseen God is the one who saves people, not the bronze
serpent itself. The fact that the God of Israel is "Savior of all" reassures his
people that his power is universal.[1] "Savior of all" was used to refer to Serapis,

---

1. This is an important theme in †Philo, who upholds both the unique calling of the Jewish people
and the universal jurisdiction of the God of Israel. See David Winston, trans., *Philo of Alexandria: The*

a popular god in Alexandria—a hint that the author is seeking to dissuade his audience from worshiping this specific false god.[2] The phrase reappears in reference to Christ at 1 Tim 4:10 and is similar to the Samaritans' title for him: "Savior of the world" (John 4:42). Even the Egyptians were **convinced** of God's power to save by his care for the Israelites in the wilderness. Some indications in the wilderness texts point to the possibility of communication between the two groups (Num 14:13–14). God's role as **you who deliver from every evil** is embodied in the Lord's Prayer (Matt 6:13) and in the Communion Rite of the Mass, where the priest virtually quotes Wis 16:8, saying, "Deliver us, Lord, we pray, from every evil."[3]

16:9–10   From Israel, the author now turns to Egypt. While the Israelites were saved by the bronze serpent, the Egyptians are plagued by **the bites of locusts and flies**. In Exodus the effect of these insects is only once described as "†death" (Exod 10:17), but here their bites are viewed as truly lethal to parallel the fiery serpents.[4] The Israelites were bitten but saved, while the Egyptians were bitten and died without **healing**. In addition, **they deserved to be punished by such things**, since they had given themselves over to the irrational worship of loathsome animals. In contrast to the fate of the Egyptians, who died from insect bites, God's **sons were not conquered** by far more deadly creatures, **venomous serpents**. Rather they were **healed** by the Lord's **mercy**.

16:11–12   Amplifying the idea that God used snakebites as teaching tools, the author explains that the snakes were sent **to remind** Israel of God's **oracles**. The pain of being **bitten** suffices to remind the Israelites of the laws of God to which they are supposed to be devoted. The **deep forgetfulness** to which they were tempted was the danger of covenant infidelity, often characterized as "forgetfulness" in the Old Testament (Deut 4:23; 2 Kings 17:38; Prov 2:17). "Forgetfulness" (Greek *lēthē*) alludes to the river Lethe in Greek mythology, from which the dead souls would drink on their entrance into †Hades and thus forget their earthly lives.[5] The same word is repeated in Wis 17:3. Without the prompting of snakebites, the Israelites are in danger of becoming **unresponsive**, numb to the promises of God.

To repeat the earlier idea that the bronze serpent itself did nothing (16:7), the author highlights that it was not natural medicine (**neither herb nor poultice**) but the mercy of God that saved the people from the serpent bites. He cites a

---

Contemplative Life, the Giants, and Selections, Classics of Western Spirituality (Mahwah, NJ: Paulist Press, 1981), 286–98.

2. Aelius Aristides 45, 20K, cited in BDAG 985.

3. *The Roman Missal: Renewed by Decree of the Most Holy Second Ecumenical Council of the Vatican, Promulgated by Authority of Pope Paul VI and Revised at the Direction of Pope John Paul II*, Third Typical Edition (Washington DC: United States Conference of Catholic Bishops, 2011), 665.

4. Josephus (*Jewish Antiquities* 2.14.3) also regards the insect bites as lethal.

5. James M. Reese, *The Book of Wisdom, Song of Songs*, Old Testament Message 20 (Wilmington, DE: Michael Glazier, 1983), 170.

Hades

Several times Wisdom refers to the place of the dead, Hades (Wis 1:14; 2:1; 16:13; 17:14). The †Septuagint uses this term to translate Hebrew *Sheol*, the gloomy gated netherworld to which all souls descend after †death in Old Testament theology (Job 7:9; Ps 49:14–15; Jon 2:3–6). In the context of Greco-Roman mythology, Hades (meaning "unseen") was divided into sections: Elysium, also called the Elysian Fields, a pleasant place for the blessed; and Tartarus, the deepest pit for the fallen Titans.[a] It was entered by crossing the river Styx, one of the five rivers that flowed through Hades, the others being Acheron (woe), Cocytus (lamentation), the fire river Phlegethon (burning), and Lethe (forgetfulness). Wisdom twice alludes to Lethe (Wis 16:11; 17:3).

The god Hades, also called Pluto, ruled over the underworld. Sometimes he is identified with Serapis, a popular god in Alexandria whom Wis 16:7 seems to mention. Hades is often depicted holding the key to the iron gates of his realm,[b] gates that Wisdom mentions (16:13). While the author of Wisdom does not adhere to Greek religion, he uses this important term, Hades, to describe the place of the dead, which Jesus will come to unlock (see Rev 1:18).

a. See Walter Burkert, *Greek Religion* (Oxford: Blackwell, 1985), 194–99.

b. See Pausanias, *Graeciae descriptio* 5.20, in *Pausanias: Description of Greece*, vol. 2, trans. W. H. S. Jones and H. A. Ormerod, LCL (Cambridge, MA: Harvard University Press, 1926), 497: "As to the key (Pluto holds a key) they say that what is called Hades has been locked up by Pluto, and that nobody will return back again therefrom." See also "To Plouton," in *The Orphic Hymns*, trans. Apostolos N. Athanassakis and Benjamin M. Wolkow (Baltimore: Johns Hopkins University Press, 2013), 18 (translation modified): "O Pluto, holder of the keys to the whole earth."

common biblical theme of the power of God's word to heal (see 2 Kings 2:22; Ps 107:20; Matt 8:16): **your word, O Lord, which heals all men**. The author is at pains to show that God's miraculous power is at work here and that the Israelites were not healed by magic, medicine, natural remedies, or the bronze serpent itself. The healing must be attributed to God alone.

The final segment specifies God's **power over life and death** as the basis   16:13–14 of his power to heal (Deut 32:39; 1 Sam 2:6; Tob 13:2). God's plenary power is illustrated by his choice to punish the Egyptians with death and to save the Israelites from death. The **gates of Hades** refer to the entry point to the place of the dead (see the sidebar "Hades," above). The "gates of Hades" appear several times in the †Septuagint.[6] They symbolize death and the moment of death, sometimes called "the gates of death" (Job 38:17; Pss 9:13; 107:18). While in Greek mythology Hades himself possessed the key, in the book of Revelation

6. Isa 38:10; *3 Maccabees* 5.51; *Odes of Solomon* 11.10; *Psalms of Solomon* 16.2.

the risen Christ declares, "I have the keys of Death and Hades" (Rev 1:18). Matthew 16:18–19 mentions the "gates of Hades," and Jesus grants the "keys to the kingdom of heaven" to Peter. The last verse of this passage (Wis 16:14) explains the difference between human power and God's power. While human beings might have the ability to take away life through murder, they **cannot bring back the departed spirit**. God's power is greater since he can both give life and take it away (see Matt 10:28). This verse asserts God's ability to raise the dead to life, a hope reflected in other Old Testament texts (Ps 16:10; Dan 12:2; 2 Macc 7:9). While God can bring death upon the powerful Egyptians with a tiny insect, he can also bring life to his snake-bitten people and even raise the dead to life.

Reflection and Application (16:5–14)

According to Wisdom, God sent fiery serpents against his own people, "lest they should fall into deep forgetfulness and become unresponsive to your kindness" (16:11). Their forgetting of his blessings, his laws, his covenant could lead to a fateful state of spiritual paralysis. Spiritual apathy, or acedia, is a common problem in the interior life today. When we forget the blessing of creation, redemption, and our eternal destiny, we can become spiritually blind and numb. Like the snakebites in the wilderness, sufferings can wake us up to the reality of who God is and what he requires of us. Instead of drifting into forgetful apathy, when we suffer we can allow the pain to teach us to turn toward God in our need.

Storms of Wrath versus Manna from Heaven

Wisdom 16:15–29

The third antithesis in this chapter, the fourth of seven in the whole architecture of chapters 10–19, contrasts two phenomena that come from the sky: the heaven-sent storms that plagued Egypt and the heaven-sent bread that blessed Israel.

Fire, Hail, and Bread from Heaven (16:15–29)

> [15]To escape from your hand is impossible;
> [16]for the ungodly, refusing to know you,
> were scourged by the strength of your arm,
> pursued by unusual rains and hail and relentless storms,
> and utterly consumed by fire.
> [17]For—most incredible of all—in the water, which quenches
>   all things,
> the fire had still greater effect,
> for the universe defends the righteous.
> [18]At one time the flame was restrained,
> so that it might not consume the creatures sent against
>   the ungodly,
> but that seeing this they might know
> that they were being pursued by the judgment of God;
> [19]and at another time even in the midst of water it burned more
>   intensely than fire,
> to destroy the crops of the unrighteous land.
> [20]Instead of these things you gave your people the food of angels,
> and without their toil you supplied them from heaven with bread
>   ready to eat,
> providing every pleasure and suited to every taste.

²¹For your sustenance manifested your sweetness toward your
      children;
and the bread, ministering to the desire of the one who took it,
was changed to suit every one's liking.
²²Snow and ice withstood fire without melting,
so that they might know that the crops of their enemies
were being destroyed by the fire that blazed in the hail
and flashed in the showers of rain;
²³whereas the fire, in order that the righteous might be fed,
even forgot its native power.

²⁴For creation, serving you who have made it,
exerts itself to punish the unrighteous,
and in kindness relaxes on behalf of those who trust in you.
²⁵Therefore at that time also, changed into all forms,
it served your all-nourishing bounty,
according to the desire of those who had need,
²⁶so that your sons, whom you loved, O Lord, might learn
that it is not the production of crops that feeds man,
but that your word preserves those who trust in you.
²⁷For what was not destroyed by fire
was melted when simply warmed by a fleeting ray of the sun,
²⁸to make it known that one must rise before the sun to give
      you thanks,
and must pray to you at the dawning of the light;
²⁹for the hope of an ungrateful man will melt like wintry frost,
and flow away like waste water.

OT: Exod 9:23–25; 16:1–36; Num 11:7–8; Pss 18:13–15; 78:23–25; 105:32
NT: John 6:31, 49; Rom 1:19–21

16:15–16 The passage begins with a sharp reminder of God's power: **To escape from your hand is impossible**. This summary of the preceding verses (16:5–14) alludes to a common biblical theme, the inescapable authority of God (Deut 32:39; Tob 13:2), which will be further justified by the observations that follow. It affirms the dual nature of God's dominion; his rule is a threat to his enemies and a consolation to his friends.

The ungodly Egyptians were not guiltless but, in fact, refused to **know** God. As argued earlier (Wis 13:1), the unrighteous are willfully blind to God as creator, so they deserve their punishment (compare Rom 1:19–21). God uses the creation he made to afflict them with **unusual rains and hail and relentless storms**. The author is extrapolating from the description in Exodus: "There was hail, and fire flashing continually in the midst of the hail, very heavy hail, such as had never been in all the land of Egypt since it became a nation" (Exod 9:24).

The next three verses (vv. 17–19) meditate on the contradictory nature of this remarkable "thunder hail." In biblical imagery, lightning and fire are interchangeable (see Ezek 1:13), so the passage explains the confusing mixture of fire and ice in this miraculous, punishing storm. The author interprets it not as a typical weather event but as a miracle that bends the laws of physics. Rather than the rainwater extinguishing the fire, **the fire had still greater effect**, as if water became a fuel for it. †Philo similarly describes the exodus storms as containing "continuous claps of thunder and flashes of lightning and constant thunderbolts. These last provided a most marvelous spectacle, for they ran through the hail, their natural antagonist, and yet did not melt it nor were quenched by it, but unchanged coursed up and down and kept guard over the hail."[1]

Wisdom's explanation for these extraordinary events matches the principles stated earlier (Wis 11:5, 16), that **the universe** (Greek *kosmos*) **defends the righteous**. Creation is not a neutral system, but rather, it is on God's team, always at work against the wicked and on the side of the righteous. Wisdom is compressing the timeline, envisioning the plagues against Egypt as simultaneous and the lightning as like a rain of fire that would destroy everything in its path. Because of this, the author must invent a solution as to how the flies, gnats, locusts, and frogs would not be incinerated: **the flame was restrained**. Again, the punishment is a lesson for the Egyptians, so that **they might know that they were being pursued by the judgment of God**. The miraculous nature of the fire and hail accompanied by the preservation of the plague insects would convince them that "this is the finger of God" (Exod 8:19). Though the fiery hail did not destroy the plague animals, it did destroy livestock: "The hail struck down everything that was in the field throughout all the land of Egypt, both man and beast; and the hail struck down every plant of the field, and shattered every tree of the field" (Exod 9:25). And the hail destroyed **the crops of the unrighteous land**—namely, "the flax and the barley" (Exod 9:31). These three verses in Wisdom (16:17–19) interpret the hailstorm plague as an example of God's use of creation to punish the Egyptians in a miraculous way that could prompt their conversion ("that they might know," 16:18). In this way his "inescapable hand" teaches his enemies.

Attention shifts at verse 20 from the raging storms of divine †wrath to the blessing of the manna from heaven, the **food of angels**.[2] The author depicts the miraculous manna with five descriptors: (1) **from heaven**, a gift from God; (2) **ready to eat**, requiring no preparation; (3) **without their toil**, not the fruit of difficult farm labor; (4) **providing every pleasure**; and (5) **suited to every taste**, changing **to the desire of the one who took it**. Exodus describes the manna as

16:17–19

16:20–21

---

1. Philo, *On the Life of Moses* 1.118 (Colson, Whitaker, and Earp, LCL 6:337).
2. The famous hymn *Panis Angelicus*, "The Bread of Angels," was composed by St. Thomas Aquinas on the basis of this verse and Ps 78:25.

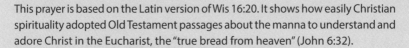

Tantum Ergo

The *Tantum Ergo* is a hymn sung or said at the conclusion of the benediction of the Blessed Sacrament. After the hymn proper, the celebrant sings a verse that invites a response:

> *V.* Panem de caelo praestitisti eis
> *R.* Omne delectamentum in se habentem.
>
> *V.* You have given them bread from heaven.
> *R.* Having all sweetness within it.

This prayer is based on the Latin version of Wis 16:20. It shows how easily Christian spirituality adopted Old Testament passages about the manna to understand and adore Christ in the Eucharist, the "true bread from heaven" (John 6:32).

"like coriander seed, white, and the taste of it was like wafers made with honey" (Exod 16:31), but Wisdom feels free to expand on the manna's significance in the †divine pedagogy. The flavor-changing nature of the manna reveals God's fatherly care for his **children**, even his **sweetness**. Like a father who knows what each of his children uniquely enjoys, God empowers the manna to change its taste miraculously for each Israelite. **Your sustenance** (Greek *hypostasis*) that **manifested your sweetness toward your children** could refer either to the manna itself or to the divine nature, perhaps as personified wisdom or †*Logos* (see Wis 7:25–26; Heb 1:3). Only from a Christian perspective can *hypostasis* ("substance" or "person") refer both to the *Logos*, the Word Incarnate, and to the manna from heaven—namely, Christ in the Eucharist (John 1:1; 6:35).

16:22–27   Now the author turns back to the comparison by explaining how the manna was similar to and yet opposite of the fire and ice of the divine storms (vv. 22–24). The **ice** from hail and even **snow** were preserved by God's power from the **fire** in their midst so that they did not melt. **Melting** then becomes a motif: the manna would melt in the sun but, like the hail, would not melt as expected when cooked in an oven or pot (v. 27; Num 11:8). The hail-fire destroyed the Egyptians' crops to teach the Israelites—**that they might know** the power of God. Indeed, in the author's estimation, all creation adjusts and yields to God's will, either to punish the wicked or to bless his righteous people. And this ongoing transformation of creation is not limited to nature following its normal course. Rather, fire **forgot its native power**, and **creation changed into all forms**. The manna and the miraculous thunder hail are only examples of this ongoing miracle put on display by the plagues. The whole purpose of the plagues then is educational: **that your sons, whom you loved, O Lord, might learn**. The lesson is the same as that of Wis 16:12, that God's word, not the bronze serpent, delivers healing.

Here God's word is what nourishes his people, not **the production of crops**. It is a re-presentation of the lesson of the manna drawn by Moses: the Lord "fed you with manna, which you did not know, nor did your fathers know, that he might make you know that man does not live by bread alone, but man lives by every word that comes from the mouth of the LORD" (Deut 8:3 ESV-CE). The fact that it is God's **word** that **preserves those who trust in** him refers to the principle in Wis 11:25 that God not only wills creatures into being but sustains them thereafter in existence. Food might seem to be what sustains us, for without it we would starve, but at a deeper level, God sustains us in being at every moment. Without his "word," we would cease to be. The manna demonstrates this principle yet again by bending to God's will—sometimes melting away **by a fleeting ray of the sun** (Exod 16:21), and sometimes resisting the heat of the Israelites' cooking fires (Num 11:8). The Targum, an ancient Aramaic expansive translation, embellishes the melting of the manna to the point that it becomes a stream that attracts hunting game for the Israelites.[3]

Again, the pedagogical purpose of the miracles is emphasized: **to make it known that one must rise before the sun to give you thanks**. Wisdom is recalling that the Israelites had to collect the manna early in the morning before the sun became hot enough to melt it (Exod 16:21). Thus, they always enjoyed a predawn breakfast of manna and gave thanks to God for it before sunrise. This sets the pattern of predawn prayer, which the author interprets as normative: "one must" pray before dawn (see Sir 39:5). The lesson is that one must **pray to you at the dawning of the light**, which could also be translated "toward the east." Jewish morning prayer toward the east is recounted in some sources contemporary with the Bible.[4] Prayer toward the east (or toward Jerusalem) became a common practice in Judaism, earliest Islam, and Christianity to the point that church buildings, altars, congregations, and priests typically faced *ad orientem*, "to the east," in worship.[5] (The Latin phrase *ad orientem* is present in the Vulgate of Wis 16:28.) The final verse of this section compares the **hope of an ungrateful man** to the melting manna—it will **flow away like waste water**.

(margin: 16:28–29)

---

3. *Targum Pseudo-Jonathan* on Exod 16:21: "So they gathered it *from* morning *time until the fourth hour of the day*, each according to what he could eat. *But from the fourth hour onwards* the sun grew hot over it and it would melt, *becoming wells of water flowing to the Great Sea. And clean beasts and animals came and drank from it, and the children of Israel were hunting them and eating them*" (Kevin Cathcart, Michael Maher, and Martin McNamara, eds., *The Aramaic Bible: Targum Neofiti 1: Exodus and Targum Pseudo-Jonathan: Exodus*, trans. Martin McNamara, Michael Maher, and Robert Hayward, vol. 2 [Collegeville, MN: Liturgical Press, 1994], 208–9).

4. The Essenes rose early to pray (Josephus, *Jewish War* 2.8.5); likewise, the Therapeutae, a Jewish sect, prayed toward the east at sunrise (Philo, *On the Contemplative Life* 89).

5. For a brief overview of the topic, see Joseph Ratzinger, *The Spirit of the Liturgy*, trans. John Saward (San Francisco: Ignatius, 2000), 74–84; see also Uwe Michael Lang, *Turning Towards the Lord: Orientation in Liturgical Prayer* (San Francisco: Ignatius, 2009), 35–47, who gives evidence of Jewish synagogues oriented to the east and of Muhammad at first praying toward Jerusalem before directing his followers to pray toward Mecca.

Matins and Lauds

LIVING
TRADITION

From ancient times Christians have preserved a tradition of prayer before dawn (Matins) and prayer at dawn (Lauds). In the revised Liturgy of the Hours, Matins is now called "The Office of Readings" and can be celebrated at any time of day, while Lauds, as "Morning Prayer," still retains its place at the hour of dawn. St. John Chrysostom aptly describes the purpose of morning prayer:

> The morning psalm is of the same sort. . . . For it kindles the desire for God, and arouses the soul and greatly inflames it, and fills it with great goodness and love. . . . But let us see where it begins, and what it teaches us: "O God my God, I keep vigil before you, my soul thirsts for you" (Ps 62:1). Do you see how it shows the words of a soul afire? Where there is love of God, all evil departs; where there is remembrance of God there is oblivion of sin and destruction of evil.[a]

a. St. John Chrysostom, *Commentary on Ps 140*, 1, quoted in Robert Taft, *The Liturgy of the Hours in East and West: The Origins of the Divine Office and Its Meaning for Today*, 2nd ed. (Collegeville, MN: Liturgical Press, 1993), 42–43.

The hope of the righteous is firmly founded in God's word, while those who reject him are left with nothing.

Reflection and Application (16:15–29)

Wisdom's meditation on the plague storms and the manna is seeking to understand what God was trying to teach through these dramatic interventions in human history. While the miraculous events reveal God's power to punish and to deliver, they also remind us of our absolute dependence on him and his goodness toward us. Our whole life, our existence, and our happiness are totally dependent on God's blessing. When describing the early morning manna breakfast of the Israelites, Wisdom concludes that gratitude is the lesson of the whole event. It declares, "One must rise before the sun to give you thanks" (16:28). When we wake up, it is fitting that we also give thanks to God for his good blessings which sustain us.

Plague of Darkness versus Pillar of Light

Wisdom 17:1–18:4

This fifth antithesis in the series of seven expounds on the plague of darkness sent against Egypt in Exod 10:21–29 and compares it to the light the Israelites experienced at the same time. Commentator David Winston says that here "the author employs all his rhetorical skill to provide his readers with a living impression of the psychological terror occasioned by the plague of darkness."[1] In this poetic meditation on the darkness, the Egyptians' fear is palpable.

The Terror of Darkness and the Brilliance of Light (17:1–18:4)

[1]Great are your judgments and hard to describe;
therefore uninstructed souls have gone astray.
[2]For when lawless men supposed that they held the holy nation in
their power,
they themselves lay as captives of darkness and prisoners of long
night,
shut in under their roofs, exiles from eternal providence.
[3]For thinking that in their secret sins they were unobserved
behind a dark curtain of forgetfulness,
they were scattered, terribly alarmed,
and appalled by specters.
[4]For not even the inner chamber that held them protected them
from fear,
but terrifying sounds rang out around them,
and dismal phantoms with gloomy faces appeared.
[5]And no power of fire was able to give light,

1. David Winston, *The Wisdom of Solomon*, AB 43 (Garden City, NY: Doubleday, 1979), 303.

nor did the brilliant flames of the stars
avail to illumine that hateful night.
⁶Nothing was shining through to them
except a dreadful, self-kindled fire,
and in terror they deemed the things which they saw
to be worse than that unseen appearance.
⁷The delusions of their magic art lay humbled,
and their boasted wisdom was scornfully rebuked.
⁸For those who promised to drive off the fears and disorders of a
    sick soul
were sick themselves with ridiculous fear.
⁹For even if nothing disturbing frightened them,
yet, scared by the passing of beasts and the hissing of serpents,
¹⁰they perished in trembling fear,
refusing to look even at the air, though it nowhere could be
    avoided.
¹¹For wickedness is a cowardly thing, condemned by its own
    testimony;
distressed by conscience, it has always exaggerated the
    difficulties.
¹²For fear is nothing but surrender of the helps that come from
    reason;
¹³and the inner expectation of help, being weak,
prefers ignorance of what causes the torment.
¹⁴But throughout the night, which was really powerless,
and which beset them from the recesses of powerless Hades,
they all slept the same sleep,
¹⁵and now were driven by monstrous specters,
and now were paralyzed by their souls' surrender,
for sudden and unexpected fear overwhelmed them.
¹⁶And whoever was there fell down,
and thus was kept shut up in a prison not made of iron;
¹⁷for whether he was a farmer or a shepherd
or a workman who toiled in the wilderness,
he was seized, and endured the inescapable fate;
for with one chain of darkness they all were bound.
¹⁸Whether there came a whistling wind,
or a melodious sound of birds in wide-spreading branches,
or the rhythm of violently rushing water,
¹⁹or the harsh crash of rocks hurled down,
or the unseen running of leaping animals,
or the sound of the most savage roaring beasts,
or an echo thrown back from a hollow of the mountains,
it paralyzed them with terror.
²⁰For the whole world was illumined with brilliant light,

and was engaged in unhindered work,
²¹while over those men alone heavy night was spread,
an image of the darkness that was destined to receive them;
but still heavier than darkness were they to themselves.
¹⁸:¹But for your holy ones there was very great light.
Their enemies heard their voices but did not see their forms,
and counted them happy for not having suffered,
²and were thankful that your holy ones, though previously
    wronged, were doing them no injury;
and they begged their pardon for having been at variance
    with them.
³Therefore you provided a flaming pillar of fire
as a guide for your people's unknown journey,
and a harmless sun for their glorious wandering.
⁴For their enemies deserved to be deprived of light and
    imprisoned in darkness,
those who had kept your sons imprisoned,
through whom the imperishable light of the law was to be given
    to the world.

OT: Wis 1:14; Exod 10:21–29; Job 4:12–21; Prov 28:1
NT: Matt 24:38–41; Luke 8:17; John 1:5

This eloquent reflection on the nature of darkness is the longest in the Bible. Like other biblical texts it speaks of a palpable darkness rather than the simple absence of light. The †Septuagint translation of Exodus refers to the plague of darkness with two consecutive nouns, which literally translated would simply be "darkness darkness" (Exod 10:22). In biblical imagery, a dark cloud, sometimes translated "thick darkness,"[2] shrouds God's presence and acts as a protective screen between the divine brightness of the pillar of fire and the Israelites.

This lengthy passage is highly structured in fifty-five lines of Greek poetry. Two rare words from the same root, "shut in" (Wis 17:2) and "imprisoned" (18:4), form an †*inclusio*.[3] A definition of fear in verse 12 stands at the very center of the passage.[4] The fifty-five lines can be divided into forty-four lines that describe the darkness (17:1–21) and eleven lines, exactly one-fifth, that depict the light belonging to God's people (18:1–4). The poetic momentum of terror at God's judgment builds from the first verse all the way until light breaks into the scene in 18:1.

This new chapter opens the fifth comparison by saying God's **judgments** are   17:1–2
hard to describe. This paradox is a repeated biblical emphasis: God's wisdom is

---

2. See Exod 20:21; Deut 5:22; 1 Kings 8:12; 2 Chron 6:1.
3. *Katakleisthentes* in 17:2 and *katakleistous* in 18:4.
4. For further examination of the literary structure of this passage, see James M. Reese, *The Book of Wisdom, Song of Songs*, Old Testament Message 20 (Wilmington, DE: Michael Glazier, 1983), 179–86.

so high above human understanding that we cannot fully comprehend it (e.g., Job 11:7; Ps 139:6; Rom 11:33). Its incomprehensibility does not mean that God's wisdom is unintelligible in itself, only that it is unintelligible to us because of our limited capacity. We need instruction and revelation to grasp the wisdom of God, which is why **uninstructed souls have gone astray**.

The confusion brought on by lack of proper instruction in God's law sets the stage for the description of the terrifying plague of darkness. The Egyptians are described here as **lawless** (*anomia*), acting without the benefit of the law (*nomos*) of God, which is described as "imperishable light" (Wis 18:4). The author's contrast between darkness and light is both literal, in reference to the plague of darkness and Israel's freedom from it, and metaphorical. On the one side are darkness, moral confusion, lawlessness, guilt, fear, and its resulting enslavement, while on the other are light, moral clarity, law, holiness, and freedom. The Israelites are God's **holy nation**, whom the lawless Egyptians enslave; but in ironic justice, the Egyptians themselves become slaves, **captives of darkness**. The author uses many terms to describe the Egyptians' spiritual condition as slaves: **captives**, **prisoners**, **exiles**.

17:3   The terrible plague of darkness becomes an all-encompassing experience of terror. It is not merely a physical experience but a visible sign of the Egyptians' guilt. When the darkness falls, they are haunted by **their secret sins**, which are not secret from God. While the darkness would seem to hide a person from God, in fact, the terrified Egyptians feel even more exposed to the danger of divine judgment. Elsewhere, the Bible describes God's "eyes" as roaming through the whole earth, seeing every good and evil act (2 Chron 16:9; Prov 15:3; Zech 4:10), a metaphorical description of his omniscience. Here the all-knowing power of God is contrasted with the **dark curtain of forgetfulness** that links the physical darkness of the plague to the Egyptians' moral and intellectual darkness. "Forgetfulness" (Greek *lēthē*) could again allude to the river Lethe in †Hades (as in Wis 16:11). In a similar vein, Jesus warns that "nothing is hidden that shall not be made manifest, nor anything secret that shall not be known and come to light" (Luke 8:17). Not only does the Egyptians' guilt haunt them, but also they are **appalled by specters**, like the apparition that appears to Job's friend (Job 4:12–21). It is as if their guilty consciences are producing visions in the dark that frighten them all the more.

17:4–5   Not even the **inner chamber** (the same Greek word is rendered "recesses" in 17:14) of the Egyptians' homes nor "their roofs" (v. 2) can shield them from the psychological torments of the darkness: the **terrifying sounds**, the **dismal phantoms**. While humans instinctually hide from frightening threats, the more the Egyptians hide, the worse their fear gets. The author is embellishing the brief description of the plague described in Exodus as "palpable darkness . . . , darkness, gloom, hurricane" (Exod 10:21–22 NETS). This supernatural darkness is so unrelenting that **no power of fire was able to give**

Philo on the Relationship of Sin to Fear   BIBLICAL BACKGROUND

†Philo also contemplates the nature of cowardice in the soul of a law-breaker and even references how the slightest sound will cause great fear. The similarities to Wis 17 are striking:

> And if with all this they [the lawbreakers] fail to learn wisdom and still go crookedly away from the straight paths which lead to truth, then cowardice and fear will be established in their souls. They will fly when no man pursues; false rumors . . . will send them falling headlong, and the lightest sound of a leaf borne through the air will cause as much trepidation and quaking as the most savage war waged by mightier enemies. So children will take no thought for parents nor parents for children, nor brother for brother, expecting that mutual help will lead to destruction, and flight, each man for himself, to safety.[a]

a. Philo, *On Rewards and Punishments* 148 (Colson, Whitaker, and Earp, LCL 8:405–7; translation modified).

light. The Egyptians could not fight back against the darkness with fire; nor was there help from the light of **the stars**. God's judgment completely surrounded them.

The terror of the darkness was amplified, not diminished, by a **dreadful,** **17:6–10** **self-kindled fire**—that is, lightning—which enabled the Egyptians to see their surroundings in brief flashes followed by total darkness. While the Egyptian magicians had been able to imitate the first few plagues, now the **delusions of their magic art lay humbled**, or, as Winston translates, "Their magical shams proved ineffectual."[5] These magicians **who promised to drive off the fears** were themselves overwhelmed by **ridiculous fear**. Rather than monsters, they hear only passing "insects[6] and the hissing of reptiles" (v. 9 NABRE). Their terror at the mere sounds of animals was so extreme that some of them died of fright! They became fearful **even at the air**, meaning the inky blackness, the gloomy cloud of darkness that enclosed them.

To conclude his embellished description of the plague of darkness, the author **17:11** draws a lesson: **wickedness** and cowardice go together. The Egyptians' childish fear of the dark is not surprising; rather, the expected interior consequence of transgression is to be **distressed by conscience**. Sin caused their courage to collapse, as it **always exaggerated the difficulties**. Proverbs says something similar: "The wicked flee when no one pursues, but the righteous are bold as a lion" (Prov 28:1).

5. Winston, *Wisdom of Solomon*, 302.
6. To align with the plagues of gnats, flies, and locusts, NABRE has "insects" where RSV-2CE translates "beasts." The Greek word, *knōdalon*, can indicate any wild creature.

St. Augustine on Sevenfold Gifts and Sevenfold Evils

LIVING
TRADITION

In a way similar to Wisdom's description of irrational fear with its attendant intellectual errors (17:12–13), St. Augustine compares the gifts of the Holy Spirit, which enlighten the soul, to the wicked spirits of hypocrisy, which darken it:

> The Holy Spirit is presented to us as sevenfold in his activity, so that he may be in us the Spirit of wisdom and understanding, of counsel and courage, of knowledge and piety, and of the fear of God. Now set against this sevenfold good the opposite sevenfold evil: the spirit of folly and error, the spirit of rashness and cowardice, the spirit of ignorance and impiety, and the spirit of pride against the fear of God. These are seven wicked spirits; who are the other seven more wicked still?
>
> Another seven more wicked still are found in hypocrisy: one evil spirit of folly, another worse one of pretended wisdom; an evil spirit is the spirit of error, another worse one is the pretense of truth; an evil spirit is the spirit of rashness, another worse one is the pretense of counsel; an evil spirit is the spirit of cowardice, another worse one is the pretense of courage; an evil spirit is the spirit of ignorance, another worse one is pretended knowledge; an evil spirit is the spirit of impiety, another worse one is the pretense of piety; an evil spirit is the spirit of arrogance, another worse one is pretended reverence. Seven were not to be borne; who could put up with fourteen? So it necessarily follows that when you add to malice the pretense of truth, the last state of a person is worse than the first (see Matt 12:45).[a]

a. St. Augustine, *Sermon* 72A.2 (on Matt. 12:41–45), quoted in Robert Louis Wilken, Angela Russell Christman, and Michael J. Hollerich, eds., *Isaiah: Interpreted by Early Christian and Medieval Commentators,* The Church's Bible (Grand Rapids: Eerdmans, 2007), 149.

17:12–13   This extended meditation brings the author to offer a definition of fear in the exact center of the composition: **fear is . . .** the **surrender of the helps that come from reason**. Adults know that fear of the dark is irrational, but here the author specifies its irrationality in a textbook-style definition. Although elsewhere the book of Wisdom acknowledges the limits of "the reasoning of mortals" (9:14–17), here it upholds reason (Greek *logismos*) as helpful. Since fear is an **expectation** of evil rather than **help**, it weakens the mind so that it **prefers ignorance** to knowledge. Aristotle (384–322 BC) similarly defines fear as the imagination of a future evil.[7]

The author is illustrating the slippery slope of wickedness, which leads to a guilty conscience (17:3), which leads to irrational cowardly panic (v. 9), which destroys hope for the good and instead expects evil around every corner (v. 11),

7. Aristotle, *Rhetoric* 2.5.

not willing to have its view corrected by investigation of **what causes the torment** (v. 13). Fear comes from ignorance and then, as a disease of the mind, devolves into further derangement. Reason dispels fear through its calm embrace of truth, giving a rational basis for hope. The emphasis on reason proposed here is like that of *4 Maccabees*, a noncanonical writing from the first century AD, which claims that "devout reason [*logismos*] is master of all emotions, not only of sufferings from within, but also those from without."[8]

After defining fear, the author returns to describing the Egyptians' experience of the darkness in greater detail. The darkness itself was **powerless** since it came from **the recesses of powerless Hades** (see also Hosea 13:14; Rev 1:18; 20:6). Wisdom 1:14 already declared that "the dominion of Hades is not on earth." In addition, God has "power over life and death" and jurisdiction over Hades (16:13). Yet in their fear the Egyptians willingly submitted themselves to the power of darkness and **slept the same sleep** as the dead already in Hades. They needlessly abandoned themselves to deathly fear.   **17:14**

Their **souls' surrender** to **fear** was brought about by visions of **monstrous specters**, already mentioned in 17:4. While the apparitions might be real, the Egyptians succumb to foolish fear, to panic induced by the dark. Their capitulation to irrational terror is so complete that it is as if they are **shut up in a prison not made of iron** as "captives of darkness" (v. 2) hiding in their "inner chamber[s]" (v. 4). Next the author emphasizes how the darkness afflicted great and small alike, as the plague of the firstborn also would (Exod 11:5). They   **17:15–17**

8. *4 Maccabees* 18.2 RSV.

Descents into Hades

Wisdom asserts God's power over life and †death with figurative language: "You lead men down to the gates of Hades and back again" (Wis 16:13). This language draws on a wider literary theme from both biblical literature and Greco-Roman mythology. For example, Hannah's prayer states, "The Lord kills and brings to life; he brings down to Sheol and raises up" (1 Sam 2:6). Similarly, Tobit's prayer describes God in such terms: "He leads down to Hades, and brings up again" (Tob 13:2). Many Greco-Roman myths depict their heroes—Orpheus, Theseus and Pirithous, Heracles, Dionysus, Odysseus, Aeneas—descending to the realm of the dead and returning. These *katabasis* ("descent") stories vividly portray the gloomy dread which besets the souls in Hades, a literary theme that Wis 17 adopts as it dramatically illustrates the fear that came upon the guilty Egyptians at the time of their judgment. In Scripture, the *katabasis* pattern is exemplified by Jonah's descent into Sheol (Jon 2:2–9), which prefigures Jesus's own descent into the netherworld (Matt 12:39–41), where he "preached to the spirits in prison" (1 Pet 3:19).[a]

a. See Richard Bauckham, "Descent to the Underworld," *ABD* 2:145–58.

---

all are imprisoned by darkness, serving "the inescapable sentence" (Wis 17:17 NABRE).[9]

17:18–19   To illustrate the fear of the Egyptians, the author returns to the "terrifying sounds" mentioned earlier (17:4). He speculates on the origins of these sounds: **wind, birds, water, rocks, animals**, echoes. These normal sounds of nature are transformed by the Egyptians' panic-stricken imagination into unseen phantom terrors that **paralyzed them**.

17:20–21   While everyone and everything else enjoyed the **brilliant light** of the sun as usual, the Egyptians **alone**, because of their sins, were shrouded in darkness. This plague of physical darkness signified **the darkness that was destined to receive them**—namely, Hades, the place of the dead to whose power they had willingly surrendered (17:14). The final line underlines the Egyptians' panic and anguished state of mind: **still heavier** (NABRE: "more a burden") **than darkness were they to themselves**. In effect, in their moral weakness they became their own jailers.

18:1   Finally, the darkness gives way to light as Wisdom turns its attention to the Hebrews in the midst of Egypt to complete the antithesis: **for your holy ones there was very great light**. The author reflects on the fact that "all the sons of Israel had light where they dwelt" (Exod 10:23) during the plague of

---

9. Here (v. 17) the NABRE renders the Greek *anankē*, a word that could mean "fate" or "punishment," in a way that takes account of the imprisonment context.

darkness.[10] According to Exodus, the Israelites lived apart in their own territory of Goshen (Exod 8:22; 9:26), where they enjoyed the normal light of the sun during the plague of darkness. The fact that at the same time and in nearly the same place the Egyptians experienced darkness and the Israelites light leads the author to imagine that the Egyptians could hear, but not see, their Hebrew neighbors, while the Hebrews could clearly see the Egyptians cowering in fear.

The virtuous restraint of the Israelites is thus put on display since their enslavers   **18:2–4** were at their mercy, but they did **them no injury**. Instead, the Egyptians "begged their forgiveness" (NETS), an expansion of the Exodus account of the Egyptians' generosity toward the departing Hebrews (Exod 11:3; 12:36). To continue the comparison, Wisdom recalls the **flaming pillar** of God's presence for his people in contrast to the darkness besetting the Egyptians (Exod 13:21). In line with the principle that divine punishment corresponds to the wrong done (Wis 11:5, 16), the Egyptians are **imprisoned in darkness** since they had **imprisoned** the Israelites, who are to be the instruments **through whom** the world will receive the **imperishable light of the law**. The idea that the law of God, the Torah, was intended as a light for all the nations and that Israel would be the instrument through which it would be disseminated is found elsewhere in the Bible.[11] Though the Egyptians sought to detain God's **sons** (see Exod 4:22) as slaves, the Israelites will now spread the law of God to free all peoples, even their oppressors, from fear. The Israelites thus become benefactors to their former masters.

Reflection and Application (17:1–18:4)

When the lights go out due to a power failure, people typically freeze in place. Our instinctive response to darkness protects us from stubbing our toes or running into walls. Sometimes when we recognize the gravity of our own sin and feel the sting of guilt, we tend to freeze in place spiritually—to condemn ourselves, to lose hope, to descend into a downward spiral. Like the Egyptians, we might try to hide "behind a dark curtain of forgetfulness" (Wis 17:3) and allow ourselves to be overcome by despair. Yet even in our darkest moments, God provides a "flaming pillar of fire" (18:3) to guide us—his word and his Spirit. In his generous love he invites us to repent of our sins and be forgiven. Thus, he gives us the light of hope even when we fail. As the New Testament teaches, "If we confess our sins, he is faithful and just, and will forgive our sins and cleanse us from all unrighteousness" (1 John 1:9). In the end, every act of repentance is an act of hope.

---

10. This statement is similar to Esther 8:16, where "the Jews had light and gladness and joy and honor" when they were delivered from their enemies.

11. Isa 2:2–3; 42:6; 49:6; Mic 4:1–2; see also *Testament of Levi* 14.4; Philo, *Questions and Answers on Exodus* 2.42.

Death of the Firstborn versus Israel's Deliverance from Death

Wisdom 18:5–25

This sixth of seven antitheses contrasts the †death of the Egyptian firstborn at the hand of the destroying angel on the first Passover (Exod 12:21–42) with the Israelites' deliverance from a terrible plague through the mediation of the high priest, Aaron (Num 16:41–50). Reading those two passages first will help one understand this section.

Death of the Egyptian Firstborn (18:5–19)

⁵When they had resolved to kill the infants of your holy ones,
and one child had been exposed and rescued,
in punishment you took away a multitude of their children;
and you destroyed them all together by a mighty flood.
⁶That night was made known beforehand to our fathers,
so that they might rejoice in sure knowledge of the oaths in
    which they trusted.
⁷The deliverance of the righteous and the destruction of their
    enemies
were expected by your people.
⁸For by the same means by which you punished our enemies
you called us to yourself and glorified us.
⁹For in secret the holy children of good men offered sacrifices,
and with one accord agreed to the divine law,
that the saints would share alike the same things,
both blessings and dangers;
and already they were singing the praises of the fathers.
¹⁰But the discordant cry of their enemies echoed back,

and their piteous lament for their children was spread abroad.
[11]The slave was punished with the same penalty as the master,
and the common man suffered the same loss as the king;
[12]and they all together, by the one form of death,
had corpses too many to count.
For the living were not sufficient even to bury them,
since in one instant their most valued children had been
destroyed.
[13]For though they had disbelieved everything because of their
magic arts,
yet, when their first-born were destroyed, they acknowledged
your people to be God's son.
[14]For while gentle silence enveloped all things,
and night in its swift course was now half gone,
[15]your all-powerful word leaped from heaven, from the royal
throne,
into the midst of the land that was doomed,
a stern warrior [16]carrying the sharp sword of your authentic
command,
and stood and filled all things with death,
and touched heaven while standing on the earth.
[17]Then at once apparitions in dreadful dreams greatly troubled
them,
and unexpected fears assailed them;
[18]and one here and another there, hurled down half dead,
made known why they were dying;
[19]for the dreams which disturbed them forewarned them of this,
so that they might not perish without knowing why they suffered.

OT: Exod 12:21–42; Num 33:3–4
NT: Acts 7:21; Heb 11:28
Catechism: "son of God," 441
Lectionary: 18:6–9: 19th Sunday in Ordinary Time (Year C); 18:14–16, 19:6–9: Ordinary Time, Week 32, Saturday (Year I)

This section begins with a taut comparison: since the Egyptians intended to cast **18:5** the Hebrew boys into the Nile (Exod 1:22), the Egyptians themselves were cast into the Red Sea (Exod 14:27–28). The punishment fits the crime. Baby Moses, however, was **exposed and rescued** as a foreshadowing of the Israelites' plight during the plague. They will be threatened and then saved.

That night was Passover, "a night of vigil" (Exod 12:42 NABRE), the night on **18:6–7** which the Israelites were delivered by the Lord according to his plan. The covenant **oaths** given to Abraham warned that his descendants would sojourn in a foreign land for a time (Gen 15:13–16). Instead of being fearful due to ignorance, the Israelites were bolstered in faith by **sure knowledge** of the promises of God **so that they might rejoice**.

18:8–9   The author now restates the key concept of the Book of History, that God uses **the same means** to punish the wicked and bless the righteous. The principle is so firm that it becomes the Israelites' expectation. Thus, the Passover event was no surprise to the Israelites. The fact that the **sacrifices** took place **in secret** interprets the rule recorded in Exod 12:46, which mandates that the meal take place "in one house," to mean that the Passover rituals must be done secretly. While the Israelites were eating the sacrificial meal of the Passover, **the divine law** (NABRE: "divine institution"), the Egyptian firstborn were being struck down (Exod 12:29). In fact, not only were the Hebrew firstborn spared, but they were **glorified**; this refers to the special consecration of the firstborn to the Lord (Exod 13:2, 15). Wisdom frequently refers to the Israelites as "holy ones" or **saints** (Wis 18:1, 5, 9), meaning that they are a people set apart for God. The singing of **the praises of the fathers**—in particular the Hallel psalms (Pss 113–18)—at the Passover Seder meal became traditional. For example, Jesus and his disciples sang after the Last Supper (Matt 26:30; Mark 14:26).

18:10–12   In stark contrast to the joyful singing of the Israelites at the original Passover, the Egyptians let out a **discordant cry** of grief at the †death of their firstborn. The sweeping scope of the plague is emphasized by the fact that both **slave** and **master** were afflicted, both **common man** and **king** (Exod 12:29). Neither royal blood nor high social status brought protection; the only distinction that mattered was whether one was Hebrew or Egyptian. The author describes how the Egyptian firstborn became **corpses too many to count**, so that there were not enough people **even to bury them** (see Num 33:3–4). The author weaves a theological meditation on the contrasting fates of Israel and Egypt at the first Passover by making one contrast after another: comparing "one child" to "a multitude of their children" lost (Wis 18:5), the punishment of the Egyptians to the glorification of the Israelites (v. 8), singing to wailing (v. 10), and the commoner to the king (v. 11).

18:13–19   At first the Egyptians **disbelieved** Moses's message because of the power of Pharaoh's magicians, who could mimic at least the first few plagues. Yet the final, deadly plague changes their minds: **when their first-born were destroyed, they acknowledged your people to be God's son**. Indeed, in Moses's commission to challenge Pharaoh, the Lord sets up the confrontation: "And you shall say to Pharaoh, 'Thus says the LORD, Israel is my first-born son, and I say to you, "Let my son go that he may serve me"; if you refuse to let him go, behold, I will slay your first-born son'" (Exod 4:22–23). Only the horror of the final plague can shatter the Egyptians' illusions and cause them to recognize the power of the true God and his people's sonship. In the end, Pharaoh surrenders and sends the Israelites away (Exod 12:31).

According to Exodus, "At midnight the LORD struck all the firstborn in the land of Egypt" (Exod 12:29). The author sets the stage for the sudden arrival of God's **all-powerful word** (Greek †*logos*), which leaps down from his throne into Egypt, by describing the **gentle silence** that **enveloped all** as the **night** ran its **course**. This *logos*, while described in terms similar to wisdom (Wis 7:23), is a further description of "the destroyer" (Exod 12:23) that wields **the sharp sword** of divine judgment against the firstborn Egyptians. The fact that this destroying messenger **touched heaven while standing on the earth** perhaps alludes to Homeric tradition in which the goddess Discord (*Eris*) is depicted with her head in heaven and her feet on earth.[1] The destroyer links heaven and earth by bringing down divine †wrath. It resembles the vision seen by David of "the angel of the LORD standing between earth and heaven, and in his hand a drawn sword" (1 Chron 21:16).

Like Lady Wisdom in chapters 6–9 and like the palpable darkness described in chapter 17, the wrath of God is personified in Wis 18 so that it becomes a character in the unfolding drama of the two parallel scenes: the Passover plague of the firstborn and the plague that Aaron confronts in Num 16. The author uses a variety of terms to denote this figure, elevating it to personal status: "your all-powerful word" (Wis 18:15); "a stern warrior" (18:15); "the wrath" (18:20); "the anger" (18:21); "the disaster" (18:21); "the wrath" (18:22); "the punisher" (18:22); "the wrath" (18:23); "the destroyer" (18:25); "pitiless anger" (19:1).

The author returns to the vocabulary of fear from his previous reflection on the plague of darkness (17:1–18:4) to describe the psychological effects of the destruction of the firstborn: the victims are terrified by **apparitions in dreadful dreams** and **unexpected fears**, and they are only **half dead**. This temporary state of injury and dreaming is meant as a moral lesson so that none of the firstborn would die **without knowing why they suffered**. Since the Egyptians had previously preferred ignorance (17:13), now they will not be allowed to die without knowing that their oppression of the Israelites brought on the punishment of God. For the author of Wisdom, knowledge is the key to righteousness (15:2–3). Here the "sure knowledge" (18:6) of the Israelites is juxtaposed with the willful ignorance of the Egyptians, which leads to their destruction, but not without a final realization of their error.

A Priest Stops a Plague (18:20–25)

> [20]The experience of death touched also the righteous,
> and a plague came upon the multitude in the desert,
> but the wrath did not long continue.

1. Homer, *Iliad* 4.443.

²¹For a blameless man was quick to act as their champion;
he brought forward the shield of his ministry,
prayer and propitiation by incense;
he withstood the anger and put an end to the disaster,
showing that he was your servant.
²²He conquered the wrath not by strength of body,
and not by force of arms,
but by his word he subdued the punisher,
appealing to the oaths and covenants given to our fathers.
²³For when the dead had already fallen on one another in heaps,
he intervened and held back the wrath,
and cut off its way to the living.
²⁴For upon his long robe the whole world was depicted,
and the glories of the fathers were engraved on the four rows
    of stones,
and your majesty on the diadem upon his head.
²⁵To these the destroyer yielded, these he feared;
for merely to test the wrath was enough.

OT: Exod 28:1–43; Num 16:41–50; 1 Chron 21:16; Sir 50:1–21

In verses 20–25 the author turns to the second half of the antithesis, the "trial of death" (18:20 NABRE) recounted in Num 16:41–50, which the Hebrews themselves had to face in the desert. The structural unity of Wis 18:20–25 is evident in the use of the keyword "trial" (Greek *peira*), which both opens and closes the section as an †*inclusio*. During the wilderness wanderings, some of the Israelites organized themselves against Moses and Aaron under the leadership of a Levite named Korah. These rebels objected to the fact that the priesthood was reserved only to Aaron and his descendants, declaring that "all in the congregation are holy, every one of them" (Num 16:3 ESV-CE). The dispute was resolved when Korah's tent was swallowed by the earth and the rebels were all consumed by divine fire (Num 16:31–35). However, afterward the people complained to Moses and Aaron concerning this deadly judgment. In response to their complaints, the Lord sent a plague against the whole people. It was halted only when Aaron atoned for the sin of the people by offering incense as "he stood between the dead and the living" (Num 16:48).

18:20-21   While both the Egyptians and the Israelites encountered a **plague** of †**death**, only the Egyptians were helpless in the face of it. They were hunted down by the destroyer (see comments above at 18:13–19), while Aaron acted as the Israelites' **champion**, an "angel of life" as it were. His priestly power, a privilege that had been under dispute, now is proven in a miraculous way as he bears **the shield of his ministry, prayer and propitiation by incense**. The author is illustrating the validity of Aaron's priesthood and the effectiveness of his intercession.

The author shows how the threat of death faced both the Egyptians and the   18:22-23
Israelites, but the Israelites were delivered from the danger by the power of
Aaron's priestly office, which is implicitly contrasted to the powerless magic
of the Egyptians (Wis 17:7; 18:13). The "all-powerful word" (18:15) that afflicted the Egyptians is the same †**wrath** that afflicted the Israelites. Aaron thus
confronts one †*logos* with yet another—**by his word** (*logos*) **he subdued the**
punisher. Though Numbers records no words of Aaron in this scene, Wisdom
recounts that he spoke, **appealing to the oaths and covenants given to our**
fathers, reminding God of his promises to Abraham, Isaac, and Jacob. Relying
on the description of the scene in Num 16:48—"He stood between the dead
and the living"—Wisdom depicts Aaron as standing in the midst of dead bodies, facing down the plague and cutting **off its way to the living**. The author
dramatizes Aaron's role as priestly mediator standing at the juncture between
life and death, like the destroyer who stood at the juncture between heaven
and earth (Wis 18:16).

Aaron's priestly apparel now takes center stage for three reasons: (1) it de-   18:24-25
picts **the whole world**; (2) it includes **the glories of the fathers**; and (3) it is
emblazoned with God's **majesty**. Each of these aspects needs to be explained.
First, the blue **robe** of the high priest symbolizes the fact that he represents all
humanity in the exercise of his office since the "whole world" is depicted on his
robe—as if the blue color imaged the air, the sky. In connection with this theme,
later Jewish tradition held that the high priest's robe was originally the clothing
of Adam, sewn by the Lord himself.[2] The sanctuary in which he offers incense
is the universal temple of creation.[3] As †Philo says, "The highest, and in the
truest sense the holy, temple of God is, as we must believe, the whole universe,
having for its sanctuary the most sacred part of all existence, even heaven."[4]

Second, the "glories of the fathers" refers to the names of the twelve patriarchs, the sons of Jacob, which were inscribed on the jewels that adorned the
high priest's breastplate (Exod 28:21). Lastly, "your majesty" refers to the sacred
name of the Lord, YHWH, which was inscribed on the front of the high priest's
headdress in the phrase "Holy to the LORD" (Exod 28:36).

The last verse in this chapter closes the scene. **The destroyer**—a personification of God's wrath (see comments above at 18:13–19)—fears the priestly
robe, the names of the patriarchs, and the name of God emblazoned on the
priest's headdress, and therefore he stands down. Aaron's priestly victory
against the plague of divine anger is now complete. The phrase **merely to test**
the wrath was enough could be translated "the single taste of his wrath was

---

2. See Gen 3:21; Sir 49:16–50:11; C. T. R. Hayward, *The Jewish Temple: A Non-Biblical Sourcebook*
(London: Routledge, 1996), 45.

3. A biblical concept shared by †Stoic writers; see David Winston, *The Wisdom of Solomon*, AB 43
(Garden City, NY: Doubleday, 1979), 321.

4. Philo, *On the Special Laws* 1.66 (Colson, Whitaker, and Earp, LCL 7:137).

enough."[5] That is, the Israelites experienced only this one plague of death, while the Egyptians would be confronted by death both at the plague of the firstborn and at the Red Sea.

Reflection and Application (18:5–25)

This chapter, which compares the condemnation of the Egyptians and the deliverance of the Israelites, brings us to face the mystery of divine providence as it relates to our own lives. We know that God has "no pleasure in the death of the wicked" (Ezek 33:11), yet his inescapable judgment does come upon those who deserve it. In repentance, we can turn away from sin and toward our Lord, laying "aside every weight" (Heb 12:1). While the Egyptians finally grasped the truth at the moment of death when it was too late to change, the Israelites were saved through priestly mediation. We have hope that we too will be saved since "God has not destined us for wrath, but to obtain salvation through our Lord Jesus Christ" (1 Thess 5:9). Christians can have confidence that when we experience our own "trial of death" (Wis 18:20 NABRE), we will have Jesus as our priestly mediator and "champion" to deliver us.

---

5. Winston, *Wisdom of Solomon*, 322.

Drowning in the Sea versus Being Saved by the Sea

Wisdom 19:1–9

This seventh and last antithesis of the Book of History contrasts the watery destruction of the Egyptians with the miraculous salvation of the Israelites by means of the same Red Sea. The series of comparisons comes to climactic close with the condemnation of the wicked and the final vindication of the righteous.

The Red Sea as Death and Deliverance (19:1–9)

[1]But the ungodly were assailed to the end by pitiless anger,
for God knew in advance even their future actions,
[2]that, though they themselves had permitted your people
    to depart
and hastily sent them forth,
they would change their minds and pursue them.
[3]For while they were still busy at mourning,
and were lamenting at the graves of their dead,
they reached another foolish decision,
and pursued as fugitives those whom they had begged and
    compelled to depart.
[4]For the fate they deserved drew them on to this end,
and made them forget what had happened,
in order that they might fill up the punishment which their
    torments still lacked,
[5]and that your people might experience an incredible journey,
but they themselves might meet a strange death.

> ⁶For the whole creation in its nature was fashioned anew,
> complying with your commands,
> that your children might be kept unharmed.
> ⁷The cloud was seen overshadowing the camp,
> and dry land emerging where water had stood before,
> an unhindered way out of the Red Sea,
> and a grassy plain out of the raging waves,
> ⁸where those protected by your hand passed through as one
>   nation,
> after gazing on marvelous wonders.
> ⁹For they ranged like horses,
> and leaped like lambs,
> praising you, O Lord, who delivered them.

OT: Exod 12:30–36; 14:4–9, 21–29; Ps 114:4–6; 2 Macc 6:14
NT: 1 Cor 10:1–2
Lectionary: 18:14–16, 19:6–9: Ordinary Time, Week 32, Saturday (Year I)

19:1–4   The final comparison set forth by the author illustrates the principle outlined in Wis 11:5 that "through the very things by which their enemies were punished, they themselves received benefit in their need." Rather than †death or darkness, now it is the Red Sea itself that constitutes the reality by which people are punished or blessed. The Israelites enjoy "an incredible journey," while the Egyptians come to "a strange death" (19:5). The miraculous nature of the splitting of the Red Sea and the resulting fates of the two groups are at the forefront here.

The dramatic personification of God's **anger** connects 19:1 to the preceding verses in chapter 18. This divine attribute comes against **the ungodly**. The translators supply **God** to make sense of the verb, **knew in advance**, but in fact the subject is the anger itself. As in chapter 18, divine †wrath is personified (see comments on 18:13–19).

Now Wisdom reflects on the double-mindedness of the Egyptians, who allowed the Israelites to depart after the death of the firstborn (Exod 12:30–36) but then changed their minds and pursued them (Exod 14:4–9). The Egyptians' pursuit becomes a kind of double sin: they should have learned their lesson from the death of the firstborn. Egyptians were famous for their **mourning** rituals and elaborate **graves**, as exemplified by their pyramids and other royal tombs. The fact that they abandoned these solemn rituals of mourning to pursue **another foolish decision** shows how they were driven to madness by their desire to capture the Hebrews. They hunted down the Israelites **as fugitives**, hoping to keep them enslaved in the pagan system of fear and domination rather than allow them the freedom to go and worship the Lord (see Wis 14:11, 21). The Egyptians' madness became an irresistible **fate** (NABRE: "compulsion") that **drew them on**. This view appears to be the author's understanding of what it means for God to "harden Pharaoh's heart" (Exod 14:4). The hardening leads the Egyptians to **forget what had happened**. Though they had endured the most grueling plagues of the †divine pedagogy, they did not learn the lessons they contained but instead became obstinate. By their obstinacy, the Egyptians **fill up the punishment which their torments still lacked**. This view agrees with earlier wisdom literature, which holds that because fools despise moral instruction, they deserve the consequences that follow (Prov 1:22–26; 5:12–14).

At last, the contrast is explicitly stated: the Egyptians underwent **a strange death**, while the Israelites were simultaneously awarded **an incredible journey**. The author again demonstrates the principle of commensurate reward and punishment by the same means. The Red Sea was the means of death for the Egyptian pursuers and the means of life for the Hebrew fugitives.   19:5–9

Next the author repeats what he said earlier—namely, that creation bends to the will of the Creator to achieve the ends he desires (see Wis 16:24). In fact, the world **was fashioned anew**; the crossing of the Red Sea becomes a kind of "new creation" event. The Creator refashions his creation to punish the wicked and benefit the righteous. The dry seabed that the Israelites traversed in Exod 14:22 recalls the creation of dry land in Gen 1:9: **dry land emerging where water had stood before**. Not only that, the dry seabed becomes **a grassy plain** (literally, "a green-grass-bearing plain"). While this observation might just be an imaginative description of the seaweed-laden floor of the Red Sea, it depicts the Exodus re-creation event as following the same pattern of Genesis, where the springing up of vegetation follows the creation of dry land (Gen 1:11–12). The whole **nation** then **passed through** this restored garden of Eden on the sea-floor. Unlike the Egyptians, who were unable to hide from God's wrath "under their roofs" (Wis 17:2) and in their "inner chambers" (17:4), the Hebrews were effectively **protected by** God's **hand**. The Bible frequently mentions how Israelites witnessed God's **marvelous wonders** at their deliverance from Egypt (Num 14:22; Pss 78:12; 95:9; Mic 7:15). The final verse describes the people's celebratory joy in terms borrowed from Ps 114:4, a psalm that meditates on the exodus events: "The mountains skipped like rams, the hills like lambs."

The series of seven comparisons is finally complete with the climactic deliverance of God's holy people and a decisive judgment of their enemies at the Red Sea. The sequence that began in chapter 11 near the beginning of the Book of History (Wis 10–19) now comes to a close.

Reflection and Application (19:1–9)

While we might not normally think of the destiny of our lives as a kind of "fate," this passage invites us to see how our own moral choices drive us toward foreseeable outcomes. Both sin and righteousness can be characterized in this way. Though repentance is always possible, sin has a tendency to snowball: one transgression leads to another, which leads to another. A small sin, left unrepented, can fester in our souls and draw us, as the Egyptians were drawn to their fate, to stray farther and farther from God. Yet, righteousness also carries a momentum with it. The more we do the right thing, the easier it becomes. As St. Alphonsus Liguori says, "When the love of God takes possession of our hearts, it drives out all sinful affections."[1] Like the Hebrews, we can avoid a "strange death" and instead find ourselves on "an incredible journey" toward the Lord. While he knows the sins we will commit before we commit them, we also believe that "those whom he foreknew he also predestined to be conformed to the image of his Son" (Rom 8:29). That is a future worth looking forward to.

---

1. Alphonsus de Liguori, "Motives for Confidence in the Divine Mercy," in *Alphonsus de Liguori: Selected Writings*, ed. Frederick M. Jones and Bernard McGinn, trans. Frederick M. Jones, Classics of Western Spirituality (New York/Mahwah, NJ: Paulist Press, 1999), 99.

Epilogue: Summary and Doxology

Wisdom 19:10-22

This final segment of the Book of History summarizes the seven antitheses that punctuate chapters 11–19 and concludes with a brief comparison of the Egyptians to the men of Sodom, a musical metaphor to describe God's sovereign power over creation, and a final doxology. The lesson of measure-for-measure punishment and reward is thus brought to an end. Here the author briefly mentions all seven antitheses of the Book of History (chaps. 10–19). These references serve to recall the comparisons and bring the composition to a satisfying close. (See also the sidebar "Structure of the Book of History," p. 119.)

19:10: "River" refers to antithesis 1 (11:6)

19:12: "Quails" alludes to antithesis 2 (16:1–4)

19:13: "Punishments" perhaps refers to antithesis 3, though a different Greek term (16:1, 2, 9)

19:17: "Loss of sight" refers to antithesis 5 on the plague of darkness (17:18–21)

19:19: "Land animals" refers to antithesis 7, the crossing of the Red Sea (19:5, 9)

19:21: "Heavenly food" refers to antithesis 4, the manna (16:20)

19:22: "Glorified" alludes to antithesis 6, Israel's deliverance from death (18:8)

Reviewing the Book of History (19:10–22)

> ¹⁰For they still recalled the events of their sojourn,
> how instead of producing animals the earth brought forth gnats,
> and instead of fish the river spewed out vast numbers of frogs.
> ¹¹Afterward they saw also a new kind of birds,
> when desire led them to ask for luxurious food;
> ¹²for, to give them relief, quails came up from the sea.

¹³The punishments did not come upon the sinners
without prior signs in the violence of thunder,
for they justly suffered because of their wicked acts;
for they practiced a more bitter hatred of strangers.
¹⁴Others had refused to receive strangers when they came
    to them,
but these made slaves of guests who were their benefactors.
¹⁵And not only so, but punishment of some sort will come upon
    the former
for their hostile reception of the strangers;
¹⁶but the latter, after receiving them with festal celebrations,
afflicted with terrible sufferings
those who had already shared the same rights.
¹⁷They were stricken also with loss of sight—
just as were those at the door of the righteous man—
when, surrounded by yawning darkness,
each tried to find the way through his own door.

¹⁸For the elements changed places with one another,
as on a harp the notes vary the nature of the rhythm,
while each note remains the same.
This may be clearly inferred from the sight of what took place.
¹⁹For land animals were transformed into water creatures,
and creatures that swim moved over to the land.
²⁰Fire even in water retained its normal power,
and water forgot its fire-quenching nature.
²¹Flames, on the contrary, failed to consume
the flesh of perishable creatures that walked among them,
nor did they melt the crystalline, easily melted kind of heavenly
    food.

²²For in everything, O Lord, you have exalted and glorified your
    people;
and you have not neglected to help them at all times and in all
    places.

OT: Gen 19:1–11; 43:31–34; 45:17–20

19:10–12   The first part of this passage continues the preceding meditation on the Red
Sea crossing (Wis 19:1–9). During their journey, the Israelites recalled the
events of their deliverance as Moses had urged them (Exod 13:3). The author
uses the Israelites' recollection of the events to present his summary of the
seven antitheses which have given structure to the book since chapter 11. They
first recall the plague of gnats and the plague of frogs, the "worthless insects"
and "dumb creatures" of Wis 11:15 (NABRE). The fact that **the earth brought**

Table of References to Genesis

BIBLICAL BACKGROUND

Wisdom 19 portrays the crossing of the Red Sea as a re-creation event by alluding to the creation narratives in Genesis. The allusions are summarized in the following table:

Wisdom	Genesis
19:7: "dry land"	1:9: "dry land"
19:7: "grassy plain"	1:11: "vegetation"
19:10: "the river spewed out"	1:20: "Let the waters bring forth . . ."
19:10: "the earth brought forth"	1:24: "Let the earth bring forth . . ."
19:11: "a new kind of birds"	1:21: "every winged bird according to its kind"
19:11: "luxurious food [*tryphē*]"	3:23 (NETS): "the orchard of delight [*tryphē*]"

---

forth these creatures alludes to three things: the creation narrative, in which God says, "Let the earth bring forth . . ." (Gen 1:24); the "dust of the earth" becoming gnats (Exod 8:16); and the †Stoic concept of the transposition of elements, which will be alluded to at the end of the chapter (Wis 19:18–21). Like the earth bringing forth creatures, the Nile **river** likewise **spewed out vast numbers of frogs**. These observations show that creation is being renewed to punish the wicked and benefit the righteous. Earlier, in 11:15, the author had been relatively indirect in his allusions to the exodus as part of his literary strategy to keep the reader guessing (see the sidebar "Why Omit Names?," p. 61), but now ambiguity is cleared away as the words for **gnats** and **frogs** are employed for the first time in the book. These terms offer a clear link to the exodus events, in case readers have not understood up to this point. The sea also produces **a new kind of birds**—namely, the quail spoken of in Wis 16:2, there as *trophē* ("delicacy"), here as *tryphē*, a **luxurious food**. The same rare term is used in the †Septuagint to name Eden as "the orchard of delight [*tryphē*]" (Gen 3:23 NETS). The listing of creatures from sea, land, and sky and the allusion to Eden illustrate the author's intent to recall the early chapters of Genesis.

Now the message of the Book of History is restated: God metes out appro- **19:13–17** priate and proportional punishments and rewards, with patience and restraint (11:5; 15:1). **The sinners** are the Egyptians, who were repeatedly warned through the plagues. The sin, as we will see in the following verses, was their violation of the obligations of hospitality. Instead of receiving the Hebrews as honored **guests**, they enslaved them. To explain how terrible their **wicked acts** are, the author compares them to **others**, the despicable men of Sodom (Gen 19:1–11), a biblical comparison for emphasizing the gravity of a sin (Lam 4:6; Matt 10:15).

Citizenship and Taxes

BIBLICAL BACKGROUND

Some scholars have detected a complex allusion to Roman-era tax disputes in the city of Alexandria in the phrase "shared the same rights" (Wis 19:16). Before the Roman takeover of Alexandria, the Jews enjoyed relative social parity with the Greeks of the city, including admission to the gymnasium. But when the city was incorporated into the Roman Empire in 30 BC, a poll tax (called *laographia*) was imposed.[a] The Greek citizens were exempt, while the Egyptians were not. The Jews were lumped in with the Egyptians and forced to pay the tax as well, to which they strenuously objected. If this connection has been correctly evaluated, it helps us date the book to after the beginning of the Roman period in Egypt (30 BC), but before it is first quoted by St. Irenaeus (ca. 140–98).

a. John J. Collins, *Between Athens and Jerusalem: Jewish Identity in the Hellenistic Diaspora* (Grand Rapids: Eerdmans, 2000), 115–17.

The men of Sodom had a reputation for sin (Gen 13:13; 18:20–21), which was confirmed when they threatened Lot's angelic guests with "homosexual gang rape . . . , something completely at odds with the norms of all oriental hospitality."[1] In Wisdom's view, the Egyptians' sin of enslaving **guests who were their benefactors** was even worse. The patriarch Joseph had saved Egypt from famine by his wisdom, and the author recalls how initially the Egyptians received the family of Jacob with a warm welcome and a feast (Gen 43:31–34). The notion that they had **the same rights** could refer to Pharaoh's promise to Jacob's sons: "I will give you the best of the land of Egypt, and you shall eat the fat of the land" (Gen 45:18). The Egyptians' friendly welcome, which gives way to the complete enslavement of their guests, makes them also guilty of betrayal. The similarity between the men of Sodom and the Egyptians does not end with their violation of the law of hospitality and the gravity of their sin but is also manifest in their punishment by God. The men of Sodom had been **stricken also with loss of sight** by the angels protecting Lot (Gen 19:11). Similarly, the Egyptians were completely blinded by a plague of **yawning darkness** (compare Wis 17:18–21).

19:18   Here at the end of the book, the author returns to a favorite theme with a new twist. While he had stated earlier that creation alternately "grows tense for punishment" and "is relaxed in benefit" (Wis 16:24 NABRE), here the same idea of God's control over nature is developed with a musical analogy: the **notes** played **on a harp** are like the elements. The sound of the notes appears to change as the key or melody changes, though in fact the notes do not

1. Gordon J. Wenham, *Genesis 16–50*, Word Biblical Commentary 2 (Dallas: Word, 1994), 55.

Public Domain / Wikimedia Commons

Figure 10. "The Great Library of Alexandria" (O. Von Corven, 19th cent.).

change.[2] **The elements** literally **changed places with one another** to punish or bless, again in accord with Stoic physical theory. Stoic physics viewed the blending of elements as the "interpenetration of two or more bodies in such a way that each preserves its own proper nature and own qualities in the mixture."[3] The constituent elements in a blended substance are not destroyed but preserved in their unique characteristics. To explain the principle of the

2. Commentators have strained to explain the argument of the verse. J. A. F. Gregg offers one of the clearest attempts: "The idea is that the relations in which a thing stands can modify completely the effect which it produces: the notes of the instrument, in whatever key they are played, are the same notes, but the alteration of their relations seems (but only seems) entirely to have altered their sound" (*The Wisdom of Solomon in the Revised Version with Introduction and Notes*, Cambridge Bible for Schools and Colleges [Cambridge: Cambridge University Press, 1922], 187).

3. Alexander of Aphrodisas, *De Mixtione* 216, 28–31, quoted in Michael J. White, "Stoic Natural Philosophy (Physics and Cosmology)," in *The Cambridge Companion to the Stoics*, ed. Brad Inwood (New York: Cambridge University Press, 2003), 147.

transposition of the elements, the author comments on water, earth, and fire but leaves out air, the common fourth element in Greek thought. If the elements are the notes on the harp, then the Creator is the harpist, and the notes bend to his will. The transposition of elements is what **may be clearly inferred**, and which will be further proven in verses 19–21 by a series of examples.

19:19–21   The **land animals** that became **water creatures** are the Israelites and their cattle, who walked through the Red Sea—a reference back to 19:7–9. The swimming creatures that **moved over to the land** are the frogs that invaded the land of Egypt.[4] When the author says **water forgot its fire-quenching nature**, he again reflects on how the fiery thunderbolts that accompanied the God-sent hail were not extinguished by the precipitation (16:17–19; also 16:22).[5] Yet at the same time, **flames** did not burn up the **perishable creatures** that God had also sent against the Egyptians. The fires of the Hebrew ovens also did not melt the **easily melted** manna (16:27; Num 11:8). The manna had been called the "food of angels" and "bread from heaven" (Wis 16:20 NABRE), but now these titles are combined into **heavenly food** (NABRE: "ambrosial food").[6] The earlier references to Gen 1 and Eden combine with the description of manna as "ambrosial food" to link it, perhaps, with the fruit of the tree of life in the garden.

19:22   In a final flourish, the author concludes with a doxology, a fitting way to end a book about God's wisdom and salvation (compare Tob 14:15: "and he blessed the Lord God forever and ever. Amen" [NRSV]; Sir 51:30: "Blessed be Yahweh forever, and praised be his name from generation to generation").[7] This doxology acknowledges God's faithful action toward his people throughout salvation history in two ways: first, the Lord has **exalted and glorified** his people by choosing them and by making them victorious; second, he has never **neglected to help them**. His fidelity is consistent **at all times and in all places**. This brief closing restates the purpose of the Book of History, which is to illustrate God's hand at work to bless his people. The final verses of Wisdom sum up the seven antitheses of the Book of History and give one last glance at the meaning of divine providence. God indeed is the source of wisdom and the Lord of history.

---

4. †Philo similarly comments, "Every place, public or private, was filled with them, as though it were nature's purpose to send one kind of the aquatic animals to colonize the opposite region, since land is the opposite of water" (*On the Life of Moses* 1.103 [Colson, Whitaker, and Earp, LCL 6:329]).

5. Philo describes the event: ". . . continuous claps of thunder and flashes of lightning and constant thunderbolts. These last provided a most marvelous spectacle, for they ran through the hail, their natural antagonist, and yet did not melt it nor were quenched by it, but unchanged coursed up and down and kept guard over the hail" (*On the Life of Moses* 1.118 [Colson, Whitaker, and Earp, LCL 6:337]).

6. In Greek mythology, "heavenly food" refers to the sustenance of the Greek gods. An early Christian reference to "ambrosial food" as Eucharist can be found in *Acts of Thomas* 36.

7. Patrick W. Skehan and Alexander A. Di Lella, *The Wisdom of Ben Sira*, AB 39 (Garden City, NY: Doubleday, 1987), 579.

Heavenly Bread in Paradise

The Sibylline Oracles are prophecies dubiously attributed to ancient Greek prophetesses called "sibyls." Some of the earliest oracles were written in the context of Egyptian Judaism, while later oracles exhibit Christian influence. This poetic fragment of uncertain date speaks of the food enjoyed by the blessed in terms similar to Wis 19:21:

> But those who honor the true eternal God
> inherit life, dwelling in the luxuriant garden
> of Paradise for the time of eternity,
> feasting on sweet bread from starry heaven.[a]

a. *Sibylline Oracles* fragment 3.46–49 (trans. J. J. Collins, *OTP* 1:471).

Reflection and Application (19:10–22)

The confidence that Wisdom places in God's faithfulness is encouraging. St. Paul urges us to "have no anxiety about anything" (Phil 4:6) and to "give thanks in all circumstances" (1 Thess 5:18). The fact that God is unfailing and that he stands by his people "at all times and in all places" (Wis 19:22) should let our hearts rest easy. The Lord even goes out of his way to miraculously alter creation for the benefit of his people—changing land creatures to sea creatures and modifying the powers of water and fire. Reflecting on salvation history with Wisdom ought to dispel our anxiety and increase our faith since we see God faithfully working for the safety and salvation of his holy people.

Suggested Resources

Scholarly Commentaries

Goodrick, A. T. S., ed. *The Book of Wisdom with Introduction and Notes.* Oxford Church Bible Commentary. London: Rivingtons, 1913. Reprint, New York: Cambridge University Press, 2012. An older, academic commentary with detailed examination of textual issues.

Mazzinghi, Luca. *Wisdom.* Translated by Michael Tait. International Exegetical Commentary on the Old Testament. Stuttgart: Kohlhammer, 2019. A translation of an Italian commentary by a Catholic priest and professor who treats Wisdom from both synchronic and diachronic perspectives.

Winston, David. *The Wisdom of Solomon.* AB 43. Garden City, NY: Doubleday, 1979. The only major academic commentary on the book in print in English, it provides a thorough introduction and extensive references to classical and ancient Jewish sources.

Popular Commentaries and Study Bibles

Hahn, Scott, and Curtis Mitch with Mark Giszczak. "Wisdom of Solomon." In *The Books of Wisdom and Sirach*, 13–44. Ignatius Catholic Study Bible. San Francisco: Ignatius, 2020. The biblical text with interpretive footnotes.

Kolarcik, Michael. "The Book of Wisdom." In *The New Interpreter's Bible*, edited by Leander E. Keck, 5:435–600. 12 vols. Nashville: Abingdon, 1997. A commentary for pastoral use by a Jesuit priest and Scripture scholar that provides both detailed exegesis and pastoral reflections.

Reese, James M. *The Book of Wisdom, Song of Songs.* Old Testament Message 20. Wilmington, DE: Michael Glazier, 1983. A pastoral commentary by a Catholic priest.

Special Studies

Collins, John J. *Jewish Wisdom in the Hellenistic Age.* Old Testament Library. Louisville: Westminster John Knox, 1997. An indispensable introduction to the thought of Hellenistic Judaism, including special attention to Sirach and Wisdom.

Kolarcik, Michael. *The Ambiguity of Death in the Book of Wisdom 1–6: A Study of Literary Structure and Interpretation.* Analecta Biblica 127. Rome: Biblical Institute, 1991. An in-depth scholarly study of the meaning of death and immortality in Wisdom.

Reese, James M. *Hellenistic Influence on the Book of Wisdom and Its Consequences.* Analecta Biblica 41. Rome: Biblical Institute Press, 1970. A thorough, academic analysis of the vocabulary and style of Wisdom.

Glossary

cultic: relating to cult—that is, to formal worship of a god or gods.

death: the separation of the soul from the body.

determinism: the belief that human beings do not have free will and that therefore all human actions are fixed in advance by outside forces, whether God, fate, nature, or others.

diatribe: a Greek literary device in which an opponent's views are given voice and then refuted, producing an essentially imaginary conversation (e.g., Rom 2).

divine pedagogy: the way God reveals himself to humanity gradually through the events of salvation history; see Catechism 53, 1950.

eschatology, eschatological: referring to the end time and last things—for example, death, judgment, heaven, and hell.

excursus: a literary digression from the main composition.

Hades: the god of the dead and his realm, the underworld place of the dead, in Greek mythology.

hedonism, hedonistic: the belief that life is primarily about seeking pleasure.

Hellenistic: relating to the spread of Greek culture throughout the known world in the era following the death of Alexander the Great (323 BC) until the rise of the Roman Empire in the first century BC.

immortality: the ability to live forever; in Platonic thought, the soul by nature would live forever apart from the body; in Christian teaching, the soul and body will be reunited forever at the resurrection of the dead.

inclusio: a Greek literary device in which a certain word or phrase is used at the beginning and end of a composition to give a sense of unity to the whole.

Logos, logos (Greek "word"): in Stoic philosophy, the rational principle of the universe; in Philo's writings, the intermediary between God and the universe; see Wis 9:1–2.

nihilism, nihilistic: the belief that life is meaningless.

pantheism: the belief that all things are divine or that God or the gods are to be identified with the universe.

Philo (ca. 20 BC–AD 50): an important Jewish philosopher in the city of Alexandria; many of his books are extant.

Plato (ca. 427–347 BC), **Platonic, Platonism**: Greek philosopher, student of Socrates, teacher of Aristotle; his many writings were very influential in the Hellenistic period.

Septuagint (abbreviated LXX): a Greek translation of the Old Testament produced in about 200 BC and the version most often quoted in the New Testament.

sorites: a playful chain syllogism; see, e.g., Wis 6:17–20.

Stoic, Stoicism: a philosophical school of the Hellenistic era that followed the teachings of Zeno (333–264 BC); it emphasized the logical structure of the universe imposed by the *logos*, the acceptance of fate, indifference to circumstances, and virtue.

syncretism, syncretistic: the mixing of religious ideas, beliefs, and practices.

synkrisis, synkrises: a Greek rhetorical technique in which two examples are compared and evaluated in order to demonstrate the argument.

wisdom: God's perfect knowledge; the knowledge of causes that human beings can come to possess; the habitual seeking of knowledge with integrity of heart.

wrath: God's uncompromising opposition to evil expressed in his just punishment of evil in the present and at the end of history; God's wrath differs from human anger in that it is motivated not by emotional reaction but by true justice and the radical incompatibility between God's nature and evil of any kind.

Index of Pastoral Topics

Index of Sidebars